Collecting
in
Contemporary Practice

Collecting
in
Contemporary Practice

Susan M. Pearce

SAGE Publications
London • New Delhi

A Division of SAGE Publications, Inc.
Walnut Creek

© Susan M. Pearce, 1998

First published 1998

SAGE Publications Ltd
6 Bonhill Street
London EC2A 4PU

AltaMira Press
A Division of SAGE Publications, Inc.
1630 North Main Street, Suite 367
Walnut Creek, California 94596

SAGE Publications India Pvt Ltd
32, M-Block Market
Greater Kailash – I
New Delhi 110 048

British Library Cataloguing in Publication data

A catalogue record for this book is available
from the British Library

ISBN 0 7619 5080 X
ISBN 0 7619 5081 8 (pbk)

Library of Congress catalog card number 97–062236

Typeset by Mayhew Typesetting, Rhayader, Powys
Printed in Great Britain by The Cromwell Press Ltd,
Broughton Gifford, Melksham, Wiltshire

Contents

List of Figures

List of Tables

Preface

The Contemporary Collecting in Britain Survey project was made possible by a grant awarded to me by the Research Grants Committee of the University of Leicester, to which I am very grateful. Valuable assistance in the planning stages was given by Nick Merriman, University College, London, and the Computer Unit, University of Leicester. Sarah Wheeler and Dominic Candelori both did essential work as the project's Research Assistants: their abilities and dedication were crucial to its successful completion. Steve Chibnall of De Montfort University, Paul Martin, Department of Museum Studies, University of Leicester, Janine Lovatt, formerly Department of Museum Studies and now at Littlehampton Museum, Sussex, and Jo Digger, Walsall Museum, all gave freely of information, ideas and discussion time. Norman Rochester, President of the Leicestershire Collectors' Club, and club members were all generous in sharing their time and experiences. I wish to record my thanks to all these people, although of course any mistakes are my own responsibility.

I am very grateful to Ann Sarson, who turned a hand-written manuscript into a word-processed text, and to Jim Roberts, who produced the camera-ready figures.

Finally, as always, my gratitude goes to Mac, my husband.

Susan Pearce
October 1997

1
Collecting Culture

At any given moment, in the contemporary western world, around a quarter to a third of all adults are willing to identify themselves as collectors (Belk 1988; see Chapter 2). Moreover, since this figure is derived from snap-shots in time, it is probable that the number might rise to about a half if it embraced all those who have had, or who will have, collecting experience. Whatever else collecting involves, we are obviously looking at a major social and individual phenomenon which may be expected to reverberate in all facets of life, and which is an interesting field of enquiry.

Although considerable recent work has been lavished on collecting practice (see below), there are some directly relevant things which we do not know: what do contemporary people collect; what kind of people are they – male or female, in families or not, old or young, poor or well-off; how do they get their things; what do they say about their collecting habit and how do they feel about having it explored? All of these are fascinating questions in their own right, but they point the way to deeper and bleaker thoughts.

For life is fragile and the creation of meaning in an uncaring world equally so. As Clifford puts it, 'In the West, collecting has long been a strategy for the deployment of a possessive self, culture and authenticity' (1986: 238), and in Stewart's words it is 'a strategy of desire' whose task is the ever-impossible effort to bridge the gap between expression and experience (Stewart 1984: 139–169). This is the gulf between imagination and reality as Lacan might have put it, or between the conception and the creation, where the shadow falls, as T.S. Eliot did put it in 'The Hollow Men' (Eliot 1954: 76). Collecting as a process works in the shadowland, making its meaning on the edge where the practices of the past, the politics of present power, and the poetic capacity of each human being blur together.

These are the thoughts which this book sets out to explore, through drawing on the witness given by living, active collectors. The book is based on a survey of collecting entitled the Contemporary Collecting in Britain Survey (see Appendix for technical detail) which was undertaken in 1993 in order to present some answers to the questions posed. The rest of this chapter will be devoted to notions of culture and collection, and the genealogy of collecting studies as a field of discipline. I shall then consider the contemporary British social context and develop some appreciation of its character. Finally, I shall discuss the nature of this study, and the shape of the book will be described chapter by chapter.

Culture and Collection

The title of this chapter, which serves as an introduction to this whole study, is deliberately double-sided. Depending upon where the stress falls, it can mean both 'how culture is collected' and 'what collections are like as culture in their own right'. This book is intended to offer some answers to both questions, as they apply to contemporary Britain. In order to justify this assertion we need to establish what we mean by both collecting and culture, what contemporary Britain is like, and what technique can be used to gather information about what is happening in Britain today; we also need to understand the mind-set within which the investigation is being carried out, and the kinds of ideas which are influencing analysis.

Much ink has been spilt over the definition of 'collection', and of the difference, if any, between 'a collection' and 'an accumulation', 'a group' and 'a hoard'. As long ago as 1932, Durost offered:

> A collection is basically determined by the nature of the *value* assigned to the objects, or ideas possessed. If the *predominant* value of an object or idea for the person possessing it is intrinsic, i.e., if it is valued primarily for use, or purpose, or aesthetically pleasing quality, or other value inherent in the object or accruing to it by whatever circumstances of custom, training, or habit, it is not a collection. If the predominant value is representative or representational, i.e., if said object or idea is valued chiefly for the relation it bears to some other object or idea, or objects, or ideas, such as being one of a series, part of a whole, a specimen of a class, then it is the subject of a collection. (Durost 1932: 10, emphasis in original)

This holds the valuable distinction between objects held for use, with a helpfully wide idea of what constitutes 'use', and objects held as part of a sequence: it is the idea of series or class which creates the notion of the collection. Probably Durost had in mind collections, like those of butterflies or cigarette cards, in which the notion of series is particularly clear, but in an extended form in which sequence is a largely subjective creation of the collector, the idea has a potentially wide application.

The 1980s have produced two further useful efforts at definition. Aristides offered: 'collection . . . [is] "obsession organised." One of the distinctions between possessing and collecting is that the latter implies order, system, perhaps completion. The collector's interest is not bounded by the intrinsic worth of the objects of his desire; whatever they cost, he must have them' (Aristides 1988: 330). This recognises the subjective element in its use of the word 'obsession', and suggests that the crucial difference between 'possession' and 'collecting' is the order and possibility of completion which collecting possesses. Alsop offered a refreshingly simple approach. He says: 'To collect is to gather objects belonging to a particular category the collector happens to fancy . . . and a collection is what has been gathered' (Alsop 1982: 70). The stress here is laid on the mentality of the collector, for essentially a collection is what he believes it is, provided there are at least some physical objects gathered together. This expresses the essentially subjective element in collecting very well.

Belk and his colleagues have arrived at the following: 'We take collecting to be the selective, active, and longitudinal acquisition, possession and disposition of an interrelated set of differentiated objets (material things, ideas, beings or experiences) that contribute to and derive extraordinary meaning from the entity (the collection) that this set is perceived to constitute' (Belk et al. 1990: 8). This definition takes on board the idea of the interrelated set, Durost's series or class, and adds to it the notion that the collection as an entity is greater than the sum of its parts, an important contribution to the discussion. It brings in the actively selecting collector, with his personal or subjective slant on what he is doing, and it recognises that collecting is a prolonged activity, extending through time.

In terms of human activity, however, rather than of outcome as perceived by an outsider, definition as such tends to be unsatisfactory, because sharp notions of seriality or of intention prove too crude to catch the play of human feeling and activity. Bearing this in mind, the best definition of a collection is simply that a collection exists if its owner thinks it does: the subjective yardstick makes good working sense, even if it too has its difficulties. One of these is relatively superficial; people change their minds about the character of their material goods from time to time. But this is inherent in any study of human behaviour which must absorb, as an essential human characteristic, human fickleness and changeability. The other is more profound. The surrounding social context – the culture – may encourage collecting and may therefore encourage people to think of themselves as collectors when they would not otherwise have attached this identification to themselves.

One aspect of the Contemporary Collecting Survey made this very clear. A small group of 27 respondents, representing 3% of all the replies, ticked the box which said 'Yes' to the question 'Do you collect?' but in answer to the question 'When did you start to think of yourself as a collector?' said either 'Never' (70% of this group), or 'Upon receiving this questionnaire' (30%, Table 1.1). Clearly the members of this group had doubts about their status and eligibility, and some were prompted to re-appraise themselves when the Survey papers arrived. Interestingly, the number of pieces which these people had in their collections was at least comparable to the sizes of the collections reported by all the respondents; in fact it tended to be slightly larger. Equally interestingly, the majority of the doubters were women (63%) in the younger age groups (81% under 45) and from the lower end of the B social grouping, roughly the 'lower middle' class (15% of this group did not give employment information). It comes as no surprise that most of the diffident are youngish women from this kind of background, where brashness and over-confidence are not seen as social assets. However, it must be remembered that this group is only a small element in the whole.

Clearly society and the individual, or the broader context and the particular action, are always interwoven and always exercise an influence on each other; life, both collective and several, is not static, but on the contrary is a perpetual state of dynamic change. Recognising this as true, the

Table 1.1   *Characteristics of collectors who were doubtful of their collector identity: analysis of Survey returns*

	% of group
Women	63
Men	37
Age	
18–45 yr	81
46–65 yr	19
No. of items in collection	
1–20	30
21–50	27
51–100	43
Social class	
A	26
B	56
C	3
Did not say	15
Thought of themselves as collectors	
Upon receiving questionnaire	30
Never	70

Note: All these respondents were under 65 years, and none of these collections totalled more than 100 items.

subjective definition of what constitutes a collection will be taken in this book, and all those who replied in answer to the Survey's first question ('Do you collect anything?') saying they were collectors will be treated as such.

'Culture' is an equally critical word, which has already been used as synonymous with 'the surrounding social context'. From an anthropological or sociological perspective 'culture' means the interaction of symbolic meaning, both traditional and novel, and individual life histories through the fields of human relationships, material culture, landscape, and knowledge and understanding, all of which operate at the two levels of theoretical perception and practical event which together make up both society and lived lives. Since the collecting of objects to make collections is part of individual social activity in contemporary Britain, it is itself part of the culture; but since what is collected *is* culture, in its material aspect, it acts also as a commentary upon culture which creates symbolic perception, knowledge and understanding in its own right. Like all activities, it is embedded in culture, but through its reflexive nature, it is active within culture.

The relationship between objects and collections, and of both in the wider whole of understanding can be illustrated through Barthes's famous analysis (1985) of the fashion system (Figure 1.1). In the first level exists a wealth of objects, each of which is primarily a symbol of itself and as such functions in the real world. So, in Alex Wooliams's collection of Thirties material (Wooliams 1995), the men's and women's clothes are inseparable from their wearers and from their social role: they are both signifier (i.e. in this case, a

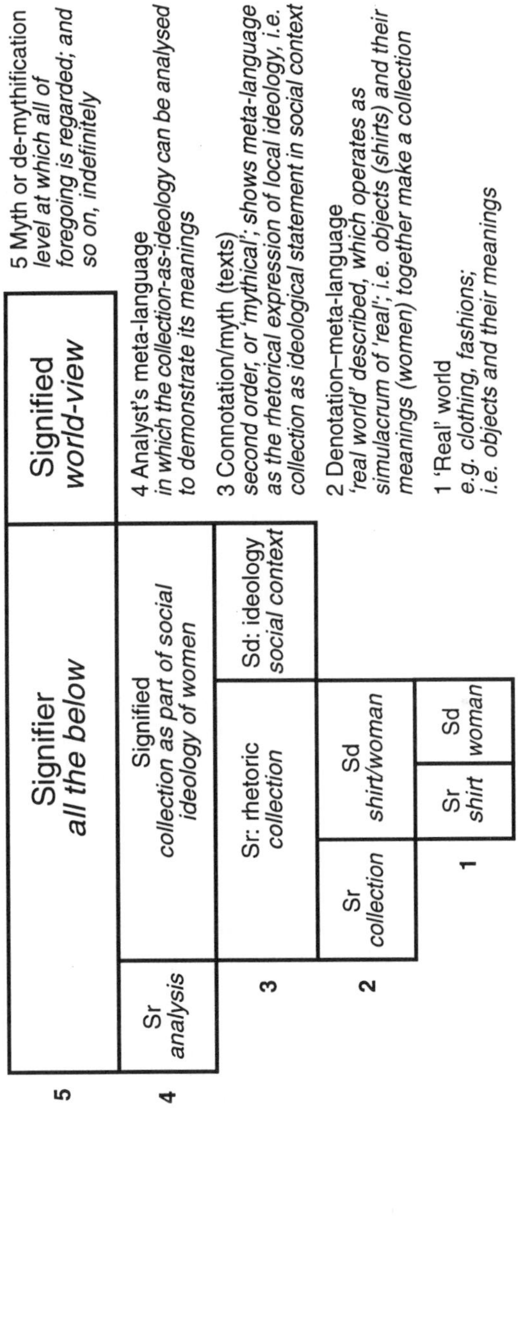

	Signifier all the below				Signified world-view
5	Sr analysis				5 Myth or de-mythification *level at which all of foregoing is regarded; and so on, indefinitely*
4	Signified collection as part of social ideology of women				4 Analyst's meta-language *in which the collection-as-ideology can be analysed to demonstrate its meanings*
3	Sr: rhetoric collection		Sd: ideology social context		3 Connotation/myth (texts) *second order, or 'mythical', shows meta-language as the rhetorical expression of local ideology; i.e. collection as ideological statement in social context*
2	Sr collection	Sd shirt/woman			2 Denotation–meta-language *'real world' described, which operates as simulacrum of 'real'; i.e. objects (shirts) and their meanings (women) together make a collection*
1	Sr shirt	Sd woman			1 'Real' world *e.g. clothing, fashions; i.e. objects and their meanings*

Figure 1.1 *Barthes's analysis of the fashion system, adapted to collecting practice*

visible, tangible object) and signified (i.e. its symbolic meaning). Level 2 is the collecting process, which brings together a range of objects and so incorporates both them and their symbolism into a body of signified, which then itself has its own signifier, that is the narrative which the collector tells about why and how he has gathered together a 'simulacrum' (Barthes's word) of the world, in this case, the past world of 60 years ago.

All of this, in its turn, becomes itself a body of signifier, the 'rhetoric' or active element through which social ideology, the signified, is expressed (level 3). In level 4 both collecting rhetoric and the ideology it expresses themselves become the signified and the signifier the body of broader analysis through which it can be analysed: but this itself is subject to signification and analysis (level 5) in a never-ending sequence of myth-making and de-mythologising from which no living person can ever detach himself. We may add that the signified, in all its progressive manifestations, is more-or-less equivalent to 'culture' and its successive degrees of reflexive perception.

In this study we shall be concerned with level 2, that of the collector and his (and her, henceforward to be understood as included) narratives. We shall endeavour to analyse these at the third level, and to understand collecting rhetoric as an active element in contemporary ideology; and, in tune with level 4, we shall endeavour to discern why and how this rhetorical ideology (or ideological rhetoric) operates. Above level 4 we do not aspire to ascend (or not often).

Some Genealogies

Mention of Barthes brings us to those critical developments over the past two decades or so which have informed and stimulated analyses of collecting practice (Figure 1.2). These can be characterised as post-war psychological studies, the appreciation of material culture as a field of study, the structural/linguistic analysis of communication, and the post-Marxist critique of ideology and the production of knowledge. Finally, we have the role of the methodology of information-gathering and of ethnography. All of these have their roots in traditional studies, and in the cultural analyses developed between 1930 and 1960.

In general, psychological studies have been disappointing, certainly those produced after the last early Freudians had stopped writing. That by Muesterberger (1994) takes a very traditional, not to say pedestrian, view and offers a limited range of case studies, most of which have been available for a long time. Leonard Bloom (1991) looked at the relationship between people and property, giving a useful overview of relevant work, and wondered if an attachment to property is essentially eccentric.

The broad structural/linguistic tradition has transformed the study of material culture in its suggestion that objects may be viewed as an act of communication, as a 'language system' like mythology and literature,

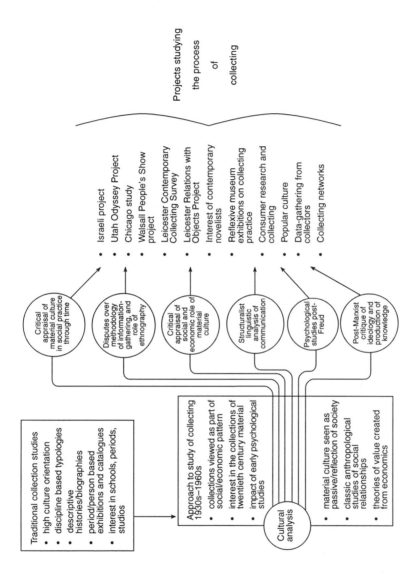

Figure 1.2 *Critical developments in collecting analysis*

kinship, the use of space, and language itself (see Hodder 1986, 1987). The system of objects in any society is seen as a text from which may be read the construction of practice in that community. Objects, like all other social constructs, it becomes clear, are fundamentally symbolic and serve not a given need but a social requirement. They are both determined by, and help to determine, a sequence of interlocking requirements which together enable the society to go on being itself. This needs a little glossing. Broad necessities certainly exist as given needs: northern Americans and north Europeans must have warm clothing if they wish to go outside in the winter (although the word 'wish' shows that even this basic act could be construed as a social construct, and hence count as a symbol). However, the specific material through which this need is satisfied is the clothes that we wear, and these are symbolic in their form and meaning. Similarly, we must eat to live (general need) but the food in our mouths is symbolic in its specificity.

Recognition of the symbolic nature of actual objects leads to an understanding that, far from being the passive relics of thought and action which have passed on, they are themselves thought and action. Symbols, in their existence as such, and in the ways in which they can be manipulated, are socially active, and so are material goods. Very roughly speaking this activity relates to the social value which is placed upon them, high value goods being one kind of effectiveness and low value ones another. Value, too, is a social construct, but one inseparable from its material content (Appadurai 1986), and from the individual histories which objects, and classes of objects, have had.

This brings us to the critique of ideology and the production of knowledge, and so back to Barthes and the network of critical theory which informs and influences all contemporary analysis of the social field. In Barthes's terms, all of this work operates in the upper levels of the plot in Figure 1.1, and indeed, has effectively created those levels. The relevant writers have, collectively, shown us how to think not about the surface social practice – as the use of objects – shows to the world, but about the processes which support the practice and which mesh in with many other processes. This involves a change of emphasis from 'collections', the focus of most earlier study, to 'collecting', the focus of the present work.

Significant here are the writings of Bourdieu, particularly his work on the workings of the social 'habitus' as a body of cultural practice (1977). Guy Debord, in his *Society of the Spectacle* (1977), was one of the first to consider 'spectacular consumption which preserves congealed past culture – whose function is to make *history forgotten within culture* – when culture becomes nothing more than a commodity, it must also become the star commodity of the spectacular society' (1977: sections 192–193, emphasis in original). This is the seed of all later writing about the commodification of memory and history as heritage.

Baudrillard similarly, difficult though some of his writing is, has explored the nature of culture and its mythologies to a depth unrivalled by anybody else (see especially Baudrillard 1975, 1988, 1993, 1994; and also Kellner

1989, 1994, 1995b). In his critique of political economy, Baudrillard argues that the construction of values in a capitalist society arises from the relationship of signified to signifier, so that the logic of meaning and value, always essentially symbolic, is itself the logic of capitalism. Value, therefore, does not exist except as capitalism's 'alibi' (Baudrillard 1988: 71) and:

> In fact the use value of labor power does not exist any more than the use value of products or the autonomy of signified and referent. The same fiction reigns in the three orders of production, consumption and signification. Exchange value is what makes the use value of products appear as its anthropological horizon. The exchange value of labor power is what makes its use value, the concrete origin and the end of the act of labor, appear as its 'generic' alibi. This is the logic of signifiers which produces the 'evidence' of the 'reality' of the signified and the referent. In every way, exchange value makes concrete production, concrete consumption, and concrete signification appear only in distorted, abstract forms. But it foments the concrete as its ideological ectoplasm, its phantasm of origin and transcendence ['*depassement*']. In this sense, need, use value, and the referent 'do not exist.' They are only concepts produced and projected into a generic dimension by the development of the very system of exchange value. (Baudrillard 1975: 30)

Similarly:

> We live in a *referendum* mode precisely because there is no longer any *referential*. Every sign and every message (objects of 'functional' utility just as much as fashion features or any televised information, polls or discussions) is presented to us as question/answer. The entire communications system has passed from a complex syntactic structure of language to a binary system of question/answer signals – perpetual testing. Tests and referenda are, as we know, perfect forms of simulation: the question induces the answer, it is *design-ated* in advance. The *referendum*, then, *is only an ultimatum*: the unilateral question is precisely not an interrogation any more, but the immediate imposition of a meaning which simultaneously completes the cycle. Every message is a verdict, delivered like the verdict of polling statistics. The simulacrum of distance (or indeed of contradiction) between the two poles is nothing but a tactical hallucination, like the reality effect on the interior of the sign itself. (Baudrillard 1993: 62, emphasis in original)

All exchange – in a shop, for labour, as a gift – is therefore symbolic and value is the value that is determined by the internal logic of these transactions. Given the contrasting value systems which contemporary collecting exhibits, these are penetrating ideas.

Fortified and stimulated by this *richesse* of critical theory, the 1980s saw a sudden spurt of interest in collecting and from a variety of angles. Belk, Wallendorf and their associates concentrated upon the field of consumer research (Belk, Sherry et al. 1988; Belk, Wallendorf et al. 1988; Wallendorf, Belk et al. 1988; Wallendorf and Belk 1989; Belk et al. 1989; Belk et al. 1990; Belk and Wallendorf 1992); Stewart (1984) on the interface between acquired objects and values of popular culture; Dannefer (1980, 1981), Olmsted (1991) and Moulin (1987) in sociology; Saisselin (1984) in art history; and Clifford (1988) in anthropology. In addition to this, there have been three data-collecting projects: that of Csikszentmihalyi and Rochberg-Halton (1981), who gathered information about domestic objects from middle-class Chicago, that of Danet and Katriel (1989), who conducted interviews with some 165 collectors in Israel, and that of Belk and his colleagues in the Odyssey Project, who did the same in the United States.

Recent writing in the area has concentrated upon relating collecting to contemporary notions of experience. Belk (1995a) has analysed the relationships between collecting and consumption. Elsner and Cardinal (1994) have gathered together a set of papers which includes one by Baudrillard (1994). Pearce has produced a study of the interrelationships between material culture, collecting and museums (1992) and a further volume (1995) which analyses collecting in Braudelian terms as an element in the European tradition of self-definition through material. Martin is concerned with networks of collecting, particularly as these are demonstrated through clubs and dealing (1997). We might mention here, too, the amazing interest contemporary novelists are showing in collectors and collecting (Edgar 1997; Wilkinson 1997).

Important here, too, is the accumulating literature of the 'People's Show', a project which has brought together contemporary collectors and museums in a new and significant way, and provided, among other things, much data about contemporary collecting (Digger forthcoming; Fardell 1995; Lovatt 1995, 1997). Similarly, the museum world has seen a series of reflexive exhibitions about the production of knowledge in collecting (National Museums of Denmark 1991), and there have been a series of museum installations by working artists aimed at deconstructing collecting meanings.

All this has given birth, in classic Kuhnian terms (1970), to a new field of enquiry, Collecting Studies, which is itself a part of material culture studies and so of social studies in general: its genealogy lies in the literature just reviewed. Its thrust, and that of this book, in comparison with earlier ways of looking at collections, can be summed up in Figure 1.3. The aim is to offer explanations of collecting rather than descriptions of collections, and these will address cultural process rather than cultural history. The thinking involved will be exploratory rather than assumptive, that is to say proceeding from an idea or an hypothesis, testing this against data, and revisiting the hypothesis on the basis of the results, rather than gathering data and scrutinising it for patterns and hence ideas (Shanks 1996: 40). This has the effect of admitting the presence of the author, rather than endeavouring to conceal him behind supposedly unengaged data, and this is an excellent thing. It is in line with much current discussion about the reliability of ethnographic (or qualitative) research as well as quantitative studies (Fink 1995a and b; Hammersley 1992; Wallendorf and Belk 1989).

All this must be justified by testing instead of by appeal to existing authority, a point particularly important in relation to value structure. This leads to a research design which is project based – the present study – instead of data-accumulation based, and intended to enable us to find out more rather than to know more. The approach is therefore quantitative, as well as qualitative or anecdotal. Finally, the rhetoric upon which all this is based is reflexive rather than assumptive, that is to say it is written in the

---

CHANGE IN THE NATURE OF STUDY

from	*to*
Focus	
Collection study	Collecting study
Rhetoric	
Assumptive/ authoritarian	Reflexive/ exploratory
Discipline of study, e.g. history	Field of enquiry, i.e. social practice, construction of identity
To learn more	To discover why
Nature (of world, humans, the past)	Culture (how ideas about world, humans, the past, are made)
Style	
Descriptive/ impersonal	Explanatory/ personal
Product	Process
Knowledge	Meaning
Research	
Data accumulation	Project design
Interest in content, i.e. what	Interest in form and style, i.e. how

---

Figure 1.3   *Shifting paradigms of study, from collection to collecting*

light of Barthes's sequence of inescapable mythologies in which answers are never reached because subjectivity can never be discarded.

Contemporary Britain

Contemporary collecting operates within the context of the broader culture, and in terms of its effect on feelings and social practice how it is perceived is its most important aspect. Perceptions of this kind are moulded in part by individual experience, in part by a perspective, either active or lacking, of what Britain was like in the recent past, and in part by the media, which includes television selection and presentation of the news, the slants of the popular press, and some input from traditional 'heavy' publications. Perceptions of the present are, of course, as complex as perceptions of the past and in what follows some of the more obviously relevant themes are picked out. All collectors are likely to have experienced some of them; probably no collector has experienced all of them; but all have become part of our contemporary mental landscape.

Over the past decade personal insecurity appears to have grown, as the heavy state-subsidised industries and state-financed bureaucracies have disappeared to be replaced (in so far as they have been) by private concerns, small businesses with an uncertain base and changing job structures. Similarly, the ideal of a near-universal property-owning democracy seems to have dissolved into debts and negative equity. Family values are still stressed, and there is no agreement on the ethical basis of unmarried partnership or single parent families, but the apparent rise of domestic violence and child abuse is frequently linked with both dysfunctional family life and the steadily growing availability of pornography and nasty violence in the various media.

Institutions, whether the monarchy, the courts, the police force, or Parliament are deemed to be facing a crisis of confidence. Meanwhile, on offer are various alternatives to established modes. We have alternative knowledge in the martial arts and assorted New Age therapies, fundamental religion, which may be Islamic, Christian, or a range of messianic cults, and new style politics which are uninterested in the traditional parties but concentrate on 'issues' – green, animal rights, the environment and the community. With all this is linked the dissolution of 'middle ground' values, which are also broadly middle class and middle aged.

As old socialism is seen to have failed, there is a new stress on individual action, which leads inevitably to a kind of latter-day philistinism, which is both anti-intellectual (certainly no new thing in Britain) and anti traditional culture. Its place is held to be taken by popular culture, street fashion, heritage nostalgia and rootless materialism for the well-off. People are joined not by the ties of blood, law, employment and community but by the virtual networks of the Internet, video and cable viewing, and tourism. These developments seem to be framed by increasing general violence, some of it racially based, and the whole takes place against the backdrop of the middle years of the twentieth century which, by general consent, appear to have been atypically quiet and law-abiding across the home front (e.g. Jewson 1991).

A range of goods which earlier generations would have found amazing are now available, thanks to refrigeration and fast travel which have eliminated the idea of seasonal foods, or distant commodities. The variety of shops has oscillated widely as department stores gave way to specialised chains and grocers to supermarkets, and High Street shopping was replaced by out-of-town malls. At the same time, personal service was replaced by check-out technology and trolley parks. These are collectively seen as a qualitative change in the experience of shopping.

Finally, we have a sea-change in the role of the media, in both pervasiveness and attitudes. The catalogue of sexual explicitness in word and image, the investigative nature of journalism, the violence, gratuitous or otherwise, and the extent to which members of the public are encouraged to offer up their private lives and their views, need not be repeated here in detail. This is paralleled by an ever-increasing range of soap operas, which now attract attention in their own right as part of popular culture.

Popular culture is an important contemporary idea which embraces most of the trends just mentioned; of course it has always existed, but it is now a critical concept whose time has come, and which has its own suite of theoretical perspectives (Strinati 1995), all of which define its nature somewhat differently. As Strinati puts it:

> Popular culture for the mass culture critics can either be defined as folk culture in pre-industrial societies, or as mass culture in industrial societies. For the Frankfurt School, popular culture is that mass culture, produced by the culture industry, which secures the stability and continuity of capitalism. The Marxist political economy perspective also comes close to this understanding of popular culture, while variants of feminist theory define it as a form of patriarchal ideology which works in the interests of men and against the interests of women. While the main tendency of semiology is to stress the role of popular culture in obscuring the interests of the powerful – in Barthes's view, the bourgeoisie – some structuralist theories see popular culture as an expression of universal and unchanging social and mental structures. Those writers who put forward a cultural populist approach tend to define popular culture as a form of consumer subversion which is precisely how they wish to evaluate and explain it. Lastly, according to postmodernist theory, popular culture embodies radical changes in the role of the mass media which efface the distinction between image and reality. (Strinati 1995: xvii–xviii)

Popular culture can be (and often is) described as 'counter culture' and is understood as a more-or-less deliberate rejection or subversion of 'high' or middle class/middle brow culture, by those who wish to disassociate themselves from the traditional moral and economic stance of the bourgeoisie. This is linked with the social changes already described, particularly the new sexual morality (or breakdown of family life, depending on your point of view), the burgeoning of eclectic taste and the virtual media culture, to suggest that contemporary culture is qualitatively different from that which went before and should therefore be described as postmodern (see e.g. Featherstone 1991; Kellner 1995b). Key characteristics of the postmodern condition are therefore seen as the abandonment of traditional values and the supposed authenticity which supported them, the willingness to explore individual personality and the belief that anything can mean whatever we wish it to mean. As Baudrillard put it in a 1984 interview:

> the characteristic of a universe where there are no more definitions possible. . . .
> One is no longer in a history of art or a history of forms. They have been

deconstructed, destroyed. In reality, there is no more reference to forms. It has all been done. The extreme limit of these possibilities has been reached. It has destroyed itself. It has deconstructed its entire universe. So all that are left are pieces. All that remains to be done is to play with the pieces. Playing with the pieces – that is postmodern. (Quoted in Kellner 1995b: 329)

Playing is taken to its logical conclusion in the multiple identities possible to those who join the Multiple-User-Dimension exchanges on the Internet sites (MUDS), and take on whatever range of sexual and social personas that they wish.

The contemporary collecting of objects can be seen to be permeated with social characteristics which may be described as postmodern. Postmodernism is about the presence of the past in the present, that is the fragmentation of the past in a belief that the narratives which connect past and present are merely the present viewing the past. Collecting is therefore an emblematic activity which ransacks the past to create a present idiosyncrasy of style. This both encourages and is encouraged by the demise of the grand shop as surely as that of the grand explanation, with their places taken by a series of market segments which differentiate groups and individuals.

All this helps the rise of new connoisseurs who can create new symbolic hierarchies of value through their gathering up of the material of mass culture, kitsch and the like, particularly when they associate this with playfulness, deliberate seriousness, or subversion. As a result, the old class-bound tastes and traditional values are made problematic. The new connoisseurship values excess – things which are 'too much' or 'over the top'. The essence (if this is the right word) of the postmodern position is irony, particularly in relation to cultural authority. It expresses itself in a fascination with discourse, with the underside of overt intention. Objects from the past amuse the sophisticated collector through their innocence of meaning. Phallic lipsticks, naive advertising, especially that featuring unreconstructed women, racist ashtrays, all these inspire satisfying mirth among knowing protagonists, and stimulate new narratives of life-style and meaning.

Social relations are seen to match. Much purchase or exchange is dense with raw humanity, in contrast to the perceived prim gentility of earlier shopping. People are scruffy, grubby, and do business in the anarchic haggling and chaffering of the open market. Trading is not apersonal, as in the supermarket, but naked eye to eye, intensive, sporadic, speculative, participatory and infinitely flexible. Many of the collectors who appear in recent discussions deal, and buy in order to sell, in order to buy more, or differently. Dealing opens opportunities, so that the dealers are often those who hold the best personal collections because they are best placed to take advantage of immediate opportunities.

Hand in hand with this goes the new approach to home, as the property market swings violently from bullish to bearish. Homes become increasingly identity cocoons as junk shops and remnant sales are rifled to create a sense of identity, which often rests in unexpected object combinations. Much of what is on show would seem bizarre to previous generations. Homes look more and more like old-fashioned museums, while modern museums look more and more like homes, so lines are blurred and authenticity dissolves.

Many contemporary collectors, especially in north America, were brought up in the abundance of the later 1950s and 1960s. Their mass accumulations as children of hoards of toys created the sense of possession as reassurance. The kind of education they received was most concerned to promote self-expression, and encouraged the development of special areas of expertise untrammelled by traditional value structures. This can easily become an interest in collecting and dealing, seen as rational economic activity which is fun too. It is also a 'comfort blanket', for its nostalgic character offers security as well as identity; something which, within postmodernism, can relieve the fracturing pains of the postmodern condition.

This point of view is tellingly illustrated by *Baby Boomer Collectibles*, subtitled *The Pop Culture Magazine*. This is published monthly from an address in Waupaca, Wisconsin, USA in order to bring together those who collect material from the Baby Boom generation, themselves usually Baby Boomers born in the years immediately following the Second World War, and connect them with each other and with suppliers. The first issue appeared in October 1993. It lists 64 advertisers, offering material from Pedal Car Graphics to Big Guys Toy Trucks, and special articles featured collectable Fiesta Dinnerware and Fifties Board Games. As John Koenig says in his introductory editorial:

> The closet I shared with my younger brother (yes to this day he's also a collector) was always overflowing with stamp albums and catalogs, those blue Whitman coin folders (my daughter has that habit now), and army men and Lincoln Logs and cars and trucks. Decades may have passed, but all that means is there is more stuff out there to find and collect. The next booth at the flea market may hold the treasure trove. Who knows what will be in the next garage sale? There's only one way to find out – dive in! That's what we're doing with this magazine. (Koenig 1993)

The appeal to sentiment, security and solidity together with the thrill of 'you never know', could not be made more clearly.

The perceived postmodern nature of contemporary collecting has not lacked its commentators. Martin sees it as an escapist response to the uncertainties – moral, social and economic – of the contemporary world, in a set of pairs which contrast collecting and 'real life' (Figure 1.4; Martin 1997). He stresses the permanency, cohesion and stability which collections offer through the control with which they endow their collector. Julian Walker, as a freelance artist, has undertaken a number of installations in a range of British museums. One in the Cuming Museum, London, in 1995, entitled 'Rows, Lines, Boxes', was accompanied by a sheet bearing a line of butterflies at the top, and two lines of cropped postage stamps half-way down. The text and its layout is shown in Figure 1.5. 'We make great

Collections	Real Life
Escapism	Entrapment
Fantasy	Factual
Familiar and comforting	Alien and harsh
Community (clubs)	Individualistic/atomised
Aesthetic currency	Fiscal restrictions
Real friends	Temporary acquaintances
Certainties	Doubts
Stable platform	Shifting sands
Controllable environment	Controlled by environment
Social cohesion	Social disintegration
Permanent	Transient
A known/safe past	Unknown future
Soothing/reassuring	Anxious/undermining
Actively rewarding	Passively repetitive

Figure 1.4   *Contrasting elements in Collections and Real Life*

structures out of our small repetitions', Walker says, and purchase 'with the eagerness of the panic-buyer'. The sheet itself is treated as a collector's item, signed and numbered by the artist.

The treatment of collecting as a postmodernist activity depends upon a number of premises. The first of these is that collecting is much more common, qualitatively as well as quantitatively, than it was before, say, 1950. This is going to remain a great unknown, because we have no reliable figures for collectors before current studies. Evidence from museums, local societies and similar sources suggests that as a proportion of the population, the number of collectors may not have changed as much as is sometimes suggested, but may have remained fairly constant during this century. Secondly, collecting is seen to involve now a much broader range of material, including commercially mass produced goods which are still in circulation or have only just gone out of it: the word for all this material is 'collectable', which sums up its 'invented' nature. This appears to be broadly true in that, for example, Edwardian material was not much collected in the 1920s, or Thirties material in the 1940s.

Thirdly, the new collecting scope is seen to be both a response to, and a part of, contemporary society and since contemporary society is characterised as 'postmodern' it follows that its collecting mode must be 'postmodernist'. This is clearly true in the simplistic sense that all activities are part and parcel of their own social context, whatever that context may be. However, if postmodernism is seen as an essentially self-conscious set of attitudes in which eclecticism, pastiche and assorted ironies are a necessary tone, if self-conscious participation in a sophisticated sense is integral to the postmodernist condition, then the relation of contemporary collectors to it is a matter for debate. It is a debate that will concern us as this book goes forward.

Part	of	the	desirability	of	objects
is	their	complicity	in	our	dominion
over	them,	their	willingness	to	sit
within	the	structures	we	make	for
them.	Observing	the	melancholy	of	these
lines,	columns	and	boxes	with	pleasure,
we	organise	our	knowledge	into	similar
compartments.	Our	actions	repeat	themselves,	and
always	fascinated	by	treasuries	of	smallness,
we	make	great	structures	of	our
small	repetitions;	we	construct	our	world
against	the	untutored	inevitability	of	untidiness.
Collecting	and	displaying	both	support	and
depend	on	an	ordered	view	of
the	universe,	an	awareness	of	the
set	(within	its	own	dynamics),	a
simultaneous	fascination	with	similarity	and	difference.
We	purchase	things	made	and	sold
in	limited	editions	with	the	eagerness
of	the	panic-buyer	or	the	butterfly-
hunter,	the	appeal	lying	in	the
comfort	of	the	repeated	act	as
much	as	the	exclusivity	of	the
club.	This	sheet	has	been	produced
in	a	limited	edition	of	50,
each	signed	by	the	author,	of
which	this	is	number	25	J C Walker

Figure 1.5 *Sheet accompanying installation at Cuming Museum 1995, produced by Julian Walker, a freelance artist who has carried out a number of museum installations*

The Present Study

The idea which informs this book is that collecting practice is significant in contemporary British society because it can tell us more about the nature of that society and of the individuals which comprise it; that since collecting practice is essentially an individual enterprise, understanding of it must start with the collectors themselves; and that collecting is embedded in the individual collector's emotional, economic and inter-personal life and so should be understood in these terms.

From this follows the need to identify approaches to data-gathering which are geared to the project in hand. The information upon which much of this book is based comes from a number of sources, most importantly, a nation-wide survey of contemporary collecting habits, the Contemporary Collecting in Britain Survey, mounted in 1993 aimed at gathering quantitative and qualitative information. Information has also been gathered about the People's Show Project carried out by British museums between 1992 and

1995. A second similar survey, the Relations with Objects Project, was carried out in 1996 (Pearce forthcoming), and some of the information from this has been drawn upon here with reference to particular issues. Finally, the broad collecting climate has been assessed through the gathering of material in the media, and through working with collections and collectors.

The Contemporary Collecting in Britain Survey (see Appendix) was based on a large-scale postal survey using the Total Design Method (Dillman 1978, 1983), chosen because is had proved to be very successful in a project undertaken by Merriman on the broadly similar topic of heritage awareness and visiting (Merriman 1991). The author had feared that, because collections are property and the population generally is very worried about levels of domestic burglary, suspicions would be felt about the *bona fides* of the Survey and the response rate would therefore be poor. Fortunately, this turned out not to be the case and the Survey yielded just under a 60% reply rate, considered excellent for such a subject. Presumably the respondents were reassured by the repeated assertions in the material sent to them that no record of names and addresses would be linked to replies unless the respondents themselves wished, although a number rang up to check before they replied (and so did officers of the various police forces who had been alerted to the Survey).

The Survey involved the sending of a questionnaire to 1500 randomly chosen adults (over 18) in Britain (Northern Ireland was not included). The first question asked was 'Do you collect anything?' and those who ticked 'Yes' were asked a further series of questions designed to throw light on their collecting history, practices and feelings. The final section of the questionnaire covered the usual basic personal information, and all respondents, collectors and non-collectors, were encouraged to complete this before return. The questionnaire included both the ticking of answer boxes and open-ended questions which called for a written reply, so giving both qualitative and quantitative information. It should be noted that all the percentages and charts and graphs showing percentages in this book derive from the findings of the Survey (and where percentages do not total 100% the missing element represents those respondents who failed to reply to a particular question, since this seems to represent realities best).

In its final form, the text of the questionnaire was designed to be as friendly as possible in order to encourage respondents. It was recognised that, while all this material was interesting and relevant, it would need to be organised into a different sequence for discussion, and this has been done. When the returning collector expressed a willingness to respond to a follow-up telephone interview, this was undertaken and noted: some 3% of the respondents were interviewed in this way.

The People's Show Project has proved to be a substantial source of qualitative or anecdotal information about contemporary collecting, as well as giving a range of quantitative information in its own right in relation to the project itself (Digger forthcoming; Lovatt 1997; see Chapter 4). Collectors who exhibited in the People's Shows in 1994 completed the same questionnaire as the Survey respondents (201 collectors). Their replies have been fed into the detailed discussion of individual collecting practices in this book, but have not informed any of the figures presented, or broad conclusions drawn from the figures.

Finally, a word should be said about the material relating to broader collecting practices, which – like the People's Show – are a part of the wider cultural scene. Collecting has made a major impact upon the media. National and regional newspapers now carry regular collectors columns, and frequent features. *The Antiques Road Show* on BBC1 has proved to be one of the most reliably popular programmes and has fathered a whole family of spin-offs in the shape of magazines, competitions and features in *Radio Times*, all of which have made presenter Hugh Scully a national figure (Coren 1993; Greaves 1991). Other producers and channels have not been slow to receive the message, with programmes about both collecting as such and about material culture and the significance of objects. BBC1 has offered the *Great Antiques Hunt*, and *Lovejoy* on the light drama side. BBC2 has *Small Objects of Desire, The Secret Life of* — (a given weekly object), *Signs of the Times*, the *A–B of Motoring* and *From Walpole's Bottom to Major's Underpants* (a three-part series on collectors of political satire cartoons).

Channel 4 has given us *For Love or Money* ('the magazine show that seeks to demystify the world of collecting, each week offering features and up-to-the-minute news', *Radio Times*, 15 October 1994: 81). On the same channel were *Visions of Heaven and Hell, Perpetual Motion* and *Scrimpers*. Carlton Television had *The Exchange*, an adult swap show. Radio 4 has offered *In Celebration of* — and editions of *Kaleidoscope*, and there have been innumerable features on the various local radios. *Scrimpers* had a particularly interesting focus on re-cycling, showing how a second use could be made of anything from tea bags to shirt buttons, and was seen not as personal meanness but as a way of subverting the manufacturers' wish for built-in obsolescence in a throw-away society.

The magazine publishers have not been slow to join. Millers have been publishing popular guides in the antique field for a long time, and in 1992 they launched a new 'popular' antique collectors' magazine. Marshall Cavendish launched *What's It Worth? The Complete Guide to Everyday Collectibles* in 1992. The first part featured 'The ever-popular rocking chair', 'Children's comics', and 'Is your teddy bear worth thousands?' Various groups of American collectors now have sites on the Internet and advertise their 'wants' over the web. Correspondingly, dealing is now relating to a more sophisticated market. A recently acquired leaflet, for the National Collector Corporation operating in the south-west USA, says 'Let America's Premier Collectibles Wholesaler help you with your next Acquisition or Liquidation. . . . We specialise in servicing private collectors, retail dealers, corporations, museums, restaurants and night-clubs.' The list tells us much about contemporary accounts of material culture.

This has its under-side. A quick scan of any tabloid newspaper, particularly the Sunday editions, will show a series of advertisements for sexually

Figure 1.6   *Relationship between collector and context*

explicit fetish ware in rubber latex and black leather(ette). The Anne Summers organisation, which sells fetish goods and sexual toys through home parties in the style pioneered by Tupperware (but more tupping than Tupperware) has attracted a good deal of attention. The preoccupation with fetishistic practice (in the Freudian sense) appears in pop music. Atticus quotes a lyric from American gangster rap: Nine Inch Nail's 'Big Man with a Gun', says 'I am a big man and I have a big gun, held against your forehead, I'll make you suck it, maybe I'll put a hole in your head, just for the fun of it' (Atticus 1995). All of this informs contemporary collecting and is informed by it. It is part of contemporary culture in Britain, and the debate about its nature, with which this book is concerned.

The organisation of the book is set out in skeletal form in Figure 1.6, which shows the collector as he perceives himself, the spider at the centre of the collecting web, the star-within-a-circle of individuality which interreacts with its surroundings. These surroundings are shown stylistically as a series of concentric rings each representing a sphere of activity in which the collector participates (or may participate). These embrace the relationship of gender to collecting, the role of family life, the interaction of the collector with the market, the relevance of work and play, and broad questions of social background and taste in objects. Surrounding the whole is contemporary society, which permeates all activity, and from which the material within collections is drawn. Needless to say, this is over-simplistic in every sense, because the various elements interact with each other and with the individual collector's personality in an infinite series of sequences. Nevertheless, it is a sketch which enables us to discuss the material under a series of headings which illuminate it. The range of elements have been conceived as running from the social and economic situation of contemporary society inwards through work and play, buying and giving, family and home, and gender, to the body and soul of the collector himself, represented in Figure 1.6 by the star. Some will say that this commits the sin of allowing to the collector an essential being which he does not possess, to which the reply is that, whether he does or not, each collector believes that he does, and that it is the collector's mentality which is our principle concern in the body of this book.

The following chapter asks and tries to answer the question of what things are collected, and by people from what background and social context. The next chapter asks how collectors integrate ideas about work and leisure or play into their habits, and their construction of a relationship with the 'outside' world. Chapter 4 is concerned with the relationship between the collector and the market place and with the dynamics of this aspect of consumption. Chapter 5 discusses how collecting operates within family and home.

Chapter 6 moves closer into the individual's centre by considering how collecting informs and is informed by concepts of gender. The following chapter concentrates upon the collector's inner life, of thought and feeling, especially as this relates to the physical world of body and material. The final chapter returns to the broader picture, and offers an integrated view of what collecting in contemporary Britain means.

2

Who and What

The broad parameters of this study have been set out in the first chapter and we must now move to specific questions, of which the first concerns the nature of the collectors and their collections. This raises issues about the relationship between material and the obvious broad distinctions between individuals – biographical in terms of gender and age group and status in terms of socio-economic class – as these are expressed in the collecting process. Moreover, just as populations can be (and generally are) divided into 'quality' groups which comprise 'higher' and 'lower' social classes, so material is traditionally allotted a place in the hierarchy of values, which revolve around its perceived qualities of 'high' or 'low' cultural value. We can, therefore, see that two distinct systems of character are involved, for both collector and collected. One revolves around a hierarchy of cultivation, taste or quality as this is seen to be demonstrated in the nature of objects, while the other embraces the distinctions of socio-economic and personal status which run across the human subjects.

This chapter, therefore, has two broad aims. It is intended to lay bare the proportionate relationships in the collecting group of respondents in terms of individual biographical and socio-economic characteristics, and relate these to the respondents as a whole and to the population at large. Some significant points resulting from this will be drawn out here, but the results will also be drawn on through the following chapters of the book. The second aim is focused on the relationship between class and collecting, conceived both as the socio-economic standing of humans and the traditional valuations of objects. This aspect of the discussion needs to be set in a wider context before we can embark on detailed consideration.

Analysis of the relationship between social class and taste in material has an honourable pedigree which begins with Pierre Bourdieu's seminal study of distinctions (1984), and progresses with Dittmar's studies, especially those of 1992, 1991 and, with others, 1989. Bourdieu's theory of the *habitus*, a conjunction between middle class wealth and stability and 'good' taste in which each reinforces the other and creates cultural capital to put beside financial capital, has received wide support. Cultural capital, derived from bourgeois background and traditional education, gives advantage in the job and marriage markets, and so helps to sustain the social structure. Any idea of real intrinsic material value does not greatly matter; the *social* effect of such beliefs is what counts. The notion of the *habitus* can be used to explain why popular culture is different from 'high' culture, and why their operation is class based. We can see the *habitus* working every time we switch from a symphony concert to a games show.

Dittmar's study (1991) of the meaning which men and women of different socio-economic strata in Britain attach to their personal possessions suggested that here Bourdieu's broad distinctions held good. Her business people were mostly concerned with their possessions as unique symbols which demonstrated their own personal history, and probably their good judgement and capacity as well. Her unemployed focused more upon what their possessions could do to help them in a more strongly utilitarian sense, suggesting their need for short-term economic and social security rather than longer-term investment. It should be recognised that Dittmar was here concerned with simple possessions rather than collections, and that her distinction between 'business people' and 'unemployed' is very coarse grained; however, her study throws up issues to which we shall return.

Opinions differ as to whether or not Britain is still a 'class-ridden society'. Professional sociologists usually point to the fundamental ways in which Britain has changed in the past 50 years and deduce from this that the old class basis has withered away. Most people living in Britain, however, point to the clear divisions within the education system, and the kinds of employment to which these usually lead, and take a more traditional view. Upward and downward mobility exists, it is felt, as it always did; but class perceptions and aspirations endure.

Under the old system, people were classified according to their employment: I professional, II managerial and technical, III non-manual skilled, IV manual skilled, V partly skilled and VI unskilled. Class I contains higher civil servants, doctors, lawyers and professors; II managing directors and lesser managers; and VI labourers. This roughly equated to upper-middle class (I and some of II), lower middle class (the rest of II and III); upper working class (IV and V) and lower working class (VI). In a parallel system much used by advertising and market research, letters were used in which As were I and some IIs, Bs roughly IIs, Cs III and IV, Ds V and Es VI.

This broad system is full of anomalies and lacks any coherent theoretical basis. In particular, occupation may not be a key indicator of social class but rather we should look to position within a local hierarchy and income: the supervisor of a group of manually skilled workers is arguably among the managerial class. In 1961 David Glass produced a system of classification by socio-economic groups which operates through 17 categories which can take account of employment relationships and size of organisation. This system, modified by David Rose, will be used by the Office of Population Censuses and Surveys for the 2001 Census. Perhaps the most interesting point within the plethora of technical distinctions is our abiding capacity to make sense of any, or all, of the systems. Any British person faced with any other will still make an immediate and finely tuned class assessment which is broadly compatible with, but more accurate than, any of the schemes.

Questions of class and its operation are among the most interesting in relation to a practice like collecting, which embraces a large and varied cultural capacity. We shall need to review these relationships in detail, but it is necessary first to form some view of the composition of the population of Britain in very broad terms, and relate this to both the Contemporary Collecting Survey respondents as a whole, and those respondents who declared themselves as collectors. This is a topic fraught with all manner of technical and operational difficulties, particularly in its need to define the population characteristics of contemporary Britain. This proviso must be borne in mind in what follows.

Accordingly the first part of this chapter will consider the personal and social characteristics of collectors and non-collectors, and will be followed by a brief discussion of the ethnic minority collectors as they appear in this study. The next part will consider what is collected in terms of specific types of material. The following section discusses the relationship of traditional material values to the collecting process, a very complex topic. The next part considers one of the key questions of the study, the relationship between socio-economic group and collection content. Finally, the conclusion returns to the discussion of the workings of the *habitus* in collecting, and draws together the threads.

Non-Collectors and Collectors: Personal and Social Characteristics

By the year 2025, all significant population growth will be in countries outside Europe. In Britain in 1971 one in four of the population was under 16, but by 2021 it will be only one in six, and by 2000 40% of the popularion will be over 45; correspondingly by 2021 this cohort will be over 65. Similar shifts are taking place across the rest of western Europe (Worcester 1996). In Britain, more than half the adult population is working, including the 27% of men and 11% of women who work full-time, and the 14% who work part-time, 82% of whom are women. Increasingly, and now for more than 50%, this work is structured as self-employment, short-term contract, or various forms of moon-lighting, with consequent effects upon long-term personal financial planning like house buying on mortgage, pensions and insurance (Law 1994). Within the British population 5.5% are from non-white ethnic groups. 40% of British marriages now end in divorce, 30% of children are born to unmarried parents and 30% of children are living with a single parent. Women make up 52% of the population as a whole (Smith 1994). One person in three receives some state benefit and one in four depends upon state benefit: this is often described as the culture of welfare dependency. Conversely, social security costs each working person £15.00 per day. Probably something like 45% of contemporary Britons could make a serious claim to possessing at least some aspects of traditional middle class characteristics: a very large middle class is a most salient social fact in northern Europe and north America.

If the respondents to the Survey, therefore, are broadly in line with the population as a whole, they should show a general fit to the fundamental

Table 2.1   *Relationship of Survey respondents to the general population, and of collecting respondents to non-collectors*

	Population at large (%)	All respondents to survey (%)	Collecting respondents to survey (%)
Men	48	45[b]	42
Women	52	55	58
White	94.5	98	97
Non-white	5.5	2	3
Over 45 years	36	45	36
Under 45 years	64	55[c]	64
Partnered	74[a]	64	65
Non-partnered	11[a]	32	35

[a]   Includes couples with no children, dependent children and non-dependent children, taken from the 1992 General Household Survey, Office of Population, Censuses and Surveys data.

[b]   All in this column represent percentage of those who replied to the relevant question.

[c]   Does not include any under 18 years.

parameters which constitute the contemporary inhabitants of Britain outside Northern Ireland. They should reflect the general proportions of men (48%) to women (52%), of white (94.5%) to non-white (5.5%) ethnic groups, of those over 45 years (about 36%) to under 45, and married or permanent partnered (74%) to those who live alone or as single parents (11%). Table 2.1 sets out the relevant data.

It shows that the proportion of male and female replies fits the national situation reasonably well, particularly as there is a suspicion that on this kind of topic women may be rather more willing to complete and return questionnaires than men, in spite of broad trends to the contrary. White respondents loom larger than they should (see below). Those over 45 years are over-represented as against those under 45, but it must be remembered that as selection was based on the Electoral Roll, nobody under 18 was included. It is likely that, if the population figures were similarly calculated, the relationship between the first two columns would be closer. The figures for partnered as against non-partnered, on the other hand, seem to represent the real difference made by the disproportionately heavy response from the 18–25 age group who collect but are as yet unpartnered.

The proportions of those who replied to the Survey saying that they collect compare fairly well to both the respondents overall, and to the general population, in the gender and age group categories. The figures for partnership continue to reflect the young group. Apart from this over-emphasis, the percentages do suggest that, very broadly, the replies received overall were not grossly unrepresentative of the proportion as a whole. Similarly, the percentages of those who declared themselves as collectors relate reasonably well to the replies as a whole, and to the general population. The figures encourage us to suppose that, overall, the profile of the contemporary collecting population does not differ markedly from that of the general population as a whole.

Collectors, therefore, are not a different or in any meaningful sense a particular personally characterised group either within the survey respondents, or within the population as a whole; on the contrary they are drawn proportionately from the general population. They are simply a segment, or a substantial minority of the population who happen to pursue a particular practice. This is a very significant point, and when the collecting group is broken down into its components further significances within it emerge.

Of those who replied saying that they did collect, 42% were men and 58% were women. This suggests that the number of men and women collecting in Britain today is slightly weighted in favour of women. This is in defiance of the accepted wisdom, which draws on the evidence of past museum accessions registers and the membership of a rather limited range of collectors' clubs, particularly those devoted to traditional material like stamps and coins, to suggest that more men collect than women. Evidence is now beginning to build up from work done at the Victoria and Albert Museum and elsewhere which suggests that a significant number of women were collecting material like china, postcards and the decorative arts through the twentieth and nineteenth centuries, and back into the later part of the eighteenth century. The bulk of this collecting activity, however, has to be discovered through study of diaries, memoirs and the like because (for reasons which will be discussed in Chapter 6), the collections themselves seldom survive, unlike the material amassed by men. Certainly in contemporary Britain there seem to be rather more women collectors than men.

The age of those collecting showed as fairly stable across the age range, apart from the over-65s who registered as 8%. The largest percentage of collectors came in the younger age groups with the 18–25-year-olds at 23%, the 26–35s at 22% and the 36–45s at 22%. Middle age saw a drop, firstly to 13% for the 46–55s and then to 15% for the 56–65s. This seems to make sense in terms of broad life patterns. Young people have fewer working and domestic commitments and more spending money. The thinness of the retired over-65s came as no surprise, for by this age people have frequently begun to make provision for the period of incapacity or death and to distribute their worldly goods accordingly. Correspondingly, the period between 56 and 65 is often a good time of life, with a resurgence of youthful freedom and spending power, while that between 46 and 55 is often characterised by demanding (and expensive) young-adult children and heavy workloads. In general we can see a peak of collecting in early adulthood, followed by a steady flow in the prime and early middle age, followed by a second peak in the later fifties/early sixties, followed by a sharp decline after 65.

Access to a car is, at 83% of collectors, around the national norm. Sixty-five per cent of collectors said they had a partner, and of the 35% who said they had not, a substantial proportion must fall within the 23% of 18–25 age range who are not yet living with a partner. These figures are very close to those who replied that they did not collect, among whom 67% had partners. Similarly, 61% of the collectors had children, while 64% of the non-collectors had them. The information about family situations, together with that about the cars, shows very clearly that collectors are living personal lives which do not differ from those of non-collectors, and which are 'normal' in terms of human sexual and familial relationships in contemporary Britain. The point is an extremely important one, because the stereotype of the collector is of a dispiriting, anorak-clad loner who is unable to form personal relationships, especially with the opposite sex, and who uses collecting as a substitute for personal emotional satisfaction. This image recurs in the media and in cartoons, and forms part of the mind-set of most non-collectors. It seems to stem from the studies undertaken by psychologists between 1920 and 1940, who used theories and sublimation of sexual needs (Abraham 1927), anal retention (Jones 1950) and general inadequacy (Fenichel 1945) to explain the urge to collect. We can see from the information here that this targeting of collectors is both unjust and beside the point. Whatever the characteristics of humans may be as such, and whatever special traits collectors may have which create their accumulating habit, in terms of their personal relationships they are no different from the rest of the population.

We can see, looking at this data across the board, that both men and women collect, with women rather more evident, and that they do so across the age range, but with an emphasis on the earlier part of life and with a distinct falling off after 65. Around two-thirds of the collectors had partners and families, and this matches the national pattern. The quantitative evidence shows how unhelpful it would be to over-state or over-simplify the picture which emerges. Nevertheless, broadly speaking, the third of the population who collect belong within that segment of the broader population who are young or young middle-aged adults, and live in family groups. In personal terms, it represents people who seem to have relatively stable lives which are 'normal' in the traditional sense.

All of these 'normal' collectors, of course, like the non-collectors, fit into the class or employment system previously described. Table 2.2 sets out the employment analysis list based on material which respondents provided about the principal wage earner in the family. Very mixed information was given in answer to this question, which was frequently a combination of the nature of employment used in the old scheme of numerical analysis and the socio-economic level of employment used in Rose's new scheme. Consequently, the 10 categories of employment used here try to embody this combined approach in order to reflect the collectors' perceptions of themselves as well as external judgements. Table 2.2 also shows the grouping of the types of employment into broader social categories, and uses the A/B/C/ D/E system because collecting has obvious links to advertising and consumer research. Finally, the ancient class terminology is added in order to provide an *aide-mémoire* for what the letters may mean, and to root the

Table 2.2   *Employment categories among Survey respondents and analysis of socio-economic class*

Employment	% in survey	Class definitions		
Professions (doctor, architect)	17	I	A	Upper middle class
Finance/company directors	6	I	A	Upper middle class
Scientific and technical, senior managers	15	II	B1	Middle middle class
Middle managers	12	II	B2	Middle middle class
Lower managers, clerks, clerical officers	10	III	C1	Lower middle class
General dealers, sales, shopkeepers, self-employed	11	IV	C2	Lower middle class
Construction workers, skilled workers	10	IV	D1	Upper working class
Transport drivers, postmen	7	IV	D2	Upper working class
Manufacturing, semi-skilled (in mining, quarries, agriculture, fisheries)	6	V	D3	Middle working class
Manual labourers	6	VI	E	Lower working class
unemployed	1.6	Technically E		
students	2.5	No information		
retired	0.8	No information		

discussion in the kinds of language which is still (for better or worse) commonly used to discuss class issues in Britain.

The percentage figures for the collecting groups have been added to Table 2.2. This shows that about 23% of the collecting respondents belonged within an upper middle class grouping, reckoning that this class holds highly qualified professionals and senior businessmen. The large and very complex middle and lower middle class groupings represent respectively 27% and 21% of collectors. The equally complex upper working class covers 17%, and the middle working class 6%. The lower working, or unskilled manual labouring, class comprised 6%.

Three classes of (un)employment could not be brought into this scheme: all were very small. The students (2.5%) are statistically more likely to come from middle class backgrounds, and to enter such employment, but while they remain students they are 'classless'. Those who scored themselves as retired (0.8%) gave no indication about the employment they had left. The unemployed (1.6%) might once have been counted as technically E, but now might come from any employment group. It should be noted that in the general population the unemployed group runs at 48%. However, this includes large numbers of women who are not seeking employment, and those of both sexes who are retired. It was difficult to bring this broad figure into any meaningful relationship to the way the Survey had been carried out. All of these three categories are left out of account in any subsequent discussions of employment later in the book, unless they are specifically referred to in relation to particular circumstances.

As is obvious from the figures set out in Table 2.2, the upper middle class is over-represented in the Survey, and possibly the middle middle class is too. However, given that so large a proportion of contemporary people in Britain would make a claim to middle class status, this disproportion must not be over-emphasised. Correspondingly, the D2s, D3s and Es are under-represented. This, of course, represents the questionnaire-returning habits of the British population, and will skew the answers to questions like the area in which collectors live. Over half (53%) of the collectors scored themselves as living in a small town or village, a factor somewhat at variance with national trends. Twenty per cent of the collectors said they lived in large towns and 16% in city suburbs, while 11% counted themselves as coming from city centres.

However, the under-represented groups are well enough represented for detailed comparisons of responses to be made, and these show that in areas of habit, feeling and action there is little or no difference in the approach to collecting taken by the different socio-economic groups. This is demon-strated across the Survey where the responses to individual questions plotted against occupation of respondent show that occupation is not a significant parameter in most cases, although of occasional importance, for example, in the size of collections (see below) or the readiness to belong to a collecting club (see Chapter 3). A range of key questions plotted against employment is given in Figure 2.1. In terms of the links between collections and work and home, in feelings about likely completion or closure, and inability to contemplate selling if the piece was valuable enough, it seems that people in all walks of life feel much the same. The actual percentages show the relative proportions of the different types of employment but the graph pattern shows that feelings and personage linkages which the collections embody are pretty similar for us all. The point is a very significant one: it seems that, by and large, socio-economic group is not a factor that greatly affects collecting practice.

Ethnic Minorities

The 1991 census counted a British ethnic minority population of just over 3 million, or 5.5% of the total population. South Asians make up about half this total: there are 840,000 Indians, 477,000 Pakistanis, 103,000 Bangladeshis and 157,000 Chinese. The Caribbean population numbered 500,000 and the Africans 212,000 (Peach 1996). The Chinese, African and Indian groups are highly professionalised, while at the other end of the scale the Pakistani, Bangladeshi and Caribbean populations are predominantly in manual occupations, but unemployment for Caribbeans runs at 18.6%, twice the national average. Asians usually live in tight-knit extended families with male heads, while Caribbean households frequently have female heads, often as a single parent. Unlike most of their Asian counterparts, these women frequently have white-collar and professional employment.

In the Survey overall, 72% scored themselves as white, and a further 25% did not complete this section. The remaining 3% represent the declared

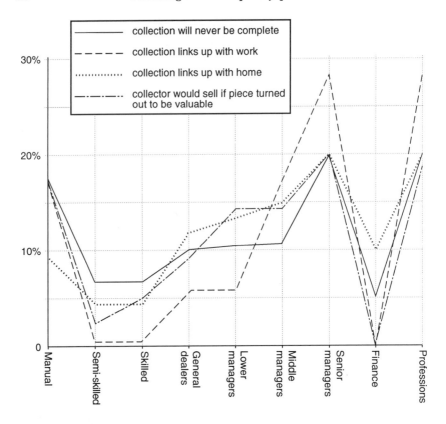

Figure 2.1 *Comparison of collecting approach among different socio-economic groups*

ethnic minority, and this split at 0.5% Afro-Caribbean, 2% Asian and 0.5% 'Other'. Clearly, the turn-out of non-whites was lower than their proportion in the general population, and they are therefore not represented fairly in the sample. It should be said, however, that among all those who did respond to this question, white non-collectors made up 95% and white collectors 97% and non-whites ran at correspondingly 5% and 3%.

The returns for non-whites are so small, in both real and percentage terms, that no effort has been made to separate them out in any of the discussions in this book. The details of their collecting habits as represented on the questionnaires (and in the sparse general anecdotal information) suggest that their collecting processes operate in the same ways as the British population at large, and they have been treated as a part of that population. Two replies may be singled out which make these points at individual level.

The Vase Collector scores herself as an Asian woman. She has under ten vases, and has them on display in the bedroom, the lounge and the bathroom. She started when she received a porcelain vase from her sister as an

Table 2.3   *Collection content types: analysis of Survey returns*

Nature of content	% in survey	Traditional value
Natural history (all types)	3	
Coins, medals, stamps (all types)	10	
Militaria (guns, weapons, military uniforms)	2	
Historical material (all types)	1	Authentic artefact
Musical instruments	1	
Jewellery and clothes	2	
Machinery (historic tractors, computer types)	2	
Toys	10	
Works of 'art' as traditionally identified	2	Authentic art
Room ornaments (detailed examination of responses suggests most belong here)	25	
Pop art (posters, memorabilia)	1	Inauthentic art
Tourist goods	8	
Sporting material (posters, trophies)	3	
Household goods (tea towels, egg cups)	15	Inauthentic artefact,
Drink and tobacco, spirit miniatures	3	as collected
Records, books, CDs, videos, photographs	13	Not easily classifiable

anniversary present. She worries a little at the cost of buying the vases, but she 'loves the way they are made different from one another'. The Coin, Stamp and Badge Collector scores himself as an Asiatic doctor. He has up to one hundred pieces and organises them by country, age and face value. They are kept in the bedroom in a chest of drawers. He regards them as both decorative and an investment, and shows the material to fellow collectors. As those who pursue this book will see, these collecting traits are so typical of collectors in general that they could almost stand as a paradigm of contemporary collecting practice in the broad sense.

What and How Much is Collected?

Collectors were considerably more specific about what they collected than they were about the occupation of their wage-earner. This enabled the creation of an amalgamated list of collection types which is set out in Table 2.3, together with the respective percentage figures. To the scheme in Table 2.3 is also added the broader (and therefore admittedly more

debatable) categories which endeavour to place material within the framework of traditional values, to which we must turn in a moment.

Records, tapes, CDs and videos were put in a group together, and books
and photographs were added to the same group. This kind of material
presents an obvious difficulty in a study of collecting. If material of this
kind is gathered principally to play or read, in other words the material is
valued as *media*, then it represents at least a particular aspect of collecting
and may, indeed, not fall into any useful collecting remit at all. If, however,
the material is treated as *object*, and collected for its historical value as first
edition or memory of a particular performance then it falls into line with
more 'normal' collecting process. In practice, most collections of recorded
and published material fall between the two, just as, for example, collections
of sporting material or militaria and firearms do. Throughout this study,
therefore, the records group has been treated just like any other, unless any
difference is made clear. This material is not, however, readily classifiable in
terms of traditional values – at least material ones – and so is recorded
separately in Table 2.3.

In terms of material, the greatest number of collections fell into two
groups: room ornaments (25%) and household goods (15%). The next
greatest was recorded material (13%). Toys came in at 10%, tourist goods at
8% and coins, medals and stamps at 10%. The other groups all scored only
a few percentages each (Table 2.3). The ornaments and household goods
between them account for 56% of all female collections, and records 24% of
male collections: these are the only peaks which show up here.

The gender difference in collecting terms was very stark. All the machinery, the musical instruments and the militaria were collected by men, who
also had 86% of the sporting material and 72% of the recorded material.
Women hold 87% of the household collections, 83% of the room ornaments
and 80% of the jewellery, with 72% of the tourist goods. They also tend to
hold the pop material. The remaining classes of material are more evenly
divided. The room ornaments are held chiefly by those between 46 and 65
years old, with the other age groups broadly evenly represented across the
age range.

Access to transport was very high across all types of collection holders,
with the exception of the musical instrument holders (who are numerically
very few) and the record collectors, most of whom belong in the youngest
age range and are generally car-less. Possession of a partner was pretty
evenly divided across the groups, although the militaria, history material
and musical instrument collectors were all partner-less, while those with pop
and paintings were generally partnered. A very similar pattern was revealed
in the analysis of possession of children.

Across the board, the collections being formed are rather smaller than
might have been supposed. Fifty-five per cent of collections involve fewer
than about 50 pieces, and of these 10% have fewer than about 10 pieces and
27% number in the twenties, thirties and forties. Forty-five per cent of the
collectors had amassed the larger collections, with over half of these (28%)

containing over 100 objects. This is more than just a quantitative difference. The larger the collection, on the whole, the larger it looms in the individual's life and that of his family. Clearly, the larger collections represent, usually, the larger investment in human capital, in terms of money spent, time and trouble taken, and space devoted; we must never forget that, collections being material, the bigger they are the more they impose themselves physically on the surroundings of the collector. This is not to overlook the fact that some collections comprising many objects – Victorian Valentines, for example – can fit into a small suitcase. It is not to deny, either, the significance of the smaller groups, many of which can be just as much the source of important feelings and, in particular, can work powerfully as memories of past events.

In gender terms, the largest collections are held very definitely by men: 63% of these are owned by males as opposed to 37% by females. Men are just ahead in the ownership of the next largest group of between 51 and 100 pieces. Women predominate in the lower registers, with 31% as opposed to 19% of collections of between 21 and 50 pieces being held by women, and 14% against 6% of the smallest groups of under 10 pieces. To put the matter in terms of the collectors, rather than the collections, Figure 2.2 shows the complementary gender based pattern very clearly. Here let us simply mark the contrast: it can be interpreted in a number of ways, which must wait until Chapter 6.

Most of the largest collections (55%) are held by the youngest (18–25) age group, with the rest of these distributed fairly evenly across the age range. The over-65s had 44% of the collections of 51–100 pieces, with again a fairly even spread of this size of collection otherwise. The smaller size collections were held in roughly even proportions across the age range. This probably reflects the very large collections of recorded material held by many of the young adults in the collecting world. Access to a car and the possession of a partner showed no significant pattern, but sizes of collection in relation to children did show a complementary pattern in which those with children possessed a decreasing proportion of the whole down the collecting scale and those without children the opposite (Figure 2.2).

The bulk of the collections were concentrated in the smaller communities, reflecting the overall pattern of replies, and most (71%) of the smallest collections were also held here. Similarly, the greatest proportion of collections of all sizes were held by the broad managerial group, among whom the medium sized collections (21–50 pieces) were most evident at 58%. The 51–100 sized collections loomed largest in the manufacturing group. These, therefore, are the two most common kinds of collections-in-ownership across the board. In terms of individual occupations, the manual workers showed an almost complete preference for the very large collections and the semi-skilled for the 21–50 piece medium-sized collections; otherwise preferences were spread relatively evenly across the occupation range.

In terms of size of collection in relation to material, the largest collections are those of historical material and musical instruments, which were all over

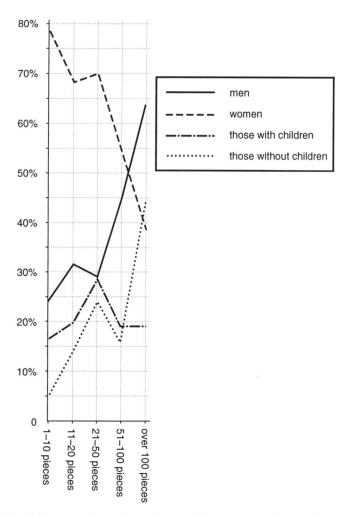

Figure 2.2 *Collectors and gender: analysis of Survey returns by size of collection*

100 pieces. Around 60% of the sporting, record and household collections were in this large group, and so were 50% of the militaria collections. The toys and the drink and tobacco came in at around 40% in the largest class. The remainder of these collections, and the rest of the collection types were divided fairly evenly across the other size groups; the machinery, for example appeared at 25% in the 1–10 pieces group, 25% in the 51–100 and the room ornaments at 20%, 25%, 27%, 17% and in the largest class, 11%. It may be worth noting that natural history, coins, history material and musical instruments made a very thin showing in the smaller groups, perhaps suggesting a commitment to more extensive accumulating in these areas.

The simple categorisation of types of material and sizes of collections, however, conceals the fact that, in terms of traditional value structures, the kinds of objects are perceived very differently. The traditional qualities of the object groups need different discussion.

Traditional Valuations

In 1970–1 the Wichita Art Museum (Kansas) put together an exhibition called 'Kitsch: The Grotesque Around Us' which toured the most important art venues in the central USA, and in 1972 formed part of the vast kitsch potpourri assembled in Kassel, Germany, for the fifth in the series of art exhibitions known as Documenta, which had an important kitsch segment. The intention of the original exhibition was to 'criticise kitsch . . . precisely because we do believe in the potentialities of ordinary people. Those so-called designers, technicians, idea-men and manufacturers who profess to provide mass man what he wants in reality perpetuate bad taste and maintain the low common denominator made manifest here' (Adlmann 1970 n.p.). Similarly, the intent of the kitsch section at Kassel was to provoke serious discussion of a bizarre phenomenon – in existence since the Industrial Revolution – namely, the proliferation of commercial objects whose function is to amuse and divert the mass consumer, feeding upon his unfortunate concept of what constitutes art, good taste, or cultivation (Adlmann 1973: 19).

There are a number of significant words in Adlmann's statements. 'Kitsch' is bizarre and grotesque; it has to do with art, good or bad taste and cultivation; it seems to involve a commercial plot against ordinary people, but these people need amusement because they have unfortunate ideas; it has been going since around the 1800s; and it needs criticism. The contents of the Wichita exhibition show what Adlmann meant. As he says, 'The purveyors of kitsch have long discovered their most successful targets. The Achillean heel of the insensitive but culturally aspiring mass consumer is foreseeably a constellation of his religion, his patriotism, his hopelessly ill-prepared approach to great art and – his sex life' (Adlmann 1970).

Religious kitsch was represented by items which, one way or another, offered bastardised versions of Dürer's praying hands called 'Hands of an Apostle'. These included a plastic 'nite-lite', a tooth pick holder in ceramic, and bookends in plaster-of-paris. Patriotism brings us American Colonial Everything from television sets housed in kitsch cupboards to electric cookers disguised as black iron wood-stoves. People buy fake walnut toilet lids emblazoned with a bronze eagle and dress up their 'home entertainment centre' with a George Washington ice bucket. Art is regularly abused by showing the Mona Lisa's face on everything from sweat-shirts to shopping bags, suitably embellished by ballooned comments of contemporary relevance. Two birds are killed with one stone when a firm offers da Vinci's The Last Supper printed on canvas ready for cross-stitching and home display.

Sex was represented by pieces like the naked female nutcracker who cracks nuts between her legs, or the garden ornament showing an indecently cute girl-child pulling up her frock (and garden ornaments are a particularly rich sub-set of this whole genre). Where sex goes, scatology will not be far behind. The innumerable figures of little boys peeing were represented at Wichita by a 'Mannequin Pis' whisky dispenser, and by a vaguely classical figure in the traditional thoughtful mode seated on a lavatory inscribed 'Congratulations on your new position'.

We see that kitsch combines or contains elements like mild indecency intended to raise a snigger. It involves an inappropriate use of an image or a shape, what Adlmann describes as the 'gross transposition of the function or concept of an object for novel effect' (1970). Kitsch is fake and reproduction, using the wrong colours and the wrong materials for the subject matter; it is 'mechanical and operates formulas. Kitsch is vicarious experience and fake sensations . . . kitsch is the epitome of all that is spurious in the life of our times. Kitsch pretends to demand nothing of its customers except their money – not even their time' (Rosenberg and White 1957: 102).

The success of kitsch in the market place is assumed to be a result of the 'aesthetic insensibility of the urban masses . . . feeding upon that insecurity that mass man feels in the face of genuine culture, the authors and manufacturers of kitsch fabricate their vague approximations of high art [as] "what the public wants"' (Adlmann 1970) but, as Macdonald points out '"I like what I get" is not the same as "I get what I like"' (Macdonald 1952). Commercial design then becomes a matter of giving the public what they unfortunately desire, pandering prostitute-like to their sadly meretricious tastes, or of educating them towards better things, but, in either case, of taking responsibility.

The meaning of the word 'kitsch' has been much debated (Dorfles 1969). The original German may have come from *kitschen*, to collect rubbish in the street, or *etwas verkitschen* to 'knock off cheaply', or to put together sloppily. It is worth noting that in the English of England, German words, unlike those of French, Spanish or Hindi, are only used to describe qualities or events (*Blitz, Schwärmerei, Schadenfreude*) for which the locals like to feel that they are innocent of native vocabulary. But given that kitsch exists as a category separable from other artefacts, and that it has these characteristics, why is it bad? How do design, mode of manufacture and raw material come to be moral qualities?

Kitsch has been with us since the mature phase of the industrial revolution, or put another way, one reason why the factory revolution happened was because there was a steadily growing appetite for consumer goods mass produced quickly and cheaply, the origins of which lay further back in English history (Campbell 1987). At this point, runs the story, culture, particularly material culture, began to diverge into its two streams, high and low (and perhaps a third, if middle-brow is counted). High maintained its aesthetic and moral qualities, low degenerated and disintegrated into the mass production which we see. Goodness then becomes bound up with education, with the opportunity for broad experience especially travel, and with the money to afford all these things, together with the cost of craft goods made of proper materials, in a word, Bourdieu's *habitus* of cultural capital (1977).

In the great tradition of high culture, authenticity and value is held to reside within a series of paradigms or vector valuations upon which objects can be placed as in a grid of worthiness (Figure 2.3). If an object scores highly in several vectors, it is correspondingly important, so a Roman bronze, for example, is made of quality material, rare, authentic, craft wrought and so on, while the Mona Lisa tee-shirts are none of these things. In practice, much of the argument hangs on material made from plastic, which lends itself particularly to cheap, coloured reproduction and near-reproduction artefacts (Mossman 1997).

In some collecting practice, however (and perhaps in other kinds of practice too), kitsch is not as simple as this. For many people it has a subversive, ironic capacity which is innate in its cultural awfulness. Such people compete to find objects which over-reach all others in bad taste, using this as a mental vehicle with which to comment upon the nature of society and human nature. 'Society' may be conceived as the custom and class-bound community which a postmodernist outlook sees itself as leaving behind. Kitsch can be seen as the bits and pieces of an old culture, which, eclectic and pastiche as they are, have the capacity to take on new meanings in which history is dead and all things are to be re-created from the *bricolage* which lies to hand.

This might be called the 'camp' aspect of kitsch, and of collecting it. Stewart quotes the *American Heritage Dictionary*'s definition of camp as 'an affectation or appreciation of manners and tastes commonly thought to be outlandish, vulgar or banal . . . to act in an outlandish or effeminate manner' (1984: 168). In popular parlance 'camp' means chiefly self-conscious and affected effeminacy, and it is interesting here to note one recent discussion of culture by the journalist Brian Sewell where he remarks 'it is odd how many collectors have been homosexual, and how many homosexuals have collected kitsch' (Sewell 1991). The first suggestion – that collectors tend to be homosexual – is, as we have seen, untrue. The second is untested, but seems to involve as many or more people who find it amusing to affect a kind of effeminacy in one aspect of their lives, as those who might count themselves as actually homosexual. This kind of flirtation can, of course, mean a degree of suppression elsewhere, but this may not be as helpful as it seems because most studies make it clear that cultural gender is more complex than physical sex, and so, presumably, gender flirtation can have a wide appeal. What is important here is that 'camp' is taken to mean 'self-conscious kitsch' with all the flirting that this involves, and since kitsch belongs within the male world of production but is received as part of the female world of fashionable consumption, the imaginative play embraced in treating it ironically is bound to partake of both genders.

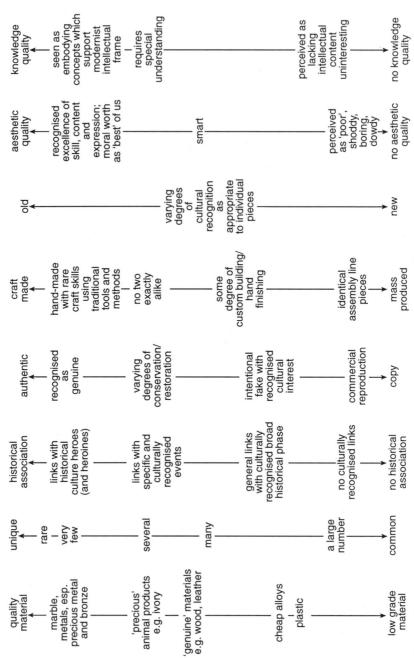

Figure 2.3 *Paradigms of value in objects and collections*

The world of kitsch is complemented by that of rubbish, using the word in its loosest sense. This, like kitsch, has stimulated its theorists as part of the postmodern examination of value structure (Carman 1990; Thompson 1979). The notion of rubbish nestles closely with the concept of commodity and the idea that objects have social life histories in much the same way that we do ourselves (Kopytoff 1986). Objects, being physical as we are (and as nothing else is apart from landscape) operate within the parameters of time and space. They have a moment when they are 'born', that is newly produced, and they run through a cycle, or perhaps several cycles, of use, and finally they, like us, must die, although their material dissolution can be very extensively delayed.

Within this life cycle objects have a period or periods when they are 'commodities', that is a thing 'with use value which also has exchange value' and which has this value not just because it is a thing but because it is 'also culturally marked as being a certain kind of thing' (Kopytoff 1986: 4). That is to say, at certain moments an object is invested with exchange value by reason of the symbolic or socially endowed values which it embraces, such as fashionable novelty and newness, or a relatively high place in the value parameters set out in Figure 2.3. At other times the object does not attract these notions of value, and is therefore said to be 'rubbish'.

Thompson (1979) argues that the state, or status, of rubbish follows hard upon that of birth, or production and entry into the market, on the assumption that nobody knowingly produces things which nobody wants. In these terms, therefore, kitsch is not rubbish, because it can command a buying public. But once the newness or fashionableness of a piece has worn off, it will be commercially worthless, another way of saying that its symbolic values have drained away. It descends into the rubbish class. There are exceptions to this sequence: some objects in the modern world, like gem stones, major pieces of ancient art, and perhaps some furniture, never slip down into rubbish, but such object groups are few and far between. For the majority of material goods, Thompson's view holds good, and it applies, of course, as much to kitsch as to everything else.

'Ordinary' or 'everyday' commodities, therefore, fall within the space of rubbish once they have been purchased. The act of buying a sweat-shirt or a spice jar turns it immediately into 'second-hand', the monetary value of which is much less than its original shop price. As it is worn or used, its value declines until it has dwindled to next to nothing. Collections composed of this kind of material, whatever they may mean to their owner, lack social symbolic content and are therefore commodities turned into rubbish.

Somewhere between kitsch and everyday commodities stands the world of tourist goods, the huge range of objects which are sometimes 'everyday' goods masked with special logos and phrases through which tourist attractions merchandise themselves, and are sometimes pieces within the kitsch class, often small replicas of a famous piece, again often suitably inscribed. These follow the life path of all other goods: once they are bought they sag immediately into the rubbish class. Tourist objects, as Stewart points out, represent an appropriation of the exotic, seen as distant or old, into the interiority of one's own life (1984: 147–150). This involves an estrangement of the piece from its own use context into the appropriator's display context.

This is particularly true of tourist material from the developing or (in north America) the First World, which often take the form of replicas of indigenous cultural material. As Graburn showed, such material often comprises miniatures of traditional artefacts, which gives them an 'applicability for decorative use, economy of materials, and a doll-like folkloristic quality not associated with the real article' (Graburn 1979: 15). Similarly, Bascom has found that in African tourist art the stylistic trends can be discerned: the replacement of traditional stylisation by European conventions of naturalism, realism and the picturesque; equally, a tendency towards the opposite extreme of the grotesque; and finally a tendency towards giganticisim, in which things are made much bigger than tradition dictates (Bascom 1979: 313–314). Much the same is true of contemporary Inuit 'art'. All this helps the distancing and de-contextualising process, although the irony is that what the tourist supposedly most values, 'real' contact with a 'really different' culture, is that most subverted by the demands of the tourist market.

Griemas and Rastier (1968), followed by Clifford (1988) and Pearce (1995: 288), have devised a scheme through which the valuations given symbolically to material by society can be expressed (Figure 2.4). This is structured by the two axes of authentic/non-authentic or spurious and masterpiece/artefact, which produce four quadrants giving, respectively, authentic masterpieces, spurious masterpieces, authentic artefacts and spurious artefacts. The first of these contains accredited high art and applied art (e.g. early silverware), together with spectacular natural history specimens ('God's masterpieces'). The second holds everything which pretends to be high art but is not, like kitsch, much giftware, airport art, and much pornography, whether collected sincerely or in fun. Here, too, belong the perverted natural history collections of unpleasant taxidermy.

The artefact classes need to be considered more carefully. Obviously all artefacts are 'authentic' in the sense that they were all made for a genuine reason which, for 'non-art', is a mingling of symbolic function or perceived utilitarian function. Here, it seems, lies the difference between authentic and spurious artefacts. Authentic artefacts are those which, when collected, are deemed to be of value because they offer insights, however flawed, into the society which made and used them originally. Into this category, therefore, falls 'historical' and 'anthropological' material, that is material culture from societies other than that of the collector. Here, too, are the bulk of the national specimens, collected for their knowledge value rather than their aesthetic properties. Knowledge value overall is the key to the authentic artefact quadrant.

Non-authentic artefacts are those currently available in the western world which are collected not in order to study aspects of contemporary society

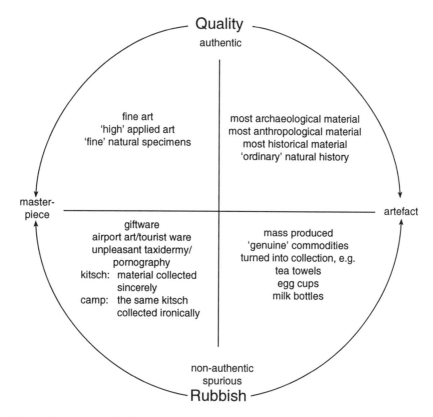

Figure 2.4 *Axes of value in objects and collections*

but for the sake of collecting as such. Mass produced commodities are given a spurious character in terms of social values through the process of collecting, that is that they are treated as if they had a cultural value, although society traditionally denies this value to them. Here they contrast with kitsch, to which society does accord cultural value, either genuinely admiring or ironic.

We can see, then, that contemporary collecting involves several modes in relation to this broad band of material. Kitsch is collected quite sincerely for its perceived attractiveness. It is also collected ironically as camp. Tourist pieces, spiritually close to kitsch, are similarly collected sincerely and in fun. 'Ordinary' commercial objects are also intensively collected, without much regard to intrinsic attractiveness or subversive parody, but because they can serve the collector in other ways. All this material, once acquired, becomes rubbish in terms of traditional value structure.

The relationship between all these categories and the broad classes of 'rubbish' and 'quality' are shown in Figure 2.4. All the material below the horizontal line becomes rubbish as soon as it is bought and incorporated into a collection. Everything above it, usually also in collections of one kind or another, belongs in the quality class, unless, in the case of the 'knowledge' material it has lost its knowledge quality by becoming de-contextualised, in which case it too stands in danger of dropping down to the bottom of the plot.

When the four criteria expressed in the figure are applied to the surveyed collections, some interesting characteristics emerge. The criteria used are those which have already been described, so that, for example, the collection of pictorial plates from firms like the Franklin Mint counts as kitsch, and collections of bookmarks are put in the inauthentic artefact class with mass-production commercial material turned into collectable. Authentic artefacts include the historical and natural historical material and collections like machinery, musical instruments and militaria.

Typical of the kitsch or inauthentic art segment is the collection of Pocket Dragon pieces. These are small dragon figurines showing dragons in a wide range of characters and situations, intended for display as household ornaments. The firm producing these figures runs its enterprise as a club issuing *Pocket Dragon Gazette: from the Collectable World Studios*, described as 'the official magazine of the pocket dragons and friends collector's club'. The Winter 1993 issue, for example (the Christmas issue), features two people, a married couple, called Real and Muff, whose 25th wedding anniversary is shown in pictures. Real and Muff are said to 'feel very lucky to still be in love after all these years'. The magazine shows the Christmas Angel, a Disney-style dragon in monk's habit and comic halo, designed by Real inspired by a photo of Muff aged 5, together with photographs of shops and collectors, competitions, a collectors' hot line, letters and an offer of the new, 40-page catalogue. Pocket Dragons operate on both sides of the Atlantic and collections emerge in surveys both in Britain and the USA.

Kitsch like this is collected quite seriously and genuinely. One collector in the Survey reports a small collection of Lilliput Lane models. These, as she rightly says, are expensive. By coincidence the *Radio Times* for the week of writing (March 1996) carried an advertisement for the new Lilliput range, Lilliput Facades featuring Georgian buildings. These retail for around £20.00 each, and it takes eight models to make up the set. Such material combines features of kitsch, thought not its ultimate excesses, with the miniaturising and de-contextualising character of airport art. Tourist material strictly speaking is represented in the Survey by some 11 collections of stamped bookmarks which are generally spoken of as 'attractive and ornamental'. Collections valued as camp for the dreadfulness of the taste involved are relatively rare, but the Pub Mirror Collector has nearly 20 examples and seems to value them in this way. He is joined by another collector who has fifties style mirrors with brass designs around them. This mirror collector is a woman, and she enjoys the designs but reports that other people find the collection strange.

A typical inauthentic artefact collection is that of the Carrier Bag Collector (collections of bags are relatively common). These objects are intended, perhaps about equally, to advertise a shop and to carry its goods home. They are not strongly made and therefore include a planned obsolescence; to keep them is to prolong their lives artificially beyond their socially recognised span. Carrier bags not only become rubbish quickly and easily if left to themselves, they also through their association with bag ladies and the life rhythms of the down-and-out, have come to symbolise human 'rubbish', the flotsam of the consuming world. To collect them, therefore, is to cherish rubbish self-consciously.

Authentic art is the rarest category, but characteristic of its collectors is the Art Collector, who is himself an artist and who collects all kinds of art but for 'no single reason – a piece has to move me in some way. Pieces are sometimes chosen because of ground in common with my own work and ideas.' This collector's favourite piece is a small piece of eighteenth century Chinese silk with a dragon embroidery. The Early Pewter Collector represents the applied art aspect of this group; again the collector's work is involved, because he is a dealer, and the reason why he gathers the material is because 'I like the look and feel of Victorian/Georgian pewter'.

This group also include collections like those of the Crystal Collector, who finds geological specimens on field trips in his native north-west America and who also purchases them from across the world. The specimens are treated as art rather than science. They are displayed artistically on shelves or window-sills without any labelling but so that the light as it falls on them can bring out their particular beauties. The collector reports that the unusual and curious mineral formations create ethereal feelings within him, and this, for him, is their most valuable characteristic.

Authentic object collections comprise the history material. The Farm Tractor Collector has around ten machines; he lives in Coventry, which was the home of the principal British tractor manufacturer, Massey Ferguson. The broadcasting engineer collects electronic equipment related to sound and vision entertainment, like jukeboxes, films and hi-fi. He says he collects 'to keep them in use and to keep period examples of engineering practice', but they also 'have a style (appearance and function)' which is important.

Some collections are, of course, extremely complex. Howard French, writing in the *Guardian* reported upon the fashion for designer coffins in Ghana. These are made by Largen Okai and his colleagues in the shapes of birds, fish, giant crabs and man-sized pods of cocoa and ears of corn (French 1995). The coffins are elaborately covered and painted, and are ordered to taste, sometimes well in advance of death, so that they can be displayed as a decoration at home. The root idea is 'authentic': Okai is a member of the Ga community who have been engaged for generations in the creation of exotic burial vessels for chiefs, for whom this honour was reserved. The new coffins are made for Ghana's *nouveaux riches*, but they are also sold to collectors in Europe and the United States. A case could be made for the inclusion of such a collection in perhaps any (or all) of the quadrants, and although the choice might light upon inauthentic art, this is certainly arguable.

Mercifully, however, the great majority of contemporary collecting in Britain seems to have a simpler nature. As Table 2.3 shows very clearly, inauthentic artefacts account for 18% of all collections, and inauthentic art for 37%. Authentic artefacts make up 31% of the collections, and authentic art 2%. The authentic art collections are divided evenly across the sexes, but the inauthentic art shows more women collectors than men (56% *v.* 44%), and authentic artefacts are much the same (55% *v.* 45%). Most telling are the figures for inauthentic artefacts, which show an overwhelmingly female collecting bias at 69% as opposed to 31% for men. The age profiles do not show up any significant patterning except that 50% of the authentic art belongs within the 36–45 age group and 42% of the inauthentic art in the 56–65 age group, but peaks are unlikely to have a broad significance in view of the small size of the art group overall.

Relationships between Socio-economic Group and Collection Content

One of the most interesting, and unexpected, facets which the Survey revealed was the relationship between socio-economic class and content of collection. The percentages scored (based on all those who gave both pieces of information) of employment types/class against collection content/authentic-inauthentic value are given in Figure 2.5. This shows that the collections of room ornaments feature proportionately largely across the social spectrum, as do coins and stamps, and toys, featuring model vehicles for men and cuddly animals or dressed dolls for women. Similarly, the possession of inauthentic art material is spread proportionately across the As, Bs, Cs, Ds and Es, as are the authentic and inauthentic artefacts; only the authentic art is concentrated in the upper reaches of the chart.

Individual examples drawn from the detail of the replies are compelling. Of the seven Cat Image Collectors, one is unemployed, one living with an accountant, one married to an engineering company director, one to an insurance broker, one is herself a personal assistant, one a teacher and one is married to a telecommunications manager. All are women. Between them, these women cover a large spectrum of contemporary British society. The three Doll Collectors, again all female, have as their main family wage-earners a driver, an electrical manager and a flight engineer. All the dolls are dressed in foreign costumes or items like bridal dresses. The Teddy Bear and Cuddly Toy Collectors (again all women) make their family livings from cleaning, the police force, electronics engineering, selling and quantity surveying. The two Lilliput Lane Collectors are married respectively to a postman and a lawyer.

Among the men, the two Football Programme Collectors are a salesman and an accountant. The Model Car Collectors are a carpenter, a factory worker and a car salesman. Three men collected early wireless sets and related material. All are long-term collectors of at least ten years' standing, and all seem to have started as a result of family inheritance and gifts from

Employment category and socio-economic group		natural history	coins, medals, stamps	militaria	historical material	jewellery and clothes	musical instruments	machinery	toys	works of art	room ornaments	pop art	tourist goods	sporting material	household goods	drink and tobacco
A	Professions	0.8	2.5		0.8				0.8	1.6	5.5			0.8	0.8	0.8
A	Finance		2.5			1.6				0.8	1.6		0.8			
B1	Senior managers	2.5	3.3		2.5	1.0		0.8	4.2	1.6	5		0.8	0.8	3.3	
B2	Middle managers	0.8			0.8					0.8	5.5				0.8	1.0
C1	Lower managers		0.8							1.6	3.3				1.6	
C2	General dealers		0.8		0.8					0.8	5			0.8		
D1	Skilled workers		1.6	0.8						2.5	2.5		0.8		1.6	0.8
D2	Drivers		0.8	0.8						0.8	1.6			0.8		
D3	Semi-skilled		0.8								3.2	0.8	0.8			
E	Manual			0.8						1.6	2.5		0.8		1.4	
	Classification of collection content by traditional value	39.4%								4.0%	44.5%				12.1%	
		authentic artefacts								authentic art	inauthentic art				inauthentic artefacts	

Figure 2.5 *Relationship between employment categories and socio-economic class, and collection content types*

friends. One of the three is an electronics engineer for whom there is a professional link; one is a mechanical design engineer who may have a different professional interest; and the third is a coal-handler in the Liverpool area. The three Coin Collectors all have substantial collections of the 50–100 magnitude. Two of them refer to their coins as a potential investment and all are interested in their historical and decorative value. Of the three, one is a heavy-goods vehicle driver, one is a plumber and one is a doctor.

We have to conclude that the particular category of object as the focus of collecting practice is not primarily a class-based interest. This contradicts the popular image of the collector as portrayed in much of the media, where the collector is usually male collecting varieties of fine art or artefact, vintage cars, for example. Most collecting is not of this kind and probably never has been. More significantly, it runs in the face of contemporary cultural analysis which takes as its base-line the social cleft between 'high' and 'popular' culture, as exemplified most tellingly in Bourdieu's notion of the 'habitus' in which cultural 'good taste' is both a class-learned formula and a form of personal capital leading to good jobs and marriages, through which class distinctions are maintained.

It seems that contemporary collecting does not function as, for example, television viewing, home furnishing or choice of leisure activity (collecting itself aside). In any of these areas it would be possible to make an informed guess about an individual's tastes and habits once his or her occupational status was known, and the tastes would exhibit a socio-economic class difference. Guessing games of this kind cannot be played successfully in relation to collection content, where somebody who is technically a C or a D may have an 'authentic' and 'important' collection, while an A or a B may be accumulating the most ordinary mass produced tourist wares.

Conclusion

The information presented here suggests that collectors are simply proportionately representative of the population as a whole, in broad terms; collectors are merely a segment or a minority group of the whole, and not a separate caste with personal or social defining characteristics. This is an extremely important point which cannot be laboured too heavily.

About a third of the population in contemporary Britain are willing to count themselves as collectors, and these are divided substantially between the two sexes, although women outnumber men by perhaps 10% so that the split is roughly 45% men and 55% women. Roughly two-thirds .of all of these collectors are in the younger group, between 18 and 45 years old, although interest in collecting picks up again to a certain extent in later middle age (56–65). Around half of all these collectors thought they lived in the smaller communities, although a third (36%) came from larger towns and suburbs. These life-styles are matched by 'normal' or 'traditional' family lives. The notion of the lone, socially inadequate, male collector as typical must be abandoned. In socio-economic terms, the middle class, especially towards its upper end, was over-represented in the responses. However, sufficient detail was presented in the replies from the rest of the social range to allow the development of some probable implications.

Collecting practice across the socio-economic groups seemed not to differ much, apart from some clear exceptions such as belonging to a collectors' club. In key areas, collecting habits and attitudes seem to match across the classes. This is also a very significant point, which suggests that relationship to collected material does not operate like most cultural behaviour.

Slightly less than half (45%) of the collections were relatively small, with the other half on the larger side, and half of these again being very large, with more than 100 pieces. Generally speaking, the larger collections belong to men and the small ones to women. Two kinds of material, the room ornaments and the household goods, account for approaching half (40%) of all collections. Records came next, with 13%, and the other collection types ranged down from this. Women hold the great bulk of the household/ ornament collections, and most of the jewellery and tourist goods, and the ornaments are collected chiefly by those in early middle age (46–56). The converse is also true in that most women are holding this kind of material. Male collections are more various in content and size. The material was all collected across the social range.

The figures show that inauthentic art is a large collecting area in itself, and particularly important for women, for this group is both proportionately and numerically very significant. The group included the primarily room ornaments collections, together with the tourist material. Inauthentic collecting of this kind is distributed roughly evenly across the age range of young adulthood, middle age and the elderly. Most significantly of all, ownership of these collections showed up across the range of types of employment, and therefore across the social range. Inauthentic artefacts, chiefly household goods, also loom large, and are also collected chiefly by women, without class distinction. The collection of authentic artefacts – coins, militaria, natural history material – appeals primarily to men, again of all classes. Only authentic art has a gender balance and a class imbalance, appealing mostly to those in the upper social groups. By and large, social situation does not affect collection content, any more than it does collecting practice.

If there is a 'characteristic', or 'typical' collector, she emerges as a youngish or young middle-aged woman who comes from a very broadly middle class or upper working class background, lives a traditional family life in an area which is not a city centre, and has a fairly small collection of domestic material (room ornaments and household goods). Almost equally characteristic, however, are men in the same age ranges, who are living the same kind of lives. These have collections which vary across the types of material and tend to be on the larger side. These two broad trends are interrupted by the youngest group of both sexes and all classes who are collecting record material, and by the male manual workers, who seem to be living comparable 'family' lives in cities, and whose collections are large and tend to be concentrated in the machinery, sport and drink/tobacco areas. Most of the collections held by the majority of the women – and therefore by the majority of collectors – fall within the 'inauthentic' or 'spurious' classes when judged against traditional value judgements. Some of these are what might be called 'kitsch', some are tourist material, and some are commercial objects turned into inauthentic artefacts by virtue of the collecting process which treats them as if they were endowed with value which, however, traditional values do not recognise.

One of the most interesting aspects of the whole collecting process is the way it cuts without distinction across the class structure. This is at variance with most cultural practices, and in defiance of received wisdom which assumes that all cultural practice is class-bound. Clearly, something is happening in collecting which is not based on socio-economic class, that is, either on income or on ideas about what is appropriate to status, educational standing and family 'tradition'.

The most likely reason why this is so is the closeness of objects to us. They, and our bodies, which are closely bound up with them, constitute our material world of tangible experience. They are our other selves, in the sense that none of us can exist without them. They are, in a sense, paralleled by our families. Everybody, regardless of class, has a mother, and a grandparent, and probably all the other socially normal range of blood and marriage (or partnership) kin, and feels about them in much the same kinds of ways, which, moreover, are understood by all. In the same way, we all make our lives out of material culture, and quite a lot of it is much the same material culture, which we use and feel about in the same ways. There is a 'great divide' in collecting, but it is gender, not class based.

3

Work and Play

One of the over-arching social narratives of modernist times has been the anti-thetical nature of work and its opposite, leisure or free time. Work can be defined as 'the effort or activity of an individual that is undertaken for the purpose of providing goods or services of value to others and that is considered by the individual to be work' (Hall 1994: 5). Historically speaking, the antithesis has crept up on us more gradually than we sometimes believe. The factory system, with its clear-cut opposition between home and workplace, began in the later eighteenth century, but it affected only a relative few for a long time, even in Britain, mostly in the textile mills of southern Lancashire and Yorkshire. Even in the classic heavy industries of the Midlands, pottery making and metal bashing, a large amount of the work was, and still is, put out amongst a huge variety of small firms operating at, or not much above, the cottage industry level. Exactly the same was true of the steel industry around Sheffield and the northern centres of ship-building. It was not until the effects of British prosperity began to create the huge lower middle class and its taste for consumer goods in the second half of the nineteenth century that a preponderance of the population began to be employed in institutionalised work, as blue collar operatives or white collar clerks and sales people.

With this was linked a developing application of the nuances of class difference: snobbery was at its most intense between around 1850–1950. A clear distinction was made between 'jobs' and 'careers'. Jobs required the same work through life, with little opportunity for the development of new or superior skills. Once adult levels were reached, jobs paid the same through life. But jobs also offered a place to go to which structured the day, provided opportunities for meeting partners and friends and for male (and sometimes female) bonding, and the support of a recognisable identity. Careers worked to a certain extent in the opposite way. They offered the chance of great personal development with steady increments of pay, responsibility and influence. They were also competitive, and correspondingly less conducive to an easy mateyness. But, like jobs, they structured life and provided for self-identity. Both gave that crucial sense of belonging to an 'in-group' with its shared language, history, grievances and jokes.

This pattern of work has not proved to be eternal, because it contained within itself the seeds of its own transformation (Curtice 1994; Law 1994). The clear-cut system of factory, office and shop continued in its 'classic' form perhaps until the 1980s, and therefore lasted little more than a century. Even during its heyday, in fact, many people were relatively loosely tied down as sales representatives, employees in the transport industry, and travellers generally: these jobs were often valued for their 'freedom'. Meanwhile the development of Taylorian and Fordist assembly line principles at the beginning of the twentieth century, which made the consumer revolution possible in industrial terms, developed apparently inexorably into steadily increasing automation, and so to the search for new approaches to efficiency which have given us the micro chip, data-base information availability, and Internet-style global communication.

The workplace begins to turn into the workstation: the Henley Centre has calculated that 50% of the jobs in London could be done, at least in part, by wired-up outworkers using computers, and perhaps 15% of the total salaried British workforce is working at home already (Girling 1994). In its turn, this tends to break down the boundaries between 'job' and 'career' and also between consumption and employment, just as the distinction between employee and consumer blurs as a result of expectations that everybody, in all aspects of life, must be calculating, enterprising entrepreneurs both inside and outside work (du Gay 1995).

These capacities, in turn, together with intense market competition, have deskilled many whose grandfathers and often even fathers considered themselves to be skilled tradesmen. They have created what now appear to be the characteristic employment patterns of the 1990s, the fragmentation of specialist work groups, the growth of part-time jobs and short contract appointments, and the development of freelancers who work where and how they can, at all levels of expertise from window-cleaning to leisure industry consultancy. With this, of course, is linked the great increase of women in the work force, driven by perceived low family incomes, single parenthood and principles of equality. All this is perceived to be producing much less security, and engenders a workaholic culture in which family relationships and personal stability are endangered (Cooper 1996). Stress at work and stress management are now major issues (Newton et al. 1995).

The new work practices are connected to the new approaches to personal banking and finance, with its range of mortgages, loans, savings and credit, and its concomitant risks of associated re-possession. Political parties of the right and left across the western world assume that this insecure employment style will continue after 2000, with unforeseeable consequences for house purchasing, pensions, health and health care, the relationships between men and women, and the up-bringing of children.

If, therefore, proto-capitalism is seen as the invention of money-handling techniques (including big lotteries) in the decades either side of 1700, and early capitalism as the development of the factory system from around 1750 to 1850, then classic capitalism ran from the mid-nineteenth century to around 1980, to be succeeded by what has been variously called postmodern or late capitalism (Jameson 1991). We can now see that the classic dichotomies between work and non-work set out in Figure 3.1 have only limited historical application, one which, of course, coincided with a period of

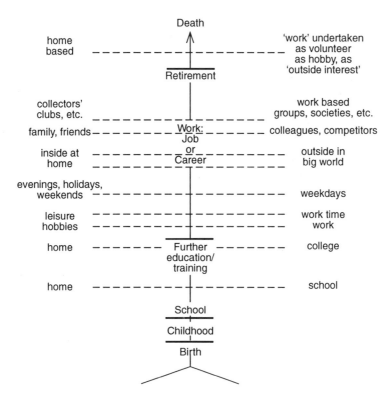

Figure 3.1 *Classic dichotomies between work and non-work*

considerable moral and social coherence in Britain, not withstanding the fact that it included two bitter wars and an appalling depression. These distinctions still make up a large part of the mental landscape of most people over 40 or 45, whatever their personal experiences have been, although these may be accompanied by a kind of folk memory of previous grim conditions. Similar notions probably still represent the pattern of security to which the younger generation aspire, perhaps with increasing wistfulness as employment steadily fragments.

Leisure time, the period when one does not have to 'work', is as much a social construct as any other cultural trait. The notion of 'leisure' that grew up alongside that of work in the capitalist sense, has concentrated upon concepts of 'escape', 'freedom' and 'choice': what we might still call the language of the travel agent (Kelley 1982). An important part of the structuring of leisure is its space: it happens at home (Kron 1983) or 'away', but not at the workplace. Two analytical trends in thinking about leisure have arisen in traditional critiques of modernist work (Crandall 1980). On one hand, it is seen as a form of social control which imprisons the individual and reinforces conformity; on the other, it is seen as liberating, as it is in popular response. This may now be inadequate. Rojek (1996) has suggested that leisure practices have responded with some difficulty to living in a risk society. 'Free' time becomes something different when simulation and nostalgia are at the heart of everyday experience.

The implications of what is set out in Figure 3.1 therefore work on two levels. For some of the population, probably the older (i.e. over 45) generation, these represent the living norms that have shaped their experience, while for the younger group they represent nostalgia, seen, as always, as simpler, easier and more comforting. A life of work progressed from its forerunner, school, through any period of training, to the 'proper' job which represented the passage to adulthood, and to a wife, home and family of one's own. Work ran its course throughout life and concluded with honourable retirement, which pre-figured physical death. Meanwhile, the job had divided home from the workplace, family from work people, work time from 'free' time, and work itself from leisure time activities, including collecting. It was a distinction which structured the space, time, human contacts and personal habits of all workers.

This has had an important implication for the way in which collecting has been treated in analysis. It can be seen as an aspect of investment or leisure (Olmsted 1991). It has been seen as at the heart of the private person, helping to create a unique *persona* and existing in a privileged position in relation to other activities which entitles it to be described as 'sacred' (Wallendorf et al. 1988). Here it is detached from the mundane, and from the economic in the normal sense; as the biography of collector after collector shows, collections are treated as unalienable, as separate from the world of socially determined value which permeates 'work'. 'Hobbies', including collecting, are assumed to be enjoyable, self-pleasing and nurturing, and are defined as such by contrast with work, seen as unpleasant, geared to satisfying others and destructive. This reflects the notion of work as alienation from self, which has run through so much of the discussion since Marx and his immediate followers that it has become a truism of analysis, and part of the mind-set of every commentator. As we shall see, this approach to the nature of collecting suffers from superficiality, and an important element in our understanding revolves around a better idea of the psychology of work and its satisfactions, both for those who experienced its late modern form, and for those who are living its postmodern experience.

The objective of this chapter is to explore those areas where collecting practice spans the leisure–work divide. At its simplest, this can be conceived as a straightforward mingling of human activities; since both work and collecting usually involve elements of spending and acquiring in the least elaborate economic sense, it is likely that there will be a relatively large area of grey between them. At a rather more profound level, there is the question of how any mix of leisure (collecting) and work is a sign of our times, an activity implicit in a world seen as postmodern in which categories dissolve, emotional purity becomes meaningless and 'work' for many increasingly becomes the construction of nostalgia with a price tag, an activity all too prone to seduce its own purveyors. Finally, there is the question of the collection as the sacred manifestation of the self, seen as separate and inviolate. This need not necessarily involve a vision of the collected self as therefore apart from the world of economic necessity and work, although traditionally it does do so; in a postmodern vision of the world in which work and leisure mingle, it is possible to imagine the emergence of a third element seen as related to, but separate from, both. Family and home both seem to belong here, and so do many of the activities which support them, like shopping.

With these thoughts in mind, this chapter will look firstly at the ways in which the collecting process, and the material collected, links up with the collector's paid employment. This will be followed by an analysis of how collectors see fit to use their materials for other 'leisure-time' activities, as a bridge to the 'world outside'. Membership of collectors' clubs is a specific aspect of this social aspect of collecting. Collecting as dealing is an extremely important element in this whole area, and is discussed at appropriate length. Finally, there is the question of the relationship between collectors and museums. This brings us round full-circle because for a collector his interest in collected objects and in visiting a museum is leisure, while for a curator care of the museum collections and attention to the visitor is work. Moreover, in the modernist system, museums function as the institutions to whom the legitimatising of object quality and significance is entrusted, which constitutes an important element of the sacred (see Figure 3.5) in contrast to lay collectors and their material seen as the profane (see Figure 3.6).

We end up with a paradox in which paid work done by the collector counts as profane while his collection counts as private sacred; but for the curator this collection counts as work, while the museum collection counts as public sacred, even though it is sustained by an aggregate of work. The categories of sacred and profane slide against each other as they articulate with those of private and public, points to which we shall return. The chapter ends with a conclusion in which the threads are drawn together.

Links with Work

Across the board 10% of collectors felt that their collections had links with what they defined as their employment (Figure 3.2). Among these, 14% were men and 8% were women, a figure which bears a general relationship both to the rather larger number of men who are in employment at any one time and to the nature of the jobs that men have tended to fill. Those for whom work and collections relate are distributed fairly regularly across the age range, with the 56–65 years age group (who scored in relation to previous employment) scoring lowest at 5% and the 26–35 group highest at 16%. The proportions of those for whom work and collecting related were similar across most of the various occupation areas, where around 15% felt

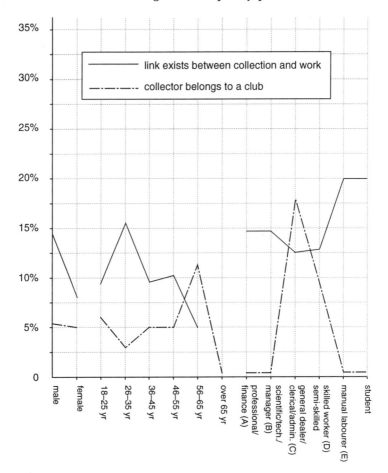

Figure 3.2 *Link between collecting and work, and membership of a collecting club: analysis of Survey returns*

there was a link. Surprisingly, however, those living in city centres reversed this trend: 24% of this group felt there was a link while 9% felt there was not.

Across the board, those in manual occupations, especially agriculture, and students, scored highest in terms of collection involvement with work, at around 20%. Here, too, is the greatest concentration of the relatively small range of responses from students. The professional groups came in at around 15% and the general dealers and semi-skilled at around 12%. This is borne out by the cross-question which asked what percentages of those within individual occupations felt the link: public services and professions (58%) and technical and scientific (41%) towered above all the rest. While 91% of those with cars were counted in the ranks of those who did not see a collecting link, and only 9% of car users did, roughly three-quarters of those who did see a link were car users (76% against 84%), suggesting that both access to a car in itself, and membership of the general car-using class are significant in the work–collection link.

In the same way, while out of those collectors who have partners, overall only 9% felt the link, 60% of the work-related collectors were in a partnership. These figures were broadly reflected in the possession of children: of the work-collectors, 71% have children, while overall 88% of the collectors with children and 93% of those without are not interested in work-related collection. Meanwhile, of those who had another collector in the family, 11% work-collected, while of those who did not have such a familiar collector, also 11% collected in relation to their occupation. Both for those who work-collected and who had other collectors in the family, and those who did not and did not have other family collectors, the scores were much the same (52% and 50%).

When the same issue is viewed from the standpoint of the collected material, it is clear that work was an important element in the collections of historical material (100%) and musical instruments (100%) (see also Willcut and Ball 1978) and a significant element in the collections of paintings (50%) and machinery (50%). All the other types of material scored much lower, with natural history material at 20%, drink and tobacco at 17% (but perhaps not to be taken too seriously), and household material at 10%.

Overall, a fairly consistent picture emerges. Those collectors for whom their work is important tend to be in a relatively youthful age group and not older than 35. This group may be living anywhere, but a significant proportion of them are in city centres. These factors probably link up with the large student presence in the group, although interestingly, agriculture, and so those living in the country, figured quite largely. Those in the very broad middle class occupations were important in the group overall, and, of course, most of these have cars, partners and children. It seems that most work-related collectors are in the 'greater' middle class with frequently stable family situations and living wherever their work takes them. A significant group are the grown-up children of this group, now living as inner-city students, whose collecting habits link up with the course that they are studying and their projected career.

Nevertheless, the anecdotal material shows how this rather clear-cut view needs softening. The Post Office Memorabilia Collector, for example, who is now around 50, has spent his life as a postman in Glasgow: this is a public service occupation, but not generally regarded as a middle class one. Another life-long postman in Bangor, Gwynedd, collects postal ephemera for 'reference and research'. The Early Cigarette Packet Collector, similarly, runs a pipe shop in Richmond, Surrey. The Goss China Collector used to work for a firm of auctioneers, and he now sometimes gives talks about his china to local groups, and shows his material to members of the Goss Collectors' Club. The Vintage Motor Cycle Collector makes his living as an antique dealer, the American Comic Collector as an arts editor, and the Coin Collector as a coin dealer, while the Medicine Measure Collector has been a nurse all her life.

The Children's Book Collector worked as a children's librarian, and the Chemistry Book Collector taught chemistry. The Medieval Militaria Collector taught politics at a university, and the Cow Cream Jug Collector was a herdswoman. The drainage worker, who collects agricultural clay fittings, writes 'my passion is soil drainage . . . [the materials] are evidence of the industry, skill and hard work of my predecessors'. A Radio Collector worked as an electronics test engineer. The retired Ambulance Control Superintendent sums all these details up when he describes his Ambulance Collection as 'a living, visual history of a noble order . . . it is my life'. What comes across most clearly in the record is the interest and enthusiasm – sometimes, indeed, passion – which unites the worker and his work.

As a corollary to the linkage with work, runs the extent to which collections are used, and to what use they are put. 'Use' is a broad issue, and covers the utilisation of collections in some aspect of the collector's paid employment, and their involvement in other, non-working, 'outside' interests.

Using Collected Material

Across the board 39% of the collectors thought that they used their collections. This involved a fairly even split across the genders with men (44%) scoring rather higher than women (37%) (Figure 3.3). In terms of age, use of material was spread fairly evenly across the ranks, apart from a dip to 30% in the 56–65 age group. The majority of the users live in city centres (25%), city suburbs (33%) and small communities (27%), with 17% in large towns, exhibiting the regular bias towards large and small communities rather than middle-sized ones. In terms of occupation, most using collectors fell into the professional/financial and skilled/semi-skilled groups, while the general dealer/lower manager group scored low, as did the manual workers. Access to a car divided about evenly across the using group (40–33%), and so did possession of a partner (38%). Forty-six per cent of the using collectors, however, did not have children, while 43% of them do live in families where others both collect and make use of their collections.

In terms of types of material, record collections (75% of all such collections), room ornaments (19%) and household goods (15%) are much used, with 6% of the jewellery and 10% of the tourist material collections. The usage rates in terms of some collection types, however, were frequently very heavy. Of the collections of musical instruments, history material and pop material, 100% were in use; and so were over 75% of all collections of machinery and paintings. The lowest scores come for collections of coins (5%), sporting gear (14%) and toys (17%). At first sight these, especially the last two, look rather odd, but it seems that coins do not count because they are not for spending, sporting gear because the collectors see their collections as embracing primarily prizes and mementoes rather than usable equipment, and toys because this material is kept by adults who do not allow it to be played with.

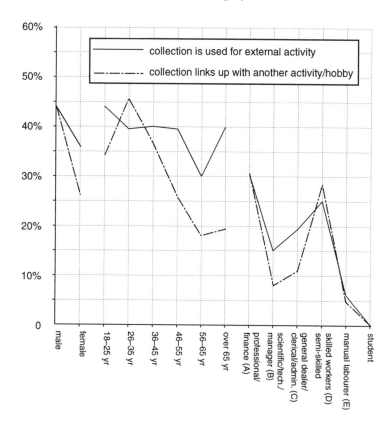

Figure 3.3 *Link between collecting and an external activity, and other hobbies: analysis of Survey returns*

The direct usage to which the collections as collections were put fell into two broad categories. Some, including obviously the music material, were simply played and listened to in the normal way. Similarly, the ornaments and household goods were in their places in the home, and this their owners, understandably, counted as use. The jewellery and some of the clothes were being worn. The other broad category can be characterised as demonstration. The Football Memorabilia Collector demonstrates his material, when requested, at quizzes and shows; the Soviet Badge Collector loans part of his material out; the Northamptonshire Material Collector gives talks to the Women's Institute; the Welsh Garments Collector supplies clothes to her daughter harpist and creates small exhibitions to accompany her performances; the Glove Stretcher Collector gives talks; the Cash Register Collector lends tills to charity shops: these are all characteristic collector activities. They show how collectors use the material as a bridge to the outside world in a way which is of use to the community and bolsters their self-esteem.

Usages of these two kinds are fairly closely mirrored in the linkages made between the collection and another specific activity. Thirty-two per cent of collectors do make this additional link, and of these men score 44% and women 26%. The highest age group is that between 26 and 35 (46%), with the lowest again falling in the 56–65 group (18%). Again, the proportions by living area are similar, with large town dwellers scoring lowest. Those in the professional and financial group, and in the skilled/semi-skilled group score highest with 30% and 27%, while the general dealer/administrator group score 11%, the scientific/technical 8%, the manual 5% and the students a bare 1%. Roughly a third of those with access to a car make the link, while a third do not, but the overwhelming proportion of the collections in use are owned by those with such access (86%). Again, possession of a partner is divided across the activity-link group (25% possession), 42% of the using group not having children, and 32% of this group live in families where somebody else is doing the same.

In terms of the material collected, 100% of the collections of militaria, musical instruments, machinery and pop material did link up with other activities, as did 73% of paintings collections, 71% of sporting collections and 61% of records. Toys (13%), drink and tobacco (1%), jewellery (20%) and household goods (16%) all scored low, although one suspects that the drink and tobacco collectors were anxious to minimise what might be seen as the vices inherent in any activity relating to their material.

The other specific activities involved frequently link up with methods of acquisition which do not fall within purchasing at shops, car boot sales, markets or jumble sales. Many people see going to auctions as a related activity (Glancey 1988), which of course means going to local house clearances and provincial auctions rather than Sotheby's or Christie's. What matters is the ever-present hope of 'picking up a bargain'. The activities also include acquisition through metal detecting, either legitimately on permitted local dumps or land like beaches, or surreptitiously on farm land or known archaeological sites. Also included in this category are those who carry out the socially permitted theft of items like ashtrays from pubs or notices from football grounds. In fact, some of the big breweries deliberately produce a range of small pub fittings, like mats, ashtrays and games pieces, in order that they can be thieved, something which gives them advertising and the drinker satisfaction. Naturally, though, the kleptomaniac collecting tendency can become a social problem if it extends, for example, beyond the relatively cheap mass produced motorway cones into individually important, one-off road signs, but both are common collecting categories.

The overall impression is that those who make use of their collections, and who link them with an outside activity, are probably in many cases the same people. Indeed, the categories are very blurred, as many of those sampled seem to have had the same effect in mind when they answered one or other, or both of the queries. These people represent about a third of all the collectors involved, a substantial proportion. They are most likely to be men, although women are also well represented. Those coming up to, or who have already taken, retirement are the least likely to belong to the group, but otherwise the practice is spread across the age range. Most are likely to live in city centres or suburbs, with small towns being proportionately well represented although smaller in numerical terms. Possession of car, partner and children did not seem to be significant, but a fairly high proportion of those involved knew that somebody else in their family was similarly engaged.

We are left with the impression that men are rather more likely to make collection links than women, and that the years between 46 and 65 represent the least likely period for either gender to do so. In social terms, it is those with very specific skills who are most likely to make the link, whether they rank in economic terms as professional, skilled or semi-skilled. As always, however, the anecdotal evidence thickens and blurs the picture. What seems clear is that all collecting has the potential to interact with other leisure activities.

A rather separate aspect of the relationship between a collector and the world outside revolves around the collectors' club, and this requires treatment in a separate section.

Collectors' Clubs

The collectors' clubs in Britain are a familiar part of the social scene. *Hoole's Guide to British Collecting Clubs* (1992) gives details of 108 collecting clubs, of which 54 have been formed since 1980 and a further 16 between 1975 and 1979; only 38 pre-date 1975. This may not be as significant as it seems. Many clubs slip through any recording net, and many might be described better as loose associations than formal clubs with elected officers and membership lists. Similarly, collecting groups tend to come and go as people move about, and particular opportunities dissolve to re-appear somewhere else. No figures for such clubs, for example, exist for the between-war years, but anecdotal information suggests that they were common. However, not all are ephemeral, of course: many of those listed have a strong structure of organisation, regular meetings and a newsletter distributed to members. The material which these clubs collect is very diverse. Martin (1995, 1997) lists 234 types, ranging from Action Man to Winnie the Pooh.

Participants and observers report that the nature and atmosphere of these clubs differ greatly, one from another. Some are characterised by relaxed good humour where the accent is on viewing each other's material and arranging exchange sessions. The Stamp Collector, for example, reports that 'At meetings a different collector presents his objects each week . . . the atmosphere of the club is very pleasant, there is some good-natured rivalry' (R. Bradley 1996: personal communication). The Leicester Collecting Club (Copp 1995) and its leading spirit, Norman Rochester, encourages a friendly atmosphere in which collectors are inspired to look out for material for each other, and to give away 'gudgies', described as 'a collectable item offered, gratis and for nothing by one member to another'. Lists of available gudgies are published and giving takes place at the monthly meetings (Rochester 1995: 11). In other clubs the tone is more competitive and more suspicious, and the conversation characterised by cryptic remarks and banter designed to baffle.

Given the very large number and various natures of the clubs, it is surprising that of the collectors sampled overall only 5% said that they belonged to one (Figure 3.2). These divided nearly in proportion between men and women, and most of those belonging fell into the 56–65 age group. Again, most of the club members lived in city suburbs. The great majority (50%) of the group did not specify their occupation, and it seems that many housewives counted themselves in this set. Apart from these, manufacturing and semi-skilled workers came in at 9% and dealing and self-employed workers were represented at around 18%. It must be remembered that the real numbers here are very small, but here we seem to touch against the considerable amount of casual and less casual dealing which collecting involves (see below). Club members do not seem to be differentiated from other collectors in terms of access to transport, possession of partner and children, and the extent to which somebody else in the family collected.

In terms of material collected, one of the highest scores was returned by the coin collectors (27%), which might have been predicted. But much more surprising were the high scores produced by the room ornament collectors (27%), and the household goods collectors (27%), with toys and pop material both coming in at 9%. This bears out the suggestion that the clubs attract large numbers of women. As Figure 3.2 shows, the patterns of links with work and membership of a club are a rough mirror image of each other. Younger people are involved with work, while in early middle age clubs figure largely; the social As and Bs and the manual workers and students favour work over clubs, while the Cs and Ds prefer clubs to work. This may be because professional and technical work lends itself to development in the collecting field more than some other kinds, but this is presumably not true for the manual workers, who are not clubbable. The general dealers and the skilled/semi-skilled seem to be attracted to both.

The club-belonging collector emerges as a person in early middle age, who lives in a city suburb and whose background belongs with socio-economic class C, probably in the upper registers of the class. Experience of collecting clubs in action shows that this figure is indeed characteristic. Membership of the more recently developed clubs tends to be female, as is that of those which are devoted to collecting as such, but these should not obscure the existence of the specialist clubs, which are usually so specialist that their members slip through any broadly based summary. These clubs, by and large, seem to be filled with men, who, typically, seem to be the husbands of the women just described. Although many individual exceptions could be found, clubableness among collectors seems to be most evident in the lower social grouping, but not in the lowest.

Collecting as Dealing

The 'market', the means by which goods leave and reach any particular individual, is a complex sequence of inter-locking movements not readily reducible to a small number of simple processes. Nevertheless, there is one helpful distinction to be made, between the mechanisms through which goods circulate in the highly organised, smooth, hard and shiny professional market place, to be discussed in Chapter 4, and the soft, hairy underbelly market through which goods move in ways that are not part of formal market procedures (and seldom trouble the Inland Revenue or the VAT Inspector). The key characteristic here is the casual nature of the trade, pursued by citizens who do not give up their day jobs, but do a bit of dealing in their leisure time.

Here we move into the world of what Martin (1997) has usefully called 'client–patron relationships' which operate between collectors and suppliers and where, indeed, the distinctions between these two identities are often blurred (Stoller 1984). The most significant venue for this kind of activity is the car boot sale, or garage sale, as they are called in north America. It was estimated in 1994 in the TV programme *Scrimpers* that two million people went 'booting' every week in Britain. The turnover involved can be considerable. Roger Morgan described in his book of 1993 how it was possible to make £500 a week from car boot sales (1993), and from the United States Hermann and Soiffer have estimated that 'there are at least six million garage sales per year, with a gross of six hundred million to one billion dollars' (1989: 401). This has been linked to the mood of shrinking expectation consequent upon the recession which in turn fuelled the nostalgia much collecting represents, and so makes legitimate a cheap, second-hand market in which collectable goods are available. One face of collecting is its capacity to put an acceptable gloss on the worn and battered, something most Americans have only had to do relatively recently (apart, of course, from those who lived through the Great Depression). Similar causal events have been experienced in Britain.

Boot trading, and similar efforts like flea markets, are now referred to as a 'service industry'. What was once a playful activity (Maisel 1974) has become 'serious leisure' (Belk 1995a: 55). The effort for both vendor and buyer to get up and drive out on a Sunday winter morning requires a substantial commitment, which is worthwhile if the one makes some good sales, and the other some worthwhile purchases. The vendors can see themselves as clever operators, preying upon the naive. Morgan says:

> If you've got something odd on the flash [stall] and you know it's not worth a carrot, as we say, you stick a ticket on it saying 'very collectable'. Some twit will pay good money and start collecting them in the hope that the stuff will go up in value . . . (Morgan 1993: 83)

In large part this cynical attitude is made possible by the obsessive desires of the collectors, and the lack of any firm valuing and pricing structure in a haggling, immediate cash-only milieu. In his study of Californian flea market dealers, Maisel says:

> Antiques, collectables, memorabilia, or 'funk' cannot be evaluated in terms of their use value or compared with their new counterparts but must be assessed in terms of highly specialised market knowledge. Further, the swiftly moving currents of fashionable interest in nostalgia reshape these markets in an almost dizzying way. (Maisel 1974: 496)

Maisel goes on to compare the regular dealers with those who have genuinely come to sell off the contents of their attics (1974: 496), and to buy and sell, to add to their holdings, and to sell off duplicates of material they feel they have 'grown out of'.

The relationship of collectors to this world is a complex one. As Figure 3.4 shows, informal sales are a common way of acquiring material across the collecting range, with women and men scoring evenly, although it is particularly popular among manual workers. Manual workers again make acquisitions through a range of informal contacts, but so do professionals and young people. Very few will admit to considering selling a piece, and manual workers are particularly clear that they would not do this. However, a number of mixed forces are at play here, similar to those which appear regularly on our televisions at showings of *The Antiques Road Show*. As Bonner shows, this is a place where the battle between 'object as sacred trust' and 'object as commodity' is played out as public spectacle, and the changes in the programme over the years show how greed and exaltation at high valuations and potential sales have become steadily more acceptable (Bonner 1995). The sad truth is that, however strongly we may feel, few of us resist the temptation to sell if tempted sufficiently. A large number of collectors do not see their collecting activity in a static way in the first place: for them dealing is an integral part of the activity, partly for the fun it brings, and partly because it makes possible a never-ending refinement of the collection.

One such collector, for example, was interested in the popular culture of the Gulf War. From boot sales, he gathered an interesting range of casual clothing, which included tee-shirts printed with an unflattering portrait of Saddam Hussein accompanied by a legend in pseudo-Arabic characters, which at first sight seemed to give the ruler of Iraq's name, but on closer inspection was seen to read 'Sod'im, the swine'. These sorts of shirts also appeared in the kiosk trade in popular seaside resorts, but apparently not elsewhere. With this civilian gear he also bought army equipment which was presented as ex-Gulf War stock. Of course, this material was being commercially made, or in the case of the War Office goods commercially sold off. The collector was well aware of this, and regarded it as adding to the interest of the stuff. However, later in the same year he decided he only wanted the civilian material, and so sold off the rest, successfully, at a boot sale himself. He felt that financially he had probably broken even, he had the material he really wanted, and the sales had been great fun in

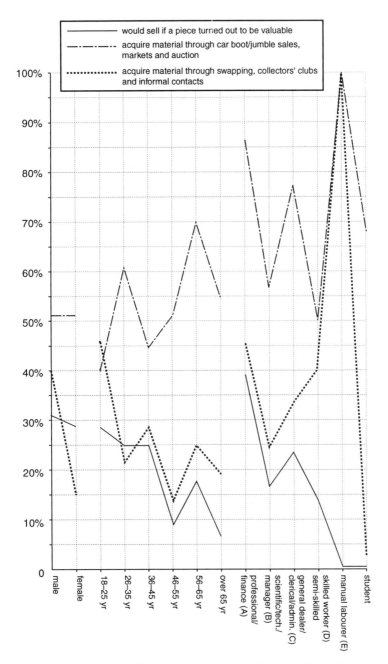

Figure 3.4 *Collecting as dealing: patterns of acquisition through car boot/ jumble sales, markets and auction, and through swapping, collectors' clubs and informal contacts; and response to finding out that a collected piece was valuable: analysis of Survey returns*

themselves. They offered a kind of freedom, a sense of being out there on the raw edge, pretending to be a street-wise barrow boy for a few hours. He thought that his accent and his gestures seemed to coarsen of themselves as a part of himself he only knew dimly came through, but that knowledge of this roughness became an important part of his self-consciousness and helped him in his ordinary life.

.If car boot sales have a predominantly masculine atmosphere, their female equivalent is the jumble sale. These, similarly, take place at weekends, usually Saturdays, across the country in a range of halls, and are organised by female committees for church organisations, Guides and Scouts, traditional charities like the Red Cross, and organisations linked with the Townswomen's Guild and the Women's Institute. They are intended to raise money not for individual dealers, but for the 'cause'; however, fringe freelancing on the same occasion is becoming much more common. Often the words 'Jumble Sale' are eschewed in favour of titles like 'Bring and Buy Sale' or simply 'Sale'. They are preceded by a collection of material gathered round the houses and taken to the central venue. The goods on offer are usually very mixed, and their organisation into separate stalls is governed by traditional ideas of what goes with what: second-hand clothes will be together, so will books, children's things, cakes, preserves, and potted plants, while assorted bric-a-brac, usually the collector's bait, will be on the White Elephant stalls. The same stalls will occupy the same positions, in the same hall, run by the same faces, year in and year out.

The atmosphere is genteel, although such events are usually packed out and the purchasing can be very determined indeed. The goods are usually genuinely 'genuine bargains' in that they are either home-made or bought originally in normal High Street shops for normal prices – here there is no suspicion of special sub-standard production or of shoddy goods shipped in especially for the sale, as there is at boot sales. Most of the (female) shoppers are looking for utilitarian material which will eke out narrow budgets, and little shame attaches to purchases, particularly when these are intended for children or for use inside the house. They offer the same kind of field for collectors that more 'street' occasions do.

These sales show the very clear workings of the local material cycle of quality to rubbish, especially in those areas like ladies fashions and children's toys, which embody change most vividly. The clothes stalls sometimes carry famous designer labels in styles several years out of date. These are the focus of much covert interest, fingered but usually not easily sold because their origins are too obvious and everybody either recognises the garment from seeing it worn, or, at the very least, could identify the particular household from which it must have come. In 1991, at a village sale I attended, a Mary Quant dress in soft grey-blue wool flannel trimmed with tucks and huge black buttons in her distinctive style appeared; it must have been bought originally in about 1963. It failed to sell, and re-appeared in the following year when its eventual purchaser made the company understand that she bought it for the sake of the particularly large buttons. The collecting potential of such events needs no stressing, although the survey gives the impression that they are a relatively under-exploited resource, probably by reason of their intensely local and relatively inaccessible character.

It would be easy to draw up a list of opposed characteristics which these two kinds of informal shopping display. Male and female would head the list, followed perhaps by shifting/stable, open air/undercover, rather strange/ deeply familiar, mixed old and new/all second-hand, dodgy material/ genuine material, and so on. Both lines reflect and reinforce the stereotyped views of men and women in our (and most other) cultures. Just as import-ant, however, is what they have in common. Both represent well understood mechanisms through which individuals can mingle their dealing and collecting for the pleasure and excitement which this brings. Maisel con-cluded that this kind of operation 'provides participants with a sense of risk, uncertainty, consequential chance and this produces experiences usually absent in ordinary social life' (1974: 503). This process offers something better than (or at least a change to) the reality of day-to-day life; it gives access to a kind of hyper-reality where life touches fantasy.

Collectors and Museums

In 1990 the Museum and Art Gallery in Walsall, a small town in the industrial West Midlands, launched what it called The People's Show, a summer exhibition created entirely by putting on show the collections of local people. The collectors were recruited by advertisements in the local press, and interviewed by curatorial staff at the museum, who then decided what would and would not be included in the Show. The material on show included collections of carrier bags, airport art, drums, posters and china pianos. The exhibition was an overnight success, attracting large numbers of visitors and extensive coverage in the national as well as regional media (Digger forthcoming; Lovatt 1997). In 1992, Walsall repeated the event and 14 more museum venues followed suit. In 1994 a nation-wide People's Show Festival was organised, in which 40 museum venues participated, all showing collections from their own areas. In 1995 and 1996 there were sporadic shows, and not a great deal of interest in the mounting of·more of the same: the staff at Walsall feel it is time to move on, and other museums are likely to do the same.

The People's Show phenomenon seems to have lived out its waxing and waning life-span between 1992 and 1996, but during those four years it posed in sharp form important questions about the relationship – actual and potential – between collectors, that is people whose collecting is seen as a leisure time activity without professional engagement, and museums curators who are perceived as professionals whose working employment is con-centrated upon museum collections. Museums are the institutions entrusted by society with the care and display of what it sees as 'key' material, that is,

CHURCH/TEMPLE	:	MUSEUM
premodernist sacred	:	modernist sacred
flight of entrance steps denoting separation from the world	:	flight of entrance steps denoting separation from the world
classical/gothic sacred building	:	neo-classical/neo-gothic institution building
sacred texts	:	labels and catalogues
priests	:	curators
'Golden Books' of saints and martyrs	:	registers of donors
relics visible to view	:	material on display
material in crypts, charnel-houses, etc.	:	material in store
ritual events	:	ritual events

Figure 3.5   *Premodernist and modernist sacred, coded in terms of church/ temple and museum*

material embodying important aesthetic, epistemological and historical information and sentiment. As such, they take on a monolithic character, expressed by their temple or church-like architectural styles, their priest-like curators, and their faithful modernist replication of the ancient attributes of the pre-modernist sacred (Figure 3.5). The contrast between this and the lay world of the collector can be equally readily summarised (Figure 3.6), and the mingling of the two was extraordinary, for here people who had their own jobs and who regarded their collecting as non-work (even if it had links with their work) brought their collections to people and institutions whose job it was to relate to them, and for whom collections *are* work.

Naturally, both sides had their own agendas. Lovatt's analysis of data she collected in relation to the 1994 People's Show Festival brought out the reasons why collectors wanted to participate in the event (Table 3.1). Most people wanted to provide enjoyment and interest to others, and to teach and share knowledge, motives presumably shadowed by the idea that exhibition of the collection also exhibited the collector in a good light. The museums' motives centred around efforts to bring the museum to the people and raise its profile in the community (Table 3.2). These motives are not, of course, incompatible, but they do reflect the different starting points of the two sides. Interestingly, a high proportion of all concerned seemed to be satisfied and pleased with the outcomes.

COLLECTOR		MUSEUM
profane	:	sacred
lay	:	professional
collector	:	curator
popular	:	elite
'low' culture	:	'high' culture
part-time	:	full-time
hobby space	:	stores, workrooms
informal display	:	formal exhibit
safe-keeping	:	collection management
interest	:	research
knowledgeable	:	qualified
private	:	public
..		..
self gratification	:	public edification
collecting = leisure		curating = work

Figure 3.6 *Contrasts between the worlds of the collector and the museum (after Martin 1997)*

Table 3.1 *Reasons for collectors' participation in People's Shows*

Response	Frequency of response	%
For enjoyment and interest of others	75	37
To teach and share knowledge	62	31
General personal aspirations (not listed elsewhere)	38	19
To support museum	26	13
Asked by museum, family, friend	23	11
Personal pride	22	11
Thought exhibition was good idea	16	8
To meet other collectors/see other collections	13	6
Encourage others to collect	10	5
To add to own collection through contacts made	5	2
Enthusiasm of museum staff	3	1
Total surveyed	201	

Source: after Lovatt 1997

Table 3.2   *Reasons for museums' participation in People's Shows*

Response	Frequency of response	%
Strengthen links within community, encourage involvement	22	56
Democratise museum	11	28
Raise profile of museum	10	27
Broaden appeal, bring in different audiences	9	23
Explore areas of collecting within local community	5	13
Past People's Show very popular with staff and community	4	10
Increase visitor figures	4	10
Stimulate popular interest	4	10
Take part in national event	4	10
Interesting concept/good idea	3	8
Enthusiasm of staff	2	5
Sounded fun	2	5
Encouragement from AMC	1	3
As a contrast to other parts of exhibition programme	1	3
Total surveyed	39	

Source: after Lovatt 1997

Digger, who was involved as a curator in all the Walsall People's Shows, has produced a socio-economic breakdown of participating collectors in all the Shows (Figure 3.7). Women were considerably better represented than men, at 59%, and the age range participation showed steady levels from 26 onwards up to the over 60s. The AB social group mustered 16%, and the C group 56%, with DE at 14%, suggesting that most of the participants belonged within the lower middle and upper working class, and were, therefore, a fairly faithful mirror of the population as a whole. Across all the years, and all the venues, the character of the material bought in for display remained very consistent (Lovatt 1997) and its character matches that recorded in the Contemporary Collecting Survey.

A number of reflections after the events are on offer. Lovatt quotes the City Museum, Lancaster as recognising that 'museums are not the only legitimate place for [the] collection of "things"'. The Dorman Museum, Middlesbrough said that 'other collectors are now recognised local "experts" in their field and provide advice to us and interested parties in the area'. Leicester Museums realised the event had been 'an insight into what ordinary people collect . . . and how this can exist alongside, and sometimes complement, the collecting done in the field by museums'. One of the collectors Lovatt collected data from said:

> To be more people orientated museums must encourage people to visit. Displays must be changed fairly often to encourage return visits. The image of a stuffy boring museum must be replaced by an expectation of something interesting to look at. The People's Shows are a really good thing as hopefully visitors will discover that collecting can be fun, interesting and not necessarily academic. Most of what we collect is historically interesting (some of it only fairly recent history)

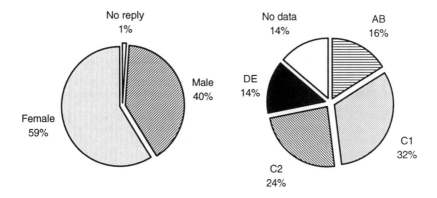

All shows: breakdown of participants   **All shows: breakdown by social groups**

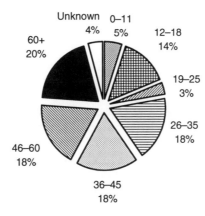

All shows: breakdown by age (yr)

Figure 3.7 *Socio-economic analysis of collectors who participated in the People's Shows at Walsall (after Lovatt 1997)*

but I think any collecting can be of interest to others. Some of our serious collecting friends felt that the People's Show was cheap and nasty. We did not agree and did not feel that because some collections were lightweight i.e. like keyrings or ducks (of all descriptions!) or sugar bags, they should be disregarded. (Lovatt 1997: 221)

This brings us to notions about how the boundary between lay collector and professional museum can be (or should be) crossed. The collectors believe that their particular expertise should be recognised in a way which is inclusive rather than patronising. The Mauchlinware Collectors' Club, for example, recognises that much material within its interest is wrongly labelled in museums (Mauchlinware was the trade name for cheap, wooden souvenir objects decorated with lithographed images made in the last century and on into the present). It tries to recruit museum staff as members as a deliberate policy. Collecting groups are able to be at the cutting edge of what may become important trends, while museums, of their nature, are usually coping with 'the backlog'. Curators are usually discouraged from collecting themselves, but this does not mean that they must sup with a long spoon where collectors and collecting groups are concerned; similarly collectors must recognise the constraints placed on those who are very properly subject to the kind of public scrutiny to which no private person must submit. 'Conflicts of interest' arise much less often if mutual under-standing and personal respect is cultivated. Clubs could be affiliated to museums, and museums could be helped by club members acting as 'spotters' for objects the museum wants to acquire. In the field of contem-porary history, in particular, cooperation between museum and collectors could have large benefits all round. The accent is upon reciprocity.

Conclusion

When this evidence of outside engagement on the part of collectors is put together, an interesting picture emerges. As we have seen, the collectors for whom their work is an important factor in their collecting tend to be fairly young – under 35 – living in cities, and engaged in broadly professional work. They were using material historical items and musical instruments to help them do their jobs better, some of them, at least, as teachers of history and cultural studies. The younger members of the group seem to be their children still engaged in formal education, at school or college, who were using their collections in project work. The group as a whole has a stable, traditional family life, and the fathers emerge as more likely to be collecting in this way than their mothers. The proportion of this group was only 10%.

The general use made of the collection was much broader, and involved 31% of all the collectors. The material used included all that just mentioned, and all the broad range of personal and household goods and playable tapes and records. These are most likely to be men, but women are well rep-resented, they belong within the broad professional group, and in the unemployed group which seems to embrace a number of housewives.

By contrast, the numbers belonging to collectors' clubs is, at 5%, very low. Here the emphasis, roughly evenly divided between men and women, is upon the youngish middle-aged. Women figure rather more obviously, but men are significant too, and both belong within the blue collar social group. Overall, it looks as if those attracted to the clubs are older, and belong within the working tradition which experienced 'jobs' rather than careers. By contrast, those who link up collection and work are younger, collect material like historical items about which non-personal stories can be told and interesting demonstrations offered, and belong within the professional class. Both groups have 'normal' backgrounds, and both are small in proportion to the overall collecting body.

We seem to touch here an aspect of the differing attitudes to employment which operate across the work force. The younger professionals are more flexible in their mental demarcations and see the distinction between work and play as fluid; their work and their collecting interlace, with the one feeding from the other. Those for whom employment and leisure are traditionally entirely separate express their need to 'tell and show' in relation to their material by joining a like-minded group. The emphasis here is not on the didactic potential of the material, but on the sociability which being with fellow collectors brings. General use made of collected material was very much broader, and seems to span some elements of both groups, but with an emphasis upon the younger professionals which probably reflects the significant record-and-tape collectors.

Many collectors dip in and out of the raunchy world of booting, and the dealing which goes with it. Many of them seem to regard this rather like an occasional vulgar day at the seaside: great fun but not worth indulging in very often. But, true to collecting form, general trends are hard to draw, because, for some, booting becomes an obsession. Garage sales are, unquestionably, a characteristic location of the time, an informal, unstructured event bringing together work, leisure, profit, fun, risk and nostalgia and the chancy business of spending and acquiring. It would be easy to see this world as male in contrast to the rummage sale as female, and the binary pairs involved (open air : undercover; individual : charity; dirty : clean etc.) compose themselves. However, although men are indeed rare at the village hall, women are common at the garages, so facile gender distinctions should be avoided.

The People's Show phenomenon was at the cutting edge of the developing interface between collectors and the museum as accredited collecting institution. It underlined another possible breakdown in the leisure–work antithesis which operates between museums and the world of popular collecting, albeit in complex form. It may help to bring about a future in which the relationship between official and unofficial collectors shows itself as capable of change.

All this has a bearing on the notion of the collection as 'set-aside', as the 'sacred' which is to be kept separate from the rest of life. If, as the data suggests, those who do keep their collections temporarily and spatially separate from their employment belong within the blue collar work force with its traditional – that is modernist – attitudes to work, then we can see here modernist notions of the sacred and the separate operating as we might expect. By contrast, those for whom work and leisure, and therefore their collecting, are more mingled seem to belong within the younger, technologically based professionals, who might be described as postmodern, and for whom all boundaries are fluid and shifting. Such people might locate the sacred within their own attitudes to themselves and their activities, irrespective of any external structures upon which these things might impinge. This is an interesting notion, and although it is not wholly borne out by the evidence, which suggests that some, at least, of the work-orientated collectors are older and in traditional jobs, it is worth bearing in mind.

What does seem clear is that a surprisingly large range of people do relate their collecting to their work. Kron (1983) has described collecting as something which 'can hold its own with politics or sport as an all-consuming organising system for one's life', and suggests that this system is linked to avocational/leisure activities rather than vocational/work activities. In Britain, at any rate, this is simply not true. Among collectors we do not see an alienated work force but, on the contrary, people who take a pleasurable interest in the history and material by-ways of their employment and who can make the most of the opportunities it offers for discovery. We do not know if this is truer than sometimes supposed for the work force as a whole, or has something to do with the temperament of the collector who will use everything that comes his way to feed his inclinations. What does seem to be true is that collecting makes work more interesting for the individual at a personal level, and at a social level makes work more satisfying and so contributes to any broader social stability. In the same zestful spirit, people dabble in the street-life version of work on offer at the car boot sale, and penetrate the holy work of the museum institution. Their own rationale for why they do all these things is because they enjoy them and this brings out the enlarging capability collecting has for an individual life, however mixed its nature.

4

Buying and Giving

Collected material has to come from somewhere, and in the contemporary world there are a limited number of mechanisms through which it can be obtained. In the last chapter we considered those – car boot sales, informal exchange, collectors' clubs and the like – which are part of a particular way of life in which social links, dealing and collecting mingle inextricably. However, important though these features are, they are not the usual way in which collectors add to their holdings. Most collected material is acquired by direct purchase in a standard market outlet, however difficult this is to define. It will be used here to mean commercial operations which are professionally run according to legal norms, and with some intention of at least medium term stability. Eighty per cent of the collectors report this as an important method of adding to their material. Correspondingly 67% also say that they receive much of their material as gifts, which themselves will have been bought in similar outlets.

The nature of collecting as a form of direct market consumption and its relationship to the world of production is a complex one. Much of the material in contemporary collections is mass produced, not particularly old (i.e. post-war) and would count as 'popular culture', which is to say low, on the traditional scale of value. And yet, it has a dynamic quality which is significant in individual lives, and which has the capacity to achieve a broader significance.

As the title of a recent collection of essays shows, acknowledging consumption (Belk 1995a, b; Miller 1995a) as a social, rather than a purely economic force has become a focus for thought, something which the theorists of media had already realised (Kellner 1995a, b; Morley 1995), and the historians (Campbell 1987; Carrier 1994; Glennie 1995) and sociologists (Campbell 1995) have had to come to terms with. The differences between the old and new perspectives can be summed up as in Figure 4.1. The whole argument has been lifted to a grander, mythical and metaphysical level, in Baudrillard's study *Symbolic Exchange and Death* (1993), a difficult book, but one which illuminates the notion of production and exchange as part of a postmodern reproduction and simulation, where death is a *'form* in which the determinacy of the subject and of value is lost' (1993: 4). We therefore 'live in a *referendum* mode precisely because there is no longer any referential. Every sign and every message . . . is presented to us as a question/answer . . . perpetual testing' (1993: 62 emphasis in original). This offers much food for thought about the nature and creation of culture and is at the

OLD PERSPECTIVE	CONTEMPORARY PERSPECTIVE

Positivist
  Quantitative
  Argument from theory
	Postmodern
	  Qualitative
	  Argument from practice

From system to individual
  Economic theory
  Management theory
	From individual to system
	  Social anthropological theory
	  Culture critique

Focus on
  purchase
  rational understanding
	Focus on
	  consumption
	  'irrational' emotion

Objects viewed as
  passive
  goods
  commodities
	Objects viewed as
	  active
	  material culture
	  possessions/collections

Figure 4.1 *Old and contemporary perspectives of the ways in which material culture has been understood*

root of relationships between collecting, the market and the production of culture which this chapter sets out to explore.

We shall look first at the broad relationship between the collector and the market, understood as the aggregate of professional commercial enterprises. We shall then turn to the nature of contemporary shopping which shows, among other things, how blurred many of the old distinctions have become. This will include a discussion of the mail order sales of collectables. The next section will discuss the nature of the collections as gift, and the final conclusion will endeavour to draw the themes together.

Collectors and the Commercial Market

The link between the collectors and the market in the broad sense is complex, and begins with how collectors view their own intentions. This is best approached by their answers to the three questions: Do you seek out pieces actively; Do you wait for pieces to appear; and, as a corollary to this, Are you offered pieces you do not want (Figure 4.2)? Only 11% of all the collectors felt that pieces were wished onto them, and this group was more-or-less evenly divided between the genders so it looks as if collectors are good at making their precise needs known, and people are aware of their predilections to the extent that unwelcome material is not a large problem; if tact needs to be exercised here it comes before, not after, the proffering, and is produced by the giver rather than the collector.

The distinction between 'actively seeking' (a phrase with unfortunate resonances in unemployment policy) and 'waiting to appear' is interesting. A surprisingly large group, of 67%, again roughly divided between the

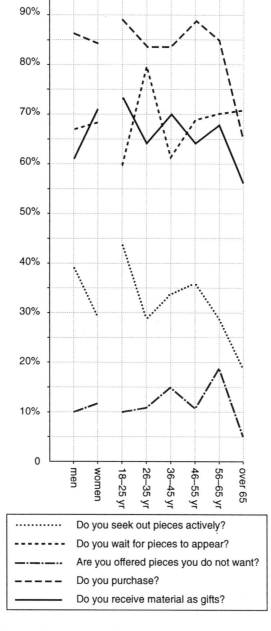

Figure 4.2 *Relationship between collectors and purchasing and receiving gifts, and active and passive seeking: analysis of Survey returns*

genders, thought that they made no especial effort to add to their material; they waited upon fate or serendipity to present opportunities. This implies a high degree of passivity, probably because, once a reasonable-sized collection has been achieved, the material generally available becomes very familiar and a little contemptible. Unfamiliar, particular and interesting material, by definition, becomes much more difficult to find, probably so difficult that there is little point in making efforts to find it; better to keep eyes and ears open and leave the new and exciting finds to chance. At the same time 38% of the men and 29% of the women out of the 33% overall who ticked 'yes' to this question box said that they actively sought out material. The difference between the scores probably represents the group of women whose collections – of souvenirs, of gifts, of inherited material – automatically rule out active acquisition.

The broad pattern described here is maintained across the age groups, with only the over 65s (understandably) giving a low score (18%) for actively; similarly the youngest group are out and about most, spending and acquiring (18–25s, 44%). Living area does not modify the pattern much, and the pattern offered by employment types, if more mixed, follows broadly the same lines, although the unemployed do not buy, and manual workers are very active. Similarly, the presence or absence of a car, a partner, children and other collectors in the family, do not make much difference.

In terms of objects collected, only those who collect records, musical instruments, tourist pieces and pop material described themselves as actively seeking. Elsewhere along the range the pattern followed that already established. It emerges that rather more than a third of male collectors, and rather less than a third of women are active in one or another aspect of the commercial market place, that these come equally from all walks of life, and that a slightly disproportionate number of them will be under 25, undoubtedly buying many of the pop pieces and records. The great majority of collectors have to be seduced into acquisition, either by spotting something desirable on offer, or by receiving a gift from somebody who is loved.

As we have noted, the machinery which makes all these acquisitions possible is heavily reliant upon commercial purchase (86% overall) and gift (67% overall). Men and women purchase nearly equally although women are rather more likely (72%) than men (61%) to depend upon gifts, and men are more ready (25%) to operate through less formal contacts than women (4%). An interesting 21% of all collectors, mostly women, used magazine mail order. This pattern is essentially consistent across the age range and all the other variables, although the retired and unemployed acquired equally through purchase and gift. In terms of the objects, the balance of purchase and gift is much the same for all except room ornaments, toys and history material, where gifts were more important, or of equal importance (history material) to purchase.

However, the sums of money involved in this purchasing were often not large. Nearly a quarter (24%) reckoned to spend no more than £1.00, and this accounted for around a quarter of those buying records, coins, room ornaments and household goods, machinery and paintings: these purchases are surely second-hand. Approaching half (42%) spend between £1.00 and £5.00: many of the object categories just mentioned were also recorded here, at levels generally around 50% of purchases. A third overall (34%) did not balk at handing over up to £10.00, and for their money they are getting pop material and history material, together with the groups just discussed. The big spenders, about 50%, clustered particularly in the militaria, history material, pop and paintings groups; here the collectors were willing to spend more than £10.00. (It should be noted here and in Figure 4.3 that numerous respondents scored more than one price range and the figures represent the total percentage for each price range.)

The pattern of spending (Figure 4.3) between the genders was reasonably similar, in that each sex showed the same curve of percentage numbers rising for up to £1.00 to up to £5.00, dropping back at up to £10.00, and rising again at over £10.00. However, across the range the proportion of males was higher by between 6% and 3%, representing both their greater willingness to spend, and to spend more. The rise and fall of these graphs was mirrored in that of age, which demonstrated a considerable similarity of pattern across the age ranges, with around 50% showing a willingness to part with over £10.00, a pattern broken only by the youngest group (18–25), of whom only 30% said they would spend that much. This is the age group which collects almost all of the contemporary pop and up to £10.00 presumably represents what they are willing to spend on a recording of whatever kind.

The pattern of spend across the communities showed similar ranges, but produced the information that city suburb and large town people were less willing than village and inner city dwellers to spend: most of these stuck at £10.00. This was reflected in social indicators like car, partner and children, where in each case the positive replies accompanied a greater willingness to spend, and presumably reflect a generally larger income enjoyed by the traditional family with at least one parent in work, in spite of the considerable financial responsibilities such families usually carry.

In the light of all this, we can see a pattern appearing, which is much the same across the field, in spite of differences of gender, community, economic conditions and family circumstances. Only about a third of collectors gather material actively, while the rest wait for it to appear. Nearly all collectors (86%) are involved in the commercial market place and are purchasing material for themselves. The money each individual was willing to part with was fairly low for about half of them, but the other half was willing to spend more than £10.00. Two-thirds of all collectors (67%) also receive material as gifts, with women showing as rather more prominent here. Since, of course, the gifts are usually also purchased, but by somebody else, it follows that a large proportion of collectors are both buying and receiving bought goods, and that most of those who do not buy themselves are nevertheless involved in the market at one remove. Very few contemporary collectors are accumulating their material without reference to the

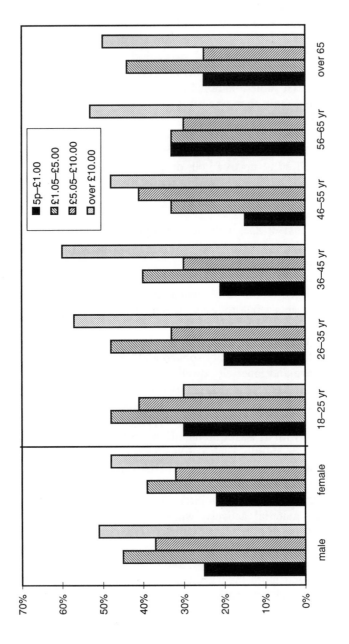

Figure 4.3   *Patterns of spending on collected material across gender and age group: analysis of Survey returns*

commercial market. It is, therefore, to notions of shopping and gift-giving that we must now turn.

Shopping

The English word 'shop' still has two meanings, both of which remain in daily use. In the form 'work shop', as in the phrase 'on the shop floor', it means the institution in which production takes place and raw materials or made-up parts are transformed into objects for sale. In the form 'corner shop' or in the phrase 'going shopping' it means the institution in which finished goods, received from the other kind of 'shop', are offered for sale. The double meaning of the word sums up much of the history of production and retail in the western world, in which the selling shop gradually became separated from the producing shop as, beginning with textiles and pottery, industry by industry almost all production became concentrated in large manufacturing concerns, linked to retail outlets by large wholesale firms, and retail concerns themselves became increasingly either department stores, or branches of large, country-wide chains. This surprisingly lengthy and patchy process has been lovingly described by a number of recent writers (Bermingham and Brewer 1995; Brewer 1994; Brewer and Porter 1993; Carrier 1994; Walvin 1996; Weatherill 1996) who suggest that the selling shop began to emerge in London and the larger provincial towns as early as the seventeenth century, particularly in relation to goods which had to be imported like tobacco, wine and brandy, tea, coffee, chocolate and sugar, and apothecary's goods. The relationship to this development of slave-worked plantations within an imperial organisation must not be ignored.

The process (Lancaster 1995) accelerated during the eighteenth and nineteenth centuries, producing the first department stores (Bon Marché in Paris 1852, Marshall Fields in Chicago 1854, and Selfridges in London 1906) and the first big chains (Woolworth's reached Britain in 1909). Meanwhile, to serve the huge hinterland of Americans beyond Chicago and the East Coast, and the huge hinterland of English people in India, the great mail order businesses of Sears Roebuck and Montgomery Ward (by 1860) and the (commercially rather peculiar) Army and Navy Stores (1871) came into operation. By the 1960s each High Street had exactly the same, predictable, run of shops, and in each large area two or three conglomerates competed for goods, as Curry's and Comet did, for example, in electrical and white goods, while the most intense competition arose between the food and ladies fashions chains.

What had looked immutable, like all of the 1950s did to those who lived through them, was in many ways the end of an era. Throughout the 1960s and 1970s shop assistants were de-skilled as most goods, including (or especially) foodstuffs, were sold pre-packaged in self-service stores. Sites changed as car-less precincts and out-of-town-centres made High Streets déclassé and deserted. Familiar names departed as mergers and crashes occurred in rapid succession, and much nastier things followed. Oxford Street, London, epitomises the change: what was once a parade of smart 'madam' dress shops presided over by Selfridges has become a distasteful straggle of grubby knick-knack bazaars and sleazy fast-food outlets.

Out of the clutter of recession and change two positive developments have emerged over the past 10 or 15 years (Morris 1988). First, the collapse of many large commercial firms and the move away from old centres has offered space to a new kind of shop, usually owner-run, and specialising in ethnic arts and crafts, jewellery and household goods, or in casual fashionable clothing aimed at the very young. These are cheek-by-jowl with the respectable second-hand shops operated by charities like Oxfam, Save the Children and Help the Aged, indeed the goods on sale often overlap and both groups have a similar caring ethos. Secondly, both these shops and the pleasure domes of the new and gleaming malls, taken in conjunction with the characteristics of postmodern society discussed in Chapter 1, are seen to have produced both a new kind of shopper/consumer, and a new attitude to shopping and consumption.

The past decade has seen a growing debate about the theory of consumption whose perspectives involve Veblen's *fin de siècle* classic study which mocked the conspicuous consumption of *nouveau riche* America, Marxist notions of commodification of producers and products, and Freudian concepts of aggressive male sexuality, drawn from earlier writers (Burkert 1985; Sherry 1995; Shields 1992). The post-war theorists are represented by Gramsci's thesis of hegemony and Debord's 'Society of the Spectacle', in which the real world changes into simple images which exercise an hypnotic effect and which motivate behaviour. Gramsci has analysed the role of ideas and value systems in modern society and shows how these shift as they enable a process of negotiation between social groups and classes, a notion which led Wilson (1989) to explore the creative relationship of women to the fashion industry and Hebdidge (1985b) to show how young people, 'mods', appropriated the motor scooter, originally a rather mundane piece of urban transport, and turned it into an important cultural symbol. These processes clearly overturn simple Marxist equations of the 'use value/exchange value' kind: goods have the value which culture places upon them and it is this symbolic meaning which fixes their monetary (or exchange) value, rather than simple notions of utilitarian or single functionalist 'use'.

The notion that the 'meaning' of goods is cultural or symbolic, rather than utilitarian, and that it is this meaning which qualifies their status and desirability, and so their exchange value, is of course one which anthropologists cut their teeth upon, but is foreign to traditional European economists who, following the norms of European thought, assume that Europeans think and act rationally and arrange their relationship with the material world accordingly. For this reason they have concentrated on production rather than retail, assuming that shoppers will follow the logic of capital based manufacture, choosing from the controlled selection on offer, and placing upon their choice the same meaning that the goods had when they left the factory. For this reason, also, Douglas and Isherwood's *The World of Goods* (1979) was so significant, because the writers showed that the European relationship to goods is no more 'rational' than that of any other community. Like everybody else, we use goods to signify position in a social pattern, to give meaning to the flow of life in a mode that can reasonably be described as ritual, and to help an existing pattern to continue or new 'subversive' pattern to emerge.

Colin Campbell has explored this line when he talks of people 'confirming' their own sense of 'character'. Campbell explores the evolution of a range of standard types – the bohemian, the aristocrat, the burgher – and suggests that for all of these modern consumption has become 'a distinctive form of hedonism, one in which the enjoyment of emotions as summoned through imaginary or illusory images is central' (Campbell 1993: 48). Campbell continues:

> The romantic ideal of character might have functioned to stimulate and legitimate that distinctive form of autonomous, self-illusory hedonism which underlies modern consumer behaviour. It does this by providing the highest possible motives with which to justify day-dreaming, longing, and the rejection of reality, together with the pursuit of originality in life and art; by so doing, it enables pleasure to be ranked above comfort and counteracts both traditionalist and utilitarian restraints on the expression of desire. (1993: 48–49)

Historically, Campbell links the development of modern consumption with the Romantic movement of the mid- to late eighteenth century, and psychologically with the tendency to romantic imaginings which seem, historically, to have always been a part of European selfhood.

Campbell's powerful analysis of consumer subjectivity needs to be brought into a relationship with the historical and hence contemporary structure which society, economic and otherwise, presents, in a model of process in which the actors are neither free nor wholly bound by determinist economic forces, but in which there is a dynamic relationship between the two. In this perpetual movement, the objects themselves are the third force, and in some ways the least predictable one. Once active human meaning has brought them into being, their physical capacity to embody symbol provokes response through which further meaning is created, meaning that can be significant to a single individual or family, a single group, or, eventually, to a whole, large, community. One obvious provoked response, and one at the heart of the consuming process, is purchase.

This leads us to the most neglected aspect of all: the practice and act of shopping. It is easy to see why it has been neglected; shopping is at the very end of the protracted process of manufacture and distribution and therefore, in the eyes of classic economists, the most constrained and simplest act in a complex, but rather mechanistic, deployment of capital, raw materials, plant and labour. An equally profound, but less overt, reason is the undoubted fact that in western society 95% of all kinds of shopping (at least) is carried out by women, who, as such, wield enormous financial power (Costa 1994; Radner 1995; Scanlon 1996). Classic thinking has shown a reluctance to admit the force of this fact and that of its corollary, that the shopper's approach to choice is actually not necessarily governed by standard rational motives, to do with utility and cheapness, although of course it may well be. The notion that the largest slice of economic influence is exercised by an aggregate of irrational females is not one which the world of economists has been able to face until recently; the customer may always be right, but not *that* right.

In a run of studies from Oakley (1976) to Wallmann (1984), the house-wife emerges as selflessly devoted to the 'moral economy of the home' (Miller 1995b: 35), for whom consumption is the means by which the traditional virtues of family life may be realised in daily practice through hot meals, warm clothes, clean floors and the like. Both housewives and material goods are essential to all other activity but their very ubiquitous necessity renders them transparent to the assessing gaze. In fact, this reading is inaccurate, perhaps grossly so. As Miller (1995b: 38) has expressed it, if, as he argues, consumption is the vanguard of history then, 'it is women in particular who have radically transformed the world'.

Advertising bears a tangential relationship to activities of consumption (Cook 1992; Goldman 1992). Advertisers consistently reject accusations of maintaining out-of-date stereotypes – the existence of the nuclear family for example – by claiming that in a commercial world they must do what producers wish and that in any case their remit is not to change the world but to hold up a mirror to it. In so far as this is true, the world which is revealed turns out to be more a sequence of mirrored images than a single reflection. Parody and pastiche have become the daily bread of advertising in which the craft feeds off itself by re-hashing old material. Reading advertisements becomes a quiz game of recognition and quotation of the kind that television loves, and so succeeds in involving the viewer/consumer in the creation of meaning. The recent advertisements for the oil firms Shell, Castrol and British Petroleum have all worked like this; so have those for McDonalds, and for Nescafé with its soap-opera style guying a now free-standing genre which began, as its name still shows, as an advertising medium.

In the same spirit, advertising exploits a 'back to the future' style of nostalgia, using the craze for the earlier post-war decades up to the 1970s with its acid rock, platform shoes and sexual politics; after the recession of the 1980s, the 1990s have wanted the reassurance of mythic past to help this decade face the coming millennium, and advertisements like those for Ribena have given it. In the same way, advertising plays up a mythical masculinity, particularly of course in the beer and car adverts, which is becoming out-dated in real life. The corresponding female image has mutated over the past few years, in that while super-mums and sex-babes are still exploited to sell goods, so are career high flyers, like the woman in the Kenco adverts, or women of the world, in those parts of the motor industry aimed at women's purchasing power.

In no sense are the advertisers afraid of flying. Increasingly explicit erotic scenes are now a commonplace, matched by the symbolic acts of air-borne products as they experience euphoric leaps and falls which mirror the agony and the ecstasy (especially, of course, the latter) of shopping and consuming. Flying equals desire and desire gives pleasure is the subliminal message of all advertising campaigns. And as air flows, so fluids splash, in soft drink advertisements, in Cool Water Cologne and Calvin Klein, and in tourist campaigns. Waves of libidinal flow create a world of consumerised lovers and eroticised products who live together in a warm lagoon of easily purchased satisfaction.

The spirit of the shopping centre is in tune with these images. Each one stands as a world-in-itself, very similar to all the others of its kind, but bearing no marks of any particular locality or context. All are 'well-planned' and 'convenient' without and fantastic within, where relentlessly optimistic colours and sounds mix in a magical mystery tour with plate glass, adult trees in pots, fountains and buying opportunities, all offering an eclectic, shiny, sexy, ever-changing but changeless world of goods. Here the Eliza Doolittle flower barrow stands next to the Kasbah, selling wooden beads made in Taiwan and the perfumes of Araby produced in east Germany, while opposite both The Blue Cockatoo offers a Peter Cheney experience of bar stools and (carefully fake) leopard skin coats. It is a human zoo of experiences, sired by the great department stores of the early part of the century and born out of the Disney worlds of its middle years.

Collecting is part and parcel of this consuming process. The shopper, usually female, whether deliberately looking to buy something for another's collection or happening upon something which she would like to add to her own, is animated by a mixture of motives towards her choice, motives at which no commercial production enterprise can do little more than guess in the broad sense. If the shopping is successful – that is, the recipients are genuinely pleased with the purchase after a short time has lapsed – then all concerned have experienced pleasure in Campbell's meaning of emotion enjoyed, and a sense of individuality enhanced. The commercial market, for all its contrived advertising and its sense that everything can mean anything, has been *appropriated* by shoppers who use the collectable items which it offers as a means of self-creation; the dialectic is essentially an internal dialogue, where the producer has to overhear as much as he can and act accordingly.

Mail Ordering

Twenty-one per cent of collectibles are purchased through mail order. A glance at the advertising columns of any local newspaper, or at *Exchange and Mart*, will demonstrate the variety and quantity of goods available through this means. *Exchange and Mart* is a nationally sold journal which comes out every Thursday, and has a circulation of over 50,000 copies.

Alongside this publication, which has a distinctly, though not exclusively, male flavour, run the mail order advertisements placed in national newspapers, especially the Sunday colour supplements and the *Radio Times*, which are, as the manufacturers make no bones about admitting, aimed at women, generally middle aged, poorly educated women who have a disposable income of their own (Jennings 1993). Between June 1993 and January 1994 some 44 such advertisements appeared in the press. Of these 10 were for plates, 22 for figurines, 8 for pseudo-antiques and speciality pieces, and 4 for pieces intended for boys of all ages (Pearce 1995: Figure 21.2).

These producers are usually anxious to emphasise the collecting element in their products, obviously with a view to maximising sales. The three principal firms are the Franklin Mint, Danbury Mint, and Brooks and Bentley, together with the Bradford Exchange, Royal Doulton, Compton and Woodhouse, Princeton Gallery and a number of small firms. Recent offerings include 'Monopoly, the Collector's Edition' with the buildings 'die-cast and plated with silver or gold . . . authorised and fully authenticated by Waddingtons' (Franklin Mint, at just £395.00); the '"Wireless", reminiscent of radios of the early 1930s, the first wooden Bush radio to be produced for over thirty years' (Rowtex Ltd, £49.99); the wall plate 'Holy Cats' created by 'Bill Bell, the world's most widely collected artist' (Franklin Mint, £19.95); 'The Lord is My Shepherd' plate ('in the tradition of the finest collectibles, this collector plate is crafted on fine porcelain, hand-mounted and bordered with 22 carat gold', Franklin Mint £19.95), and 'The Four Seasons' plates featuring cats against appropriately seasonal flowers 'destined to become a classic collection' (Danbury Mint, £19.95 each).

These examples show the key words very clearly. An association with a well-known and respected firm (Waddingtons or Bush), together with 22 carat gold, porcelain and 'die-cast' create an aura of quality and high craft. The quoted name of the artist, as somebody one should have heard of, does the same job for aesthetic virtue. These values are bolstered by the price, for none of the pieces are really cheap and a fair number are extremely expensive, a cunning profile managed well by shrewd marketing. With these go the 'adorable' or 'enchanting' designs of cats, figures, artefacts and buildings, playing on reliable feelings of nostalgia, schmaltz, religiosity and simple pride of possession. As far as can be seen, these pieces are collected at face value; they do not seem to be the subject of ironic reflection, and they do not appear very much in the second-hand market.

Sometimes pieces are accompanied by very instructive marketing literature. 'Spitfire Coming Home' had a four page letter, addressed to 'Dear Friend' and signed 'Nigel Jeffers, Managing Director', together with a special order card, and a page of 'Market Analysis Report'. This was got up like a serious market performance review, designed to demonstrate that the 'Spitfire' plate was a serious antique which would appreciate in value, complete with graph comparing issue prices and 'last UK sale' prices. Business language was used to describe these events:

As these examples show, exceptional British plates are posting some commendable gains in secondary-market trading . . . 'Spitfire Coming Home' enters one of today's most consistent market sectors.

In addition, the plate is produced by a famous name, Royal Doulton, and 'released under the sponsorship of, and officially endorsed by the RAF Benevolent Fund' to whom donations are made by the Bradford Exchange. The marketing strategy is at least as carefully crafted as the plates.

Unsurprisingly: mail order collectibles are big business. Companies like Brooks and Bentley, which has about 80,000 customers on its books, will produce between 60 and 80 new items a year, some in 'limited' editions of about 10,000. Figures are hard to get at, but yearly turn-over for one of the big firms is estimated at £50 million for the UK alone. Each page of full-colour advertising in one of the colour supplements will cost around £20,000 per issue. As Keith Yeo of Brooks and Bentley put it, 'We're part of Lenox Tableware Corporation, the fourth largest giftware company in the United States'. On 20 February 1995 the Franklin Mint advertised in the *Guardian* for a Print Buyer to help it maintain its reputation for 'distinctive, high quality collectable treasures', although the reality of the job was clearly geared more towards 'the demonstrated ability to manage complex campaigns simultaneously'. Franklin Mint, we will all be glad to know, is an equal opportunities employer.

These collectibles are a curious combination of genuine quality (the gold and silver is real) and, by 'high culture' standards, appalling taste. They are not violent, or pornographic (although one or two of the 'little girl' designs teeter on the edge of the softest of porn), and their traditional morality is that of the supposedly silent majority. The Limited Edition Plate Collector, very characteristic of the type, writes: 'The original plate as well as being decorative has jumped up in value . . . they are decorative and hold their price as an investment.' They are unredeemed by any glimpse of irony, and their mass appeal rests in the comfort which they offer, the consolation of easy emotion uncomplicated by the real world. The shopping is equally uncomplicated. The firms are very efficient in the American style, and this easefulness, coupled with the other kinds of ease, explains their popularity.

Gifts

Its is likely that the notion of gift in relation to collectors features even larger than the declared 67% would suggest. Most of the material bought by individuals for their own collections is probably regarded as gifts to themselves. The collectors use this kind of language: they talk of 'treating myself', 'buying a gift from me to me' and 'giving myself a present'. Nor must it be forgotten that those, especially women, who are collecting themselves, are probably also buying gifts which they will give to other women as additions to their collections, and which figure in the summary as 'gifts' formally speaking. In other words, a very large amount of shopping which is perceived as non-utilitarian (that is, not food and basic household goods) nor as directly self-enhancing (not clothes and accessories) is bound up in the notion of gift-giving, and the reciprocal exchange which much of this represents has been the focus of much study ever since Mauss's classic publication in 1925 (Mauss 1954).

Gift-giving, sometimes to the divine, sometimes directly reciprocal between humans, but more usually from superior to inferior, seems to have been a principal force for social continuity in European society as far back as we can see (Pearce 1995: 57–109) and continues to be so, with the charitable giving of money and (second-hand) goods now occupying the role of gifts to the divine. Traditional marriage, it should be noted, is also bound into this mind-set, as witnessed by the old question at the wedding ceremony, 'Who giveth this woman to this man?', a question usually tacitly answered by the bride's father. We are all, in fact, woven into a dense network of giving and receiving which is sometimes directly reciprocal between person and person, and sometimes more widely dispersed in a broader and looser pattern of expending and returning so that across a life-time, other large factors like war or violent economic change being equal, any given actor, within his or her particular sphere of social practice, is likely to end up with honours in giving and receiving more-or-less even.

This makes the paradoxical nature of the gift clear: on the one hand gifts are freely given for love rather than calculation, but on the other they enmesh recipients in a net of obligation, which often lies heavy on the lives of ordinary people. It requires a sacrifice of time, effort and money, often money which can be ill-afforded, on the part of the giver, but at the same time this sacrifice is not free from expectations. Belk and Coon (1993) have suggested that gifts fall into two paradigms on the strength of studying gifts as exchange and agapic love (see Figure 4.4, which draws on Belk and Coon's plot). However, in real life categories are not this distinct. The lover hopes his gift will help bind the other to him, while the young child, who receives very lavishly from his parents at Christmas, is nevertheless supposed to offer wrapped tokens in exchange, even though all the family knows that these have been bought and prepared by mother. All gifts, in fact, carry obligation, and this does not necessarily relate to the purchase value of the objects concerned.

This character carries its own profound difficulties. As Derrida has shown us, for the gift to be received as a gift it must not appear as such, because its appearance as a gift brings it into a cycle of repayment and death (1992). Since in the Christian tradition life itself is considered to be a gift to each individual and since in the same tradition the key historical and cosmo-logical act is God's gift of himself to humanity in human birth and death, repeated daily in the sacrifice and consumption of sacred bread and wine, it is clear that giving and giver, freedom and obligation are all much the same things (Derrida 1995). There really is no such thing as a free lunch. The sacredness of the gift, from highest to humblest, belongs not in its freedom from strings, but in its socially embedded nature which separates it from

EXCHANGE PARADIGM	LOVE PARADIGM
Intentional	Expressive
Reasonable	Emotional
Purposefully	Freely
Male	Female
Reciprocal	Without obligation
Controlling	Pleasing
Selfish	Selfless
Cost based	Thought based
Object directed	Person directed

Figure 4.4   *Paradigms of gifts as exchange and agapic love*

pure (or impure) monetary transactions. Like the provision of good state welfare, with which as a system it has a number of links, it is financially free at the point of delivery to the individual, but that individual is only entitled to receive it in certain specific personal circumstances which arise directly from concrete life experiences.

The moments when each individual's circumstances entitle her (the pronoun is used deliberately as any reader of the earlier part of this chapter will appreciate) to receive gifts are complex and very interesting (Figure 4.5). One cycle follows the progress of life from birth to death. Newly born babies are given presents by family and friends, usually nowadays soon after birth but sometimes still as Christening presents. Initiations into adulthood at puberty – confirmation, first communion, bar-mitzvah – are usually accompanied by appropriate gifts. Each successive anniversary of birth is marked by birthday presents, particularly those of the eighteenth, fiftieth and seventieth birthdays. A date in the sixties brings official retirement from work and may be marked by a retirement present from work mates. In fact, every end of a run of employment is usually marked, by levels of enthusiasm which depend upon length of service and the feeling of all concerned. This is one present-giving ritual which is as strong for men as for women. Finally, the individual dies and all her collected belongings become gifts themselves. Meanwhile, during the course of life she has received similar death gifts from grandparents, perhaps from some friends, and from her own parents.

A second cycle follows upon marriage or its partnership equivalent. The announcement of an engagement will be accompanied by gifts, significantly in the American world called a shower and confined to the woman and her women friends (the groom will have an all-male stag night which is very

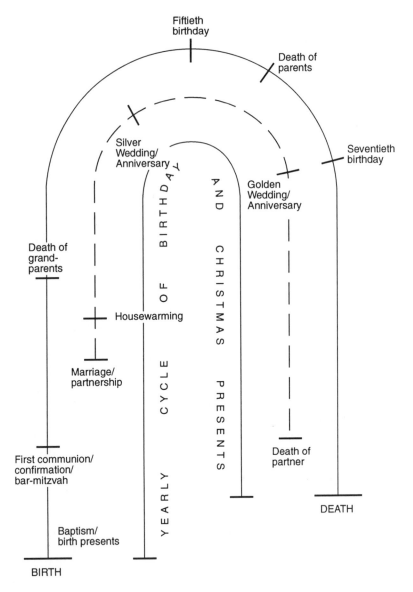

Figure 4.5   *Gifts and the life cycle*

different). The wedding brings in presents, and its non-marital equivalent is the housewarming, when the live-in couple achieve their first permanent home. The wedding anniversary is recognised every year, but is attended by special ceremonies and gifts at the Silver Wedding (25 years), Golden Wedding (50 years) and Diamond Wedding (60 years). These anniversaries cease immediately after the death of the partner, and thenceforward neither the wedding day nor the funeral day of her partner are marked by any gift-giving to the widow. The final cycle is the yearly recognition of present-giving at Christmas (Caplow 1982; Carrier 1993; Miller 1993b) and of bringing back presents from holiday, so marking the two balancing high spots of the year.

The embedded circumstances which all these occasions embody are clear. They mark a significant moment in the individual's process through life which counts as a rite of passage. The group upon whom rests the obligation of providing gifts is clear, although it is always fuzzy around the edges and hence the personal difficulties and embarrassments which accompany these occasions. The present is handed over, and received and opened with ceremony, often accompanied by a speech of presentation followed by one of thanks, formal or informal, and by hand-shakes or kisses. The presents may be displayed; this is particularly true of those relating to weddings. The occasion (these are all 'occasions' as the inscriptions upon thousands of gifts makes clear) may be marked by decorations, like paper contrivances and balloons, and displays of ancillary presents like cards and flowers. Special food and drink, recognised by the cultural group as appropriate to the particular occasion, will be provided, and this will almost always include alcohol. The presents will become elements in a personal collection, and kept with them will be mementoes like cake decorations, cards and dried flowers.

But, while some men are dying, other men are being married. In other words, rites of passage belong in a cyclic view of time in which all things come round in due season and this embraces the happy returns of one's own life and the points at which a single life inter-locks with those of others. The world of commerce, by contrast, is perceived as linear, progressive and always changing; these are functions of its character as impersonal, profane and outside. And yet almost all the presents given as ritual begin as commodities offered as goods in a shop at a monetary price. How then do these two opposed worlds come together, and how can an object be transformed from unholy sale to sacred offering?

In *The Gift Economy* Cheal (1988) argues that gift-giving marks off what he calls the 'moral economy' from the cash nexus of the market place. The moral economy exists alongside the political economy as a constant presence, but emerges most prominently at Christmas (Kuper 1993). Caplow, drawing on his study of Christmas in a town in the American midwest, makes similar points in relation to the balance of adult (office parties and New Year's Eve) and child or family orientated (Hallowe'en, Thanksgiving, Christmas) events during the winter season which buttress the family and counteract perceived weaknesses in the real social system:

> We suggest, then, that Middletown's festival cycle celebrates family matters because the family is the institution most at risk in the community. It is the institution most dependent on emotions, rather than reason, for its continuance, and in this dependence lies its vulnerability. The ritual of the festival cycle appeals to the emotions, strengthens them by assuring Middletown residents of the rightness, and so ensures the continuity of the family. (Caplow et al. 1983: 243)

Interesting although these thoughts clearly are, they avoid the central issue here, of how presents work.

The key element in presents is reckoned to be not how much they cost but how much personal effort has been expended upon them because 'it is the thought which counts'. It follows that those presents which are home-made will command the highest moral prestige. Certainly, the wool from which garments have been knitted or the wood from which they have been carpentered will have been bought in a shop, but the individual craft and the exercise of time and skill have wrought a transformation which brings commodities from the outside into the inside and in so doing changes their character; and this bears no relationship to whether the home-made piece may be regarded as attractive (or not). Something of the same kind is true of presents of books or records which offer the recipient the entry into the giver's inner world. It appears that the most precious gift is that which involves offering a part of oneself embodied in the present itself. Its maker or chooser remains with it, inhabiting it, inviting the intimate discourse of wearing or reading long after the ritual day has passed. At the opposite pole are gifts of money, the most impersonal of all things, and the one which wears away leaving nothing special behind it. For this reason money is an insulting gift, other than in special circumstances to people one knows extremely well as, for example, from a father to a young adult daughter.

Not all presents can share this close personal dimension, but all these presents share a key characteristic with the others: all are presented specially wrapped. The only exception to the wrapping rule are things brought back from holidays, which may be given in the commercial wrapping. The reason for this is probably that the name of the strange shop and town on the commercial bag validates the exotic provenance of the piece, especially if they are in a language other than English, and so does serve to mark this present's special character of home thoughts from abroad. Wrapping paper was introduced (with most of these presenting rituals) in the late nineteenth century, and the removal of price tags and the wrapping of gifts became the normal means of 'decontaminating' and 'singularising' market products. As Belk suggests, part of the role of Santa Claus may be to make things sacred, so that gifts to children are not seen in the same way by children as ordinary purchased goods and services (Belk 1993: 91).

Specially designed wrapping paper and accompanying bows and tags now exist, as do cards, for virtually all of life's special occasions, and to wrap a birthday present in holly paper, for example, is not a forgivable sin. Wrapping is now a considerable commercial enterprise on its own account, and many gift shops offer all-the-year round gift-wrapping services. The use of these, however, is felt to be acceptable only by men, whose limitations in this area are tacitly recognised. From women, presents should be hand wrapped and addressed; to have a stranger, as part of her paid job, wrap and write what should be done for love seems a meretricious denial of the honourable nature which is the essence of the gift.

At bottom, the role of the paper may, however, be at once simpler and more profound than any of this: wrapping paper is a mask. Just as masked dancers throughout the world lose their ordinary characters in a mythic transformation into forces from the Other World, so wrapped commodities lose their regular identity in a similar transformation which turns them into 'Christmas presents' or 'birthday presents' enacting their ritual identities heaped under the decorated tree or piled beside the breakfast plate. They are both surrounded by prohibitions about looking under the mask until the right moment arrives, and in both the secret is more interesting than the dénouement: notoriously presents lose their glory once they are unwrapped, just as the mighty dancer becomes again the village weaver. Justly so, for if the heightened awareness which we call ritual is prolonged for too long, it turns into weariness and loses its power.

As gifts move into the collected state they carry all this weight of significance with them. They retain the mythic quality of the rite of passage in which they were central actors, and the emotions which surrounded their transfer at that time. The collection gradually becomes the sum and visible shape of a lifetime's transactions, and the inwardness of event has transformed commercial goods into personal experience. Gifts and the collections in which they are characteristically gathered are presents indeed, the sum of all our past presents carrying us forward into the future.

Rubbish and Value

Regardless of how or where the piece is bought, usually the initial effect of purchase is a drop, often a serious drop, in monetary value. As we have seen, most collectors reckon to spend only fairly humble sums in the first place, although a minority (10%) regularly pay more than £10.00. But whatever they have spent, they will not usually be able to recover their money, because goods bought new in shops of whatever kind, or by mail order, simultaneously enter the appropriated world of the collection, and in market terms start the downward slide through second-hand into rubbish. The exceptions to this process are, of course, formal 'antiques' or goods which were second-hand to start with and which, in market terms, are classified more-or-less as rubbish throughout the process of acquisition. Such material can, and easily does, return to a junk or car boot market for resale at a price which may vary in relation to the first sale. We have therefore the paradox that the interface between public market and private possession is marked by decreasing value on the one hand, and increasing value on the other. Plainly, we are talking about two different kinds of values and yet, since all value is created by private or individual desire, the two value systems must have points of intersection and in the end, the private one must, in the aggregate if not in every individual case, be the most powerful, although the inter-reactions are likely to contain a range of tensions. It is the intersection between private and public values in market place terms and the mechanisms which turn the first into the second which we must explore.

We saw in Chapter 2 that traditional values of quality can be organised against the two axes of masterpiece/artefact and authentic/inauthentic, and that judged by these criteria the great bulk of popular collecting is concerned with objects which fall below the horizontal line. Mail order plates are characteristic of inauthentic masterworks and so is much giftware, and 'ordinary shopping' like tea towels becomes inauthentic artefact when it is treated with the seriousness of collection for which, as a class, it was not intended. Some collecting, however, belongs within the 'genuine artefact' class, like the (few) accumulations of natural history or scientific material, and a very few contemporary collections would rate an authentic masterpiece certificate of authenticity.

The scheme leads to further dimensions. As we have just seen, most purchased material, once bought falls through the value system to become 'used' and 'second-hand', and, although not necessarily immediately valueless, nevertheless steadily loses its value. It joins the broad 'junk' class of collected objects whether bought in the 'junk markets' or gleaned from beaches and rubbish tips, or stolen from pubs and sports grounds. This is the bottom zone of rubbish where prices are not fixed and exchange is in an informal one-to-one mode.

Similarly, at the top is the public collection zone wherein is gathered socially endorsed heritage in institutions like the National Trust, organisations like the Royal Palaces run by the Department for National Heritage, and the publicly owned museums. Here, as in the rubbish zone, collections are difficult to price, material does not normally come formally on to the open market, and if collections are shed this is done with discretion, and as much as possible by exchange rather than sale.

These relationships can be easily plotted (Figure 4.6), but the key element in the relationship of value and market is the dynamism created by changing desires through the passage of time. In some areas this is very simple. The scientific authentic artefacts embody what is perceived to be valuable knowledge, even though financially they are not usually priced highly. This facilitates their easy movement into the 'heritage' zone, hindered only by the large amount of duplication which is involved. Collecting here needs to be of considerable size and very well documented to achieve serious recognition. Similarly, some of the art authentic masterpiece group will 'stand the test of time' as we say, and move effortlessly upwards, while others of the group will start to appear slick or glib or pretentious and sag downwards, to inauthentic rubbish. Here we see the many complex filaments which make up artistic taste operating in relation to actual collected objects.

More interesting is the fate of rubbish. Most popular collections would be accounted (more-or-less) rubbish at the time of their collecting. However, the passing of time, the sheer enthusiasm and desperate will on the part of the collectors, and the sight of the massed ranks of material compels a kind

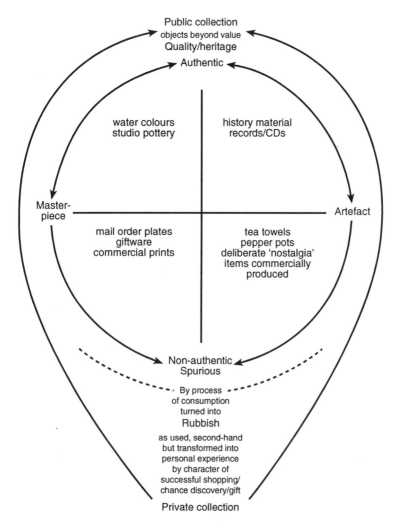

Figure 4.6 *Collecting in relation to perceived valuation*

of revisionism through which changing desires create market change. Collections of rubbish become at first interesting or amusing, then important, and finally emerge as 'significant social and historical documents in the history of material culture', with strong genuine heritage pretensions. The intense feelings of the collector over time are the mechanism through which private pastoral can, sometimes, become public value. Rubbish is the zone of transformation where the unregarded detritus of commodity is turned into personal culture, and can rise again through the system into public culture and high market value. The transformer is the collector and his or her collection; collecting is a messy, chancy, exciting affair where staggering changes can come to pass.

Conclusion

The argument offered here, while recognising the manipulative element in consumption in which the individual is the victim, or at least the target, of giant corporational productional and promotional system strategies, is essentially optimistic. In arguing that people's own fierce collecting passions can and do influence perceptions of value and hence have impact upon systems, it steers between the opposing glooms of neo-Marxism as represented by the Frankfurt School and postmodern paradoxical agony described by Baudrillard.

As early as 1947 Adorno and Horkheimer, prominent members of the Frankfurt group, could speak of culture in these terms:

> The assembly-line character of the culture industry, the synthetic, planned method of turning out its products (factory-like not only in the studio but, more or less, in the compilation of cheap biographies, pseudo-documentary novels, and hit songs) is very suited to advertising. The effect, the trick, the isolated repeatable device, have always been used to exhibit goods for advertising purposes . . . Advertising and the culture industry merge technically as well as economically. In both cases the same thing can be seen in innumerable places, and the mechanical repetition is the same as that of the propaganda slogan. In both cases the insistent demand for effectiveness makes technology into psycho-technology, into a procedure for manipulating men. In both cases the standards are striking yet familiar, the easy yet catchy, the skillful yet simple; the object is to overpower the customer, who is conceived as absent-minded or resistant. (1947: 123)

Twenty years later their colleague Marcuse wrote:

> Political freedom would mean liberation of individuals from politics over which they have no effective control. Similarly, intellectual freedom would mean the restoration of individual thought now absorbed by mass communication. (1964: 47)

But the *use* made of industrial mass production by shopper-collectors shows the resilience of the human mentality. The opposition to contemporary system-produced mass culture turned out not to be a return to detailed, particular, indigenous, historically based, local culture – the kind of thing its antagonists describe as Morris dancing – but the user used, the manipulator manipulated into genuine experience which moves across the gulf into the inside of individual life. As we have seen, the rituals of gift, of rite of passage, and of deliberate acquisition for the collection, and the shopping climax of purchase, are all important here.

Baudrillard's view is much darker than Frankfurt's: 'the factory no longer exists because labour is everywhere; the prison no longer exists because arrests and confinements pervade social space . . . capital no longer exists because the law of value has collapsed into self-managed survival in all its forms' (1993: 127) and this is actual death. A kind of human robustness, relative certainly in ultimate time and space, but immensely effective in the here and now of an individual life, answers this. We are heartened and strengthened by a carefully chosen birthday present for a daughter, or the inheritance of a china collection from a grandmother, or the acceptance of our early radio collection by a recognised museum, and, as we have seen, these personal satisfactions have a chance of playing on the wider social stage.

5

Families and Homes

'The family' has been a major – and somewhat controversial – topic of popular and academic debate over the past decades. This debate has come at its subject from a number of angles. It can be argued that the nuclear family, of two parents and their own children, is an essential element in modernity, helping to support an interlocking sequence of structuring notions which feature ideas of the 'Other' as those outside any conceivable blood kin, of investment in 'betterment and progress' for one's children, and of the binary divide between work and leisure, public and private (Benn and Graus 1983). As Talcott Parsons argued (1959), there is a functional fit between the nuclear family and the needs of classic capital industrialisation, and arguably the idea of the two grew up together. From this perspective, the supposed demise of the nuclear unit is a significant part of the broad post-modern libertarian project.

From an internal or personal perspective, the family can seem the most 'natural' field through which a many-faceted individual personality can be achieved in the structuring dimensions of time and space. In the western tradition, we should remember, individuals are assumed to be born into a 'normal' family but to leave it in order to form a sexual relationship outside the blood line which will last for life and which will be the starting point for the next blood-related group. Our kinship structure is, therefore, less like a forest tree, dominating and monolithic, and more like a strawberry bed with a dense network of cross-fertilisation and rooting runners. For most individuals in this situation the multiple roles as child, lover, parent and grandparent are how they make sense of their lives.

It is clear that the idea of the family has enormous ideological power, perhaps only equalled by that attaching to the notion of the liberty of the individual, which itself gives a good idea of the tensions involved. Ideology is one thing, and experience on the ground is quite another. We know that the kinds of family life available are shaped by political pressures brought to bear in the most direct way through tax and welfare policies. We know that the 'classic' nuclear unit does not, and probably never has, loomed as large numerically as sentiment might wish. In 1989 the Policy Studies Centre (Muncie et al. 1995: 11) noted that at any one time the population is made up of

- 1 household in 3 containing a dependent child
- 1 household in 5 consisting of a single parent
- 1 household in 4 being a childless married couple

- 3 households in 10 being married couples with dependent children
- 1 household in 10 containing people over retirement age

In 1992 the General Household Survey found that 11.1% of people live alone, 23.4% are married couples with no children, 39.9% married couples with dependent children, and 10.1% lone parents with dependent children. This suggests that the nuclear family only embraces around a third, or slightly more, of all families at any given moment; but of course, far more of us as individuals have had *experience* of living in such a family, probably as a child and perhaps as a parent, and memories are far more powerful than statistics.

Deeply enmeshed in all this, but also apart from it, is the fact that all families, whether nuclear or otherwise, are political arenas in their own right. The ramifications of these have been researched especially by avowed feminist researchers like Nancy Chodorow (1978, 1980) and Eichenbaum and Orbach (1982). Chodorow's central argument suggests that there are important causal connections between the sexual division of labour (which seems to be pretty much the same across most of humanity barring details), the fact of male dominance and the psychology of gender identity. Women almost everywhere do the main work of caring for small children, and correspondingly lack political, material and financial resources. Interlinked with all this are gender differences in the sense of the self and the capacity for relating to others.

This links with what Csikszentmihalyi and Rochberg-Halton found when they studied domestic symbols (1981). It was clear that families whose members describe their homes in warm emotional tones differ from families in which such descriptions are lacking. Warm families have close personal relationships because these are concretely represented in special household objects. These families have an internal focus, but paradoxically this produces surplus energy to direct towards external goals and activities. There is, however, one nagging ambiguity in this picture that mars its idyllic character – the position of the mother in the warm family constellation (1981: 168). The evidence all suggests an asymmetrical husband/wife relationship in such warm households whereby the husband has an orderly, self-disciplined personality and invests his energy in external, productive goals, and his wife gives herself to the nurturance of family and home. This may reflect traditional values, but would now be considered an immoral sacrifice of (female) self which will sow its own harvest of psychological weeds (1981: 166–171).

This is an interesting finding in relation to the present study. In this chapter we shall endeavour to see how collecting relates to the family scene in broad terms, and if and how collectors in families differ from those outside them. 'Family' here is used as meaning a man and a woman living together on what is intended to be a permanent basis, whether in marriage or partnership, together with any children of either of them who are living with them. In practice, the statistics for childless couples and couples with children are very similar, so both types of group should be understood in the text which follows unless attention is specifically drawn to differences, and, in order to keep the discussion as simple as possible, the figures show only the information relating to those in partnerships, with or without children, and those not in partnerships. We shall start by looking at the family relationships of collectors, and the bearing this seems to have on what material and what kinds of collections are involved. We shall then investigate the role of collecting in relation to the physical home. As 'home' is the relevant spatial field, so 'family time' is the equivalent field for time, and this is next discussed. Analyses of care and record, and getting and spending, are discussed next. The interesting angle which the effect of other collectors within the broader family, including those members belonging to the earlier generation, have on the genesis and development of collecting is pursued, followed by a consideration of links outside the home and family circle. Next, we shall discuss the bearing single parent households have on family collecting issues. Finally some concluding threads are drawn together.

Familiar Things

Of all those who replied to the Contemporary Collecting Survey, 34% had a partner and collected, while 35% said that they did not have a partner and collected; and correspondingly, 66% were with partners but did not collect and 65% were non-collectors without partners. From this we might conclude that the one-third or so of the population who do collect are divided in proportion between the partnered and the partnerless, without favouring either state: the possession of a partner has no bearing on the likelihood of forming the collecting habit. The figures were very similar for the possession of children, where 33% of those with children collected, while 36% did not, so again the collecting population relates proportionately to the generation of offspring. When those with partners and children who responded to the survey were asked if they collected, however, the figures were reversed, with around 65% replying that they did. It seems that in terms of the survey, the most likely state, by two-thirds as against one-third, is to be a collector within a family comprising sexual partners and the children of at least one of them.

It is worth noting as a matter of interest, that human members of the family, like children, spark off relatively few collections apart from those which consist of memorial objects, added to from time to time. Pets, however, do stimulate active collecting. The Black Labrador Collectors (husband and wife) collect images of 'dogs [which] have to resemble our own, real, live ones. We own two black labs. which are our pride and joy. Our daughter will carry on where we leave off. She is daft about them too.' Several Cat Image Collectors reported similar compulsions.

Those collectors in families showed a distinct tendency to have the smaller collections, although this was more marked on the smallest end of

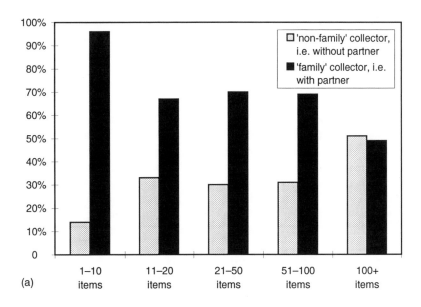

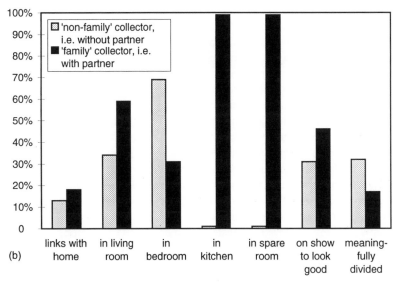

Figure 5.1 *Size (a), location and arrangement (b) of collections by partner possession: analysis of Survey returns*

the scale (see Figure 5.1). The bulk of the collections of up to 50 pieces were held by family people (96%, 67%, 70% and 69%) but when the largest size collection was reached of over 100 pieces, 49% of these collectors did have partners, and 51% did not (Figure 5.1). Where there were children, the over 100 piece collections percentage holding dropped to 39% as opposed to 61%

in childless couples. It looks as if on the whole collections in families are generally rather smaller than the others, but where a collector is deeply committed to the collection, family circumstances are not significant. Complementary evidence (see Chapter 6) suggests that these large family collections are likely to be held by men, who tend to favour the bigger accumulations.

The patterns shown in the distribution of authentic and inauthentic material across those with and without partners, and with and without children are much the same. They suggest that possession of family does not much affect collecting by inauthentic/authentic mode (except that the authentic art is concentrated in the families, but, as we have said, the actual numbers here are very few and so distortions are likely). The principal exception is the records collections, of which, unsurprisingly, two-thirds (67%) are concentrated in the partnerless/childless, that is, among the youngest group.

The range of specific object types naturally follows this broad pattern. Around 80% of all the room ornaments are possessed by those with partners, and since virtually all of these are women, we are here seeing the collections of married women, or those in equivalent relationships. The household collections come in at 16% and represent that same group, and so do the tourist collections at 72%, the household goods at 72% and the jewellery at 60%. The Gold and Silver Charms Collector, for example, displays the charms on bracelets, which she wears, and the Blue and White China Collector likes a lot of things around her. However, it seems likely that there is nothing particularly conjugal about the nature of these collections. They do not seem to show a tendency on the part of partnered women, because unpartnered women collect much the same material; rather this is a reflection of the fact that most women most of the time are in a relationship regarded as permanent. The same is true of the character-istically male preoccupations: 75% of the machinery collections and a surprising 57% of the sporting material are held by men in partnerships. All these figures are matched closely by the returns for those with children, so we are here looking at those 'normal' families that still make up the bulk of the population for those aged under 50.

From all this it appears that tastes in object collection among the family men and women are much the same as among those outside families. This could be expressed more strongly: since to be part of a family is still the most likely situation for a mature adult (and, from the different angle of 'child' status, for young ones as well), it might be said that it is the family people who set the collecting norms against which the population as a whole is judged. This is true, but perhaps not the fundamental point. At bottom, and with the exception that the largest collections seem to be outside families, it seems that likes and dislikes among objects are shaped not by the family that one forms oneself, but, to a large extent, by the family from which one came (as, of course, almost all of us did). We would, therefore, expect to see the pattern which does in fact appear, in which the same range of collecting tastes are spread across the population at large, while the incidence of families within this population is itself large enough to perpetuate the pattern.

Making Homes

To English-speakers 'home' is one of the most emotionally charged words in the language, and so the fact, frequently pointed out by commentators, that a word with this meaning only really exists in English and its immediate linguistic relations (mainly German, Dutch and the Scandinavian languages) always comes as a surprise. As Csikszentmihalyi and Rochberg-Halton have put it: 'In Italian, for instance, *casa* is the nearest equivalent, yet it is much closer in meaning to "house" than to "home". The same is even truer of the French *maison* . . . in all languages there are circumlocutions that convey the psychological meaning of "home" but these are often somehow awkward and not commonly used . . . the French *chez-nous* [does not have] the concreteness and the wide-ranging content of "home"' (1981: 121). And yet to the native Germanic speakers across the world, the word sums up crucial feelings of security, privacy, comfort and childhood roots, which are a densely interwoven net of emotional and material well-being (or, if one's home was unhappy, the corresponding negative feeling of deprivation). The language question reminds us that this need and its satisfaction is not universal, but belongs within one particular development of human culture, that of northern Europe, with its long, cold, dark winters, its domestic work rhythms and its social, kinship and land-allotting arrangements, all of which run back deep into prehistory.

The upshot of all this gives us a characteristically 'English' idea in which the group of parents and their children are matched by the single place in which they live together, people and place forming the single unit of family-and-home. In this thinking 'homeless' families are not proper families at all, and similarly 'proper' homes are those in which children and parents live together. For the Money Box Collector, the piece which had started her off was a box in the form of a wooden house bought for her by her husband while they were saving for their own home. The typical child's drawing of a home – a house with or without attached neighbours but standing on the ground with two floors, a front door, windows, and a pitched roof – mirrors the idea of the normative, or at least the desirable, pretty well, particularly if a back garden and some pet animals are added. The fact that council tower blocks make such an impact on our city-scapes has modified this image hardly at all, presumably because the real numbers of those who live in them is not a large proportion of the population overall. In terms of historical depth, the image is relatively recent and forms part of the great upsurge of the English upper working/lower middle class which gathered momentum from the last decades of the nineteenth century. Its significant artefacts were the typewriter, the adding machine, the small car and the sewing machine, and its typical houses the successive waves of 'semis' (for the gardens of which see J. Roberts 1996). It should be added that, in terms of the most of the rest of the world, these living quarters would count as luxurious, with their range of rooms, space, running water and reliable electricity, and their fittings, furniture and soft furnishings.

Putting this together, we arrive at the notional idea of a home embracing a living room, kitchen, bathroom and main bedroom, with probably one or two more bedrooms, and perhaps an extra living room ('best' room, dining room or study), more bedrooms and a garage. This formed the framework of the information-gathering relating to the physical home (Pearce forthcoming), but respondents were given an opportunity to indicate which rooms their own house actually had.

In the work carried out on individual objects (Pearce forthcoming) respondents were asked in which room they felt most at home. The living room scored by far the highest at 51%, followed by the respondent's bedroom at 17%, and the kitchen at 12%. Men tended to feel slightly more at ease in the living room than women (57% *v.* 55%), and women more at ease in the bedroom (19% *v.* 15%). Women definitely felt more at home in the kitchen (14% *v.* 9%). These indications were not modified by the area situation of the home, or by ethnicity, possession or otherwise of partner and children, or by possession of a car or occupation, which is to say by socio-economic class. The only substantial modification across the range revolved around the 18–25 group who live in the family home without partners and who prefer their own bedrooms to the family living room. We can see that most mature people, partnered or otherwise, prefer their living rooms, although some women preferred their bedroom and some the kitchen. Young people, particularly young women, have a predictable tendency to prefer their bedrooms.

This matches fairly well what Csikszentmihalyi and Rochberg-Halton found in Chicago (1981: 137–139). They discovered that children from 8 to 14 had their most important objects in their own bedrooms, but that the importance of the bedroom declined continuously into adulthood, and then became important again in old age. In this way, the role of the bedroom traces the course of the self over the life cycle. In childhood and adolescence it is valued because 'it enables the child to cultivate a sense of autonomy through interactions with an environment charged with personalized meanings'. At adulthood the sense of personal autonomy is internalised and can be expressed through the home as a whole in its full social sense. Finally, in old age, one's own room re-asserts itself as the private sphere in which autonomy can be cultivated through the objects of a lifetime.

People describe their homes in various ways (Pearce forthcoming). They are described equally happily as 'old', in which case character is stressed, or 'recent' in which case convenience is highlighted. The recurrent words are 'cosy', 'comfortable' and 'restful': one respondent summed this up in her description of her home's atmosphere as 'restful, comfortable, fresh and welcoming; a haven from outside pressures'. A heavy-goods vehicle driver described his home as 'normal happy family home'. Discordant notes were mostly struck by the under-25 age group. One young male said his home was 'natural and cosy downstairs – cold and dark upstairs'. A woman of the same age group said it was a 'very modern home but with lots of arguing and shouting'. This chimes in with the way in which different family members use the available space, and with what we know of the difficulties of adolescence. It reminds us (if we needed reminding) that 'home' embodies tension as well as refuge.

But does the shell shape the hermit-crab or the crab work to find a suitably shaped shell? The home itself is a psychic entity, invested with a life of its own through the feelings, energies and objects with which it has been endowed, and which then work their own powerful influence upon subsequent emotions and accumulations. Homes are living culture, in which all members share a symbolic environment but endeavour to create their own personal version of it. A home is many homes both at once and over time; its personality, like all personalities, changes over time and it is both active and receptive in relation to other personalities. Again, like all personalities, it operates within a broad cultural programme, which helps to explain how the different individuals live in it differently, for the final decisions about exactly how social culture will be realised in each actual home are up to the individuals living in it.

The tension between wanting to feel at home in the home and wanting to assert each of ourselves as a unique individual – so characteristic of family life – was revealed very interestingly when collectors were asked if their material directly linked up with their homes, and clearly the respondents saw this as meaning an integral link rather than a broad one in which the collection was kept at home. Overall 16% answered yes to this question, with 84% saying the collection had no link with their homes. The comparative figures for those with and without partners (and children) who answered 'yes' were very similar, so it would seem that membership of a family makes very little difference to the direct relationship people perceive between the material and their home (Figure 5.1). Predictably, probably, women related their collecting to their homes rather more than men, but the difference was not very large (18% *v.* 13.5%). The linkage was strongest among the younger middle-aged (46–55) and among the over-65s, and lowest among the youngest people. Those in large towns made the link least, but occupation made little difference except that the retired group scored high (50%), reflecting the showing made by their age group. Understandably, collections of room ornaments figured largest in the relationship with home, but not overwhelmingly so, for only 67% of such collectors made the link. Household material came surprisingly low, with only 20% making the link, but paintings (67%) and jewellery (67%) scored high.

Our impression is that the home link is made by some of the women collectors, typically gathering room ornaments and probably in the older age groups. The Pink Glass Collector was typical: 'My mother had owned the first piece of my collection. I found it after her death. The collection fits in with the colour scheme in my house.' The figure for paintings, mostly gathered by men, comes as no surprise, but the high score for jewellery is surprising, and the nature of the direct link rather obscure; perhaps the largely women collectors see it as linked to the home through celebratory events which took place there and which the gifts of jewellery commemorate. However, these groups are very much a minority. Most of the younger women and men do not see their collections in terms of their home, even though the collected material is of domestic character, like household goods. Family people seem, like others, to be using their collections primarily to make statements about themselves as individuals rather than in terms of a home-and-family collective identity: but the desire to create an individual home in the broader sense can be an important part of this individuality.

All life operates through the parameter of space, but material life does so in a particularly clear and cogent way, and to this collections are no exception. We might expect that the division of space within the homes of family collectors might differ from that in non-family contexts. Collectors were asked where in the home they kept their material, whether it was stored away or out on display, and, if on display whether this was in no special order, on show in order to look good, or divided up in a particular way. These three questions obviously bring related features together and create a sliding scale which starts with material stored away in a spare room and moves to material on display in the main living room of the home.

In general, it seems that most collectors have all or most of their material in either the living room (50%) or the bedroom (45%), although a substantial percentage of collected material is kept in the spare room (17%), and about the same percentage in the kitchen. Interestingly, the breakdown of this trend is uneven in relation to family circumstances: those with partners are much more likely to have their material in the living room (59% *v.* 34%) while those without are more likely to have it in their bedrooms (69% *v.* 31%). This must reflect the practices of the young unmarried living in the family home, who treat their bedrooms like living rooms. Kitchen collections are almost all held by those in partnerships and so are those in spare rooms (Figure 5.1).

As we would expect from this, most collections are on display, at 65% among families and 59% among non-family collectors, although in both cases about a quarter have their material in boxes, and a further tenth or slightly more have it in chests of drawers. It looks as if most of the living room, and a fair number of the bedroom collections and probably the kitchen collections are on show, but some of the bedroom material and the material kept elsewhere is in storage. Overall, around 80% of all collections are organised on show in no special order and only 20% are divided up in a particular way. In terms of families there is an interesting distinction. Those outside families are much more likely to be among the fifth who divide up their material in a meaningful way (32% *v.* 17%). On the other hand, family collectors are rather more likely to have their material on show to look good (46% *v.* 31%) (Figure 5.1).

Overall, we can see a distinct tendency on the part of family collectors to have some or most of their collection on show in the family living room, arranged according to the collector's idea of how it looks well. The Embroidered Cover Collector, for example (who said that she 'can't stop') has things 'all over' the house. Evidence to be discussed in more detail later (Chapter 7) shows that these collectors include virtually all the family women, and a good proportion of the men as well: the kitchen collections also belong with the women. A second group are the young of both sexes, who have their material in their bedrooms, sometimes on show and sometimes packed away out of sight. A substantial proportion of this group must be among those who also divide up their material in a particular way, whether on show or in store.

Family Time

Family time structures individual time in a number of ways, all of them probably crucial to the sense of significance in time passing which we all feel. In a horizontal or cyclical sense, family time structures the turning year, which, within its formal shape, harbours family-specific dates of birthdays and anniversaries (Figure 5.2). These relate to partners in gift-giving, which we shall consider shortly. We should remember that, just as the locational notion of 'home' is peculiar to the northern Europeans and their descendants, so is its temporal equivalent, the notion of 'Christmas' which, whatever its antecedents, is now the major family focus of the northern year. Family life also provides a vertical structure which organises the relationship of the passing years. This takes shape as a helix with broad belly and narrow points (Figure 5.3). We usually begin as children within a structure created by one or two immediate adults, our parents, and with varying numbers of siblings. As we grow through childhood and young adulthood, we tend to grow away from our families until our life spiral broadens to form an adult partnership and children of our own. As these children, in turn, grow up, our spiral turns again to embrace the core adults, or perhaps one single adult, ourselves. The two temporal planes come together in the kind of complex structure already described in Figure 4.5.

Reaching back before our own birth is the personal prehistory of the family, outside individual memory but within the scope of anecdote from parents and grandparents. In the great majority of families, this seems to extend no further back than the early days of the grandparents, with perhaps just a few family stories about their parents. Stretching before us is the future which follows our own death. The family stake here rests with grandchildren, or perhaps great-grandchildren, who, in their turn, will hear stories of their grandparents. Sometimes collectors understand this quite explicitly. Both Egg Cup Collectors allow their grandchildren to choose

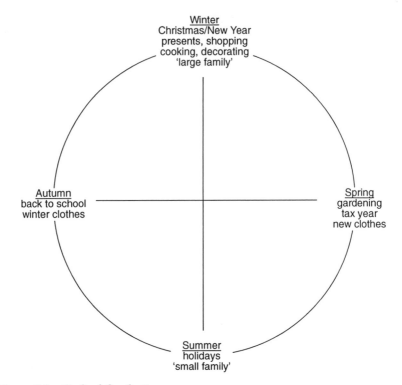

Figure 5.2 *Cyclical family time*

which cup they will eat their boiled eggs from, so building up a store of family anecdotes linked with the collections. With reasonable luck, the period of 'history', that is of direct personal experience or first-hand parental recounting – of our own babyhood, for example, or of their childhood – runs for about a century, while before and after lie different kinds of darkness to which we are tied through sequences of umbilical cords.

The unique capacity of collected objects to carry the past into the present has often recently been discussed (e.g. Belk 1988; Pearce 1995: 235–254). Collected material culture alone has the ability to be a genuine, intrinsic part of past action and to exist in a continuing series of presents, so that the past continues to exist with all its capacity for perpetual re-interpretation. This re-interpretation is so normal for family collections that we scarcely notice it, so close are we to the objects as our other selves. Pieces of kitchen equipment hoarded from the grandparents' home become sitting room ornaments in a late twentieth century home, or deeply treasured but over-elaborate porcelain from the same home's front room becomes 'naff but amusing' in the grandchildren's bathroom.

Anecdotal evidence makes it clear that a substantial number of collections, perhaps as many as a third, arise through the inheritance of one or more particular objects associated with the personal prehistory or very early

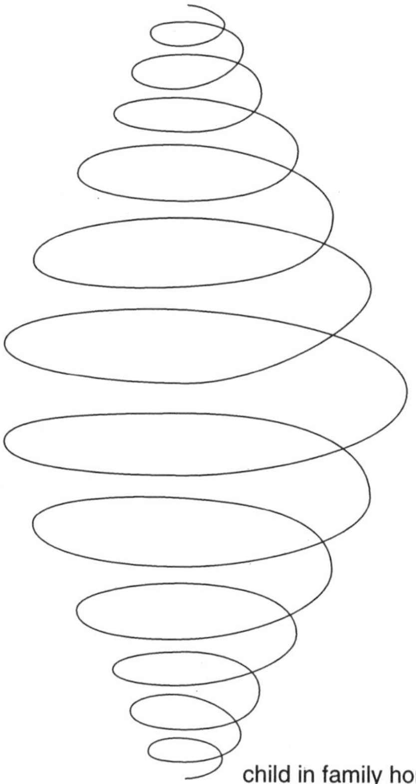

retirement, widow(er)hood,
small home, family flown

fullest family life
partner, children,
bigger home

child in family home
departure, independence

Figure 5.3 *Vertical family time*

history of the collector. Interestingly, the great majority both of original owners, and of recipients, are women. The objects themselves are seldom of the kind that feature in any official paperwork, and are usually either simply passed hand to hand in the older person's final life phase, or are collected from the old home at death, with varying degrees of acrimony. What stands out, however, is that, by and large, collections are matrilineal and form the material culture aspect of the female obligation to remember, commemorate and sustain through the passing of time. Indeed, it would be easy to feel, and perhaps not untruly, that in the accumulation and transmission of material culture generally, as opposed to property or money, male members of the family are accidental and insubstantial.

Across the collecting group overall, roughly a third had not given any thought to what would happen to their collection after death. The corresponding age range analysis shows, unsurprisingly, that these belong mostly in the younger group, with a very clear graph showing a curve from 64% of 'not thought' under 25 to 13% in the over 65s. The corresponding curve shows 5% of under 25s intending to bequeath their material, against 63% of the over 65s. This expresses the principal views, and their impact is strengthened if, as is likely, 'pass it on', with a steady 20–25%, is regarded as a less formal version of 'bequeath'. The other possibilities, of selling, 'other plans' and giving to a museum, all score a steady under 13%, with donation to museum at 5% or less. Across the age range, approaching two-thirds (59%) of the women said they would bequeath/pass on, as opposed to 46% of the men. In discussion, some of the male collectors made it clear that they had worked through these boxes chiefly because they were there, while the women were clear about which family member – usually a daughter, granddaughter or niece – they would pass their things to. All this was born out by the family figures: 63% of those in families intended to bequeath or to pass material on, while only 38% of those not in families intended to, reflecting the younger collectors (Figure 5.4). Clearly, material continuity within the family line, with emphasis on the distaff side, is the favourite form of personal collecting closure.

It would also be unsurprising if absorption in family life had a bearing on the individual collector's sense of temporal structuring in his daily life. The pattern of continuous collecting in relation to family collectors is much that of collectors overall. Rather less than half (40%) of all collectors felt that they added to their collections continuously, and similarly 41% of partnered collectors felt that they did so. The same pattern shows up in the extent to which collectors felt that they thought about their collecting during time when they were not actively adding to or working on their material: four-fifths (80%) overall felt that they did not think about it, and 79% of those with partners agreed. Again, the pattern of time spent actively collecting and looking after the collection among the collectors overall is closely mirrored by the pattern of family collectors. All groups abhor equally the idea of closure: 96% of collectors overall felt that their collection would never be complete, and in verbal interview this feeling was usually expressed in the dreaming, contemplative tones of those who find it reassuring to believe that, in this area at least, there is no such thing as a final experience. Those in partnerships scored 97% in answer to the same question.

All of this seems to show that family collectors are no more, or less, absorbed in their collections in their daily lives than are collectors overall. In part, this obviously bears out the fact that most collectors *are* family collectors, just as most people live in families. But it also makes the important psychological point that there seems to be no difference to the extent to which family and non-family collectors use their material as a mental retreat within which to structure an isolationist universe. It might have been that non-family collectors are clearly using objects as a substitute for human kin, as it might have been that family collectors habitually use their collections as a refuge, both mental and physical, from family life; but in fact neither of these two things seems to be happening. Instead, collectors

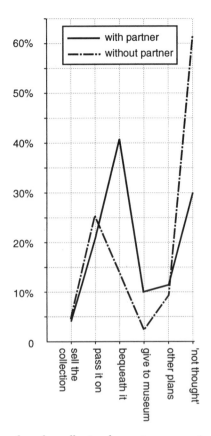

Figure 5.4   *Future plans for collection by partner possession*

generally work within the family pattern of time, both in the immediate sense of day-to-day living and in the broader sense which embraces the construction of family history.

Caring and Acquiring

How family life affects a collector's capacity to care for, and create records about his collection is an important area, but is essentially specialised information relating to the broader area of collection care and documentation in general, to be discussed in detail in Chapter 6. Here, therefore, we shall home in on the ways in which collection care seems to be directly affected by a family context.

Family collectors follow the collecting norm when it comes to remembering where they acquired a piece and what they paid for it, at 45% and 20%. They are rather more likely than others to remember how they found out about it (13.8%). All this may well have a bearing on the way in which the family system of remembering and commemorating works as a whole. We have to remember, however, that these figures are, over the collectors as a whole, rather low: half are not interested in remembering where a piece came from, and fewer still in what it cost or how it was found; it seems that for around half of all collectors, and similarly for those in families, the piece itself in the important thing.

For most people the idea of the 'piece itself' excludes the collection of related material like newspaper articles or books. Only around a quarter of all collectors were interested in doing this, and membership of a family made little difference. The quarter spread their interest around fairly evenly between knowing how, when, where and by whom the pieces were made, although, rather surprisingly, interest dropped significantly when it came to finding out how the pieces were used in the past: perhaps collectors thought that the earlier queries covered this, or perhaps they thought it was a silly question since the answer generally was obvious.

Again following general practice, most family collectors are not interested in creating a permanent record of all this collection information, although they are rather more interested than those outside families (18% *v.* 10%). Those who do do this, like all collectors, dislike both record cards and computers. If they want to make a record they use a notebook (62%) or a sheet of paper (33%), and notebooks are considerably more popular in the family than outside them (62% *v.* 24%), perhaps because they stand a better chance of survival. The sense of ownership is not generally expressed by the addition of a personal mark of any kind to the objects. Only around one in ten of all collectors – family or otherwise – do this, so apparently the sense of ownership is strong enough and the organisation of the collection sufficiently satisfying without recourse to the imposition of any signification.

One of the most significant fields of collecting practice is the patterns of acquisition, and this is also an area where we would not be surprised to find that collectors within families differ from those outside them. In terms of cash transactions, Survey analysis shows only a quarter of all males reckon to spend £1.00 or less, while over half (51%) declare themselves as sometimes spending over £10.00. Females match this pretty closely, with just under a quarter (22%) reckoning to spend under £1.00 per item, and nearly half (48%) suggesting that they will spend over £10.00. These figures mirror those of spending by family members, both male and female (20% under £1.00, 56% over £10.00), reminding us how large a feature numerically family members are in the collecting scene. By comparison, 31% of non-family collectors spend under £1.00 and only 37% spend over £10.00 (Figure 5.5). This suggests that 'general' spending patterns and 'family' spending patterns are the same, indeed one and the same, while the lower spenders are largely the young people, who in relation to spend figures come out at 30% at the low spend end and 30% at the higher. Similarly, family members show themselves as just as willing to sell a piece that turned out to be valuable as the population in general.

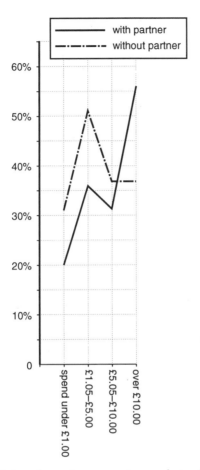

Figure 5.5 *Cost of pieces by partner possession: analysis of Survey returns*

In the collecting population as a whole, the bulk of material comes either by purchase (84% of collectors acquired some pieces in this way) or by gift (67%). The family collectors score 82% and 67% as against non-family collectors at 87% and 68%, so non-family collectors are a little more likely to purchase material. Four-fifths (80%) of all collectors, family and otherwise, acquire collection pieces in ordinary shops, followed at some distance by around 40% who get material at car boot sales and the like. It seems clear that family spending patterns aimed at the direct, personal acquisition of collection material are much the same as those in the collecting population at large. This applies to the legitimate market operating within fixed premises and fixed (more-or-less) prices, and the less legitimate, or less formal, market operating part-time and with an element of direct person-to-person exchange.

Much collected material was bought in one or other of these markets but not by the owner of the collection in which it found its permanent home; to put the point another way, almost all collected material is bought – rather than home-made or exchanged – but is purchased by a second person who then makes a gift of it to the primary collector. The nature of the gift as central social and psychological practice has already been discussed but here we are concerned with its operation within a fairly circumscribed family circle. The topic has already received some, but rather limited, consideration in print (Caplow 1982; Miller 1993a, b). As we have just noted, the pattern of gift-giving contributes considerably to the cyclical pattern of family time, and to its continuing stability through sequential time.

In the work carried out on personal relationships with objects (Pearce forthcoming) respondents were given a family tree diagram which included both blood kin and in-law relationships. Each was asked to score those from whom they received presents, at Christmas or similar occasion, and those to whom they gave presents. Figures 5.6 and 5.7 show the percentage scores of men and of women. Two-thirds of men exchange gifts with their partners, while one in ten give without receiving and only one in a hundred receive without giving. The missing 22% represent those not in partnerships at the time of the investigation. Obviously, the Christmas present to wife or partner is a crucial symbol of the marriage as a whole. About 47% of men exchange with their children, and a further 16% give without receiving; this again testifies to the symbolic importance of the present (again the missing proportion are largely those without children). Surprisingly (to this writer at any rate) exchanges between siblings also run at 46%. Exchanges between son and parents score high at 55%. In-law parents do less well, at a 34% exchange rate. Nephews and nieces participate at around half, equally divided between exchanging and receiving. Thereafter, the present-giving dwindles away.

Women record a 63% exchange with their partner, which again represents most of those in partnerships. Eight per cent give without receiving. Half of the women exchanged with their children, and 18% give without receiving. Exchanges between siblings ran at 61%, and between daughter and parents at 64%. Interestingly, the proportion of men who give their partners Christmas presents is rather higher than women, while in relation to children and, especially, parents, women are more likely to exchange or give, and they are considerably more likely to maintain present-giving with their own brothers and sisters. Both kinds of in-laws do much the same.

The point already made about partnership and parenthood holds good in the wider family sphere: present exchange or simple gift is both an integral part and a symbol of the strength of the relationship, and so its relative frequency is an indicator of the relative strength, importance and perhaps intimacy of the relationship. It emerges that partners and children loom largest for both men and women, followed by one's own parents, especially for women, and one's own brothers and sisters, again especially for women. This kinship group is the physical and symbolic heart of the contemporary British family. It matches, of course, the group of those who live together in one home, depending upon whether or not the respondent is still in his or

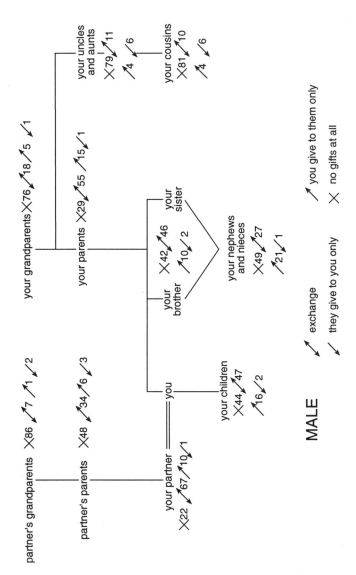

Figure 5.6 *Family gift flow for males (drawn from data in Relations with Objects Project, see Pearce forthcoming). All figures are percentages.*

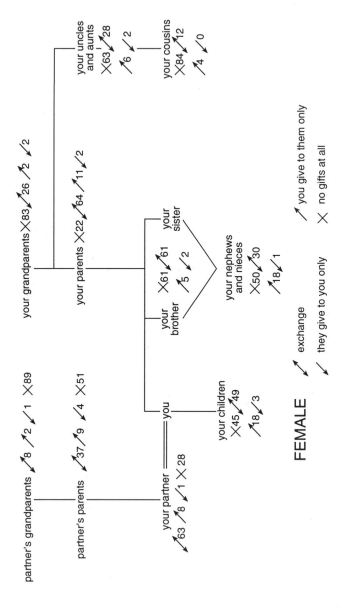

Figure 5.7 *Family gift flow for females (drawn from data in Relations with Objects Project, see Pearce forthcoming). All figures are percentages.*

her parental home, or has set up a new home with a partner. Women are rather more concerned than men to maintain what might be called the second circle of links (parents and siblings) but both sexes are anxious to sustain the core relationships of partner and children.

Patterns of acquisition are informed by mental attitudes. The majority of collectors overall (67%) wait for pieces to appear, and this includes appearing appropriately gift-wrapped, but the remaining third seek out pieces actively through all the various avenues. The figures for collectors with partners are much the same (69% v. 30%), although these collectors seem to be at greater risk of being offered pieces they do not want (12% of partnered collectors as opposed to 9% of non-partnered), presumably reflecting ill-judged presents. This chimes in with the generally relaxed attitude of collection activity overall – most of us, it seems, are happy to know that it is there without pursuing any aspect of it particularly actively. Those with partners, however, were much more likely (59%) to find one thing and carry on collecting from there, than were those without (39%). Collecting seems at first sight to be a more purposeful activity, at least in origin, for those without partners, but this may obscure the fact that the real origin of collecting, for many people, lies in a general but semi-conscious state of readiness for which the discovery of an object is a collection waiting to happen.

This brings us to the more obvious emotional considerations. Collectors with partners seem to have a clearer idea of why they like their collections than those without (69% v. 56%); partnered collectors are rather less likely to feel they 'must have' a piece (58% v. 62%); partnered collectors seem to feel that their collection is, on balance, rather less important than do non-partnered ones, although the differences in spread are fairly gentle (Figure 5.8). The message seems to be that family collectors are rather more balanced and considering than others, and that in relation to emotional attachment, they are a little, but not much, less committed: this may in large part simply reflect the youth of most of the partnerless, and in any case the differences are much less dramatic than might have been supposed.

Family Influences

An important area of the relationship between families and collecting revolves around the link between the gathering of material and the personal relationships between family members, and in particular how this has influenced collecting habits. To the simple question 'Were you encouraged to begin collecting by somebody?' 17% of collectors said they were, representing rather less than a fifth of the collecting body. The split between the sexes was fairly similar, with 47% of men and 53% of women within the 17% thinking that they were encouraged. Most of those who felt themselves to have been encouraged were young, they were spread fairly evenly across the habitation range, across the employment range and across the object range, although characteristically adolescent material like

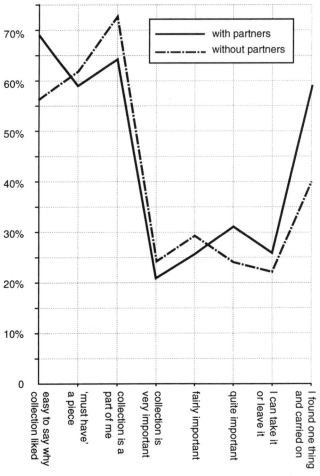

Figure 5.8 *Feelings about the collection by partner possession: analysis of Survey returns*

coins scored fairly high here (30% of these collections) and so did room ornaments.

These points must be put alongside the data revealed by the question 'Does anybody else in your family collect?' For some respondents there was a family depth of collecting which was important: one collector who herself had six separate collections reported that her husband, sisters and mother-in-law all collected also. About 62% of the collectors felt that other members of their families did the same (and 38% did not). When the question of outside encouragement was cross-referenced to that asking if other family members collected, 61% of those who were encouraged belonged to a collecting family (and 39% did not). It seems that while positive encouragement plays a relatively small part, and that usually confined to the young, family example is very important. Positive encouragement usually comes from the mother, who sees it as educationally and socially advantageous. Example can come from any part of the family, and clearly, in many families, collecting is a family tradition

The multiple collectors (i.e. those who are in a family with at least one other collector) seem to behave much like all other collectors when it comes to seeking out pieces, waiting for pieces to appear and being offered material which they do not want; their patterns of acquisition, by shop and so forth, and by gift and so on, are as those of others, and so are their spending and collection-selling habits; their linkage with a hobby is much the same and so is their membership of a collectors' club and the link-up with their work. The multiple collectors do show a certain tendency to make use of their material, with over half (55%) saying that they do use their things, while over half (53%) of the single collectors (i.e. those who are the sole collector in their family) say that they do not.

In terms of collection care (remembering acquisition details, finding out about history and use, making records and marks, collecting ancillary data) the patterns across the two groups are very similar. They are similar again across the pattern of time spent on the collection, except that those who live with other collectors are more likely to spend some time on the collection daily – 67% of these collectors do so, as opposed to 33% who do not. In terms of thinking about their collections between times, however, the two groups are very similar, neither thinking about them very much (19/20% v. 81/80%). The patterns are again very similar in answer to the question 'Who knows that you collect?', with 90% of multiple collectors and 81% of single collectors having their family know, 62/58% having friends knowing, 21/14% having many knowing and very few (1/7%) being completely secretive.

The pattern of place in which the collection is kept is also similar, although multiple collectors are rather more likely to keep their material in the family living room (51% as opposed to 47%). This probably relates to the fact that multiple collectors are considerably more likely than others to have their material on show (46% as opposed to 34%). The pattern of storage practices is similar, but 66% of multiple collectors as opposed to 61% of the single collectors have their material on display rather than put away. We can see a distinct pattern of multiple collections deliberately displayed within the main family room, matched by a certain tendency to keep collections possessed by just one family member elsewhere, although much of it is also on show. This matches the clear tendency of multiple collectors to see their material as linked with their homes: 60% of them do so see it, as opposed to 40% who do not. The comparable break between single collectors is much more closely balanced at 48% who do see a link and 52% who do not.

This leads us to the question of how the two groups feel. Guilt is fairly evenly divided, but, rather oddly, multiple collectors are marginally the guiltier at 54% (yes) and 49% (no) as opposed to 46% (yes) and 51% (no). The pattern of regret was very similar. Again, 70% of the multiple collectors felt that they would not repeat their collecting if they could start afresh, while 28% thought that they would. An interesting 58% of multiple collectors found it difficult to say why they collected, and correspondingly 53% of single collectors thought it was an easy question to answer, suggesting a certain bemusement in the multiple camp. The patterns of answers about specific reasons for collecting, however, were very comparable. Both groups did it primarily because they liked the material (85% *v.* 87%). Very few did it in order to get complete sets (11% *v.* 8%), and a surprisingly small proportion did it to bring back memories (11% *v.* 8%). Both groups intended to bequeath their material (32% *v.* 30%), but most (44% *v.* 37%) had not thought about their collection's future.

The respective natures of the multiple and single collections is important. As with family based collectors in general, there is a tendency for collections smaller than 20 pieces to belong to single collectors, while those between 21 and 100 tend to belong to multiple collectors. However, the very large collections of over 100 pieces again belong to single collectors. The multiple collectors have a certain, although not very distinctive, tendency to cluster in the object areas of natural history, history and coins (representing the young element), household goods and paintings: probably the chief significance here is the prominence of the young. The pattern of inauthentic/authentic : artefact/masterpiece shows no differentiation between the two groups.

All of this gives the impression that the inter-relationships of more than one collector in the same family are potentially as complex as we would expect any family relationships to be. It is clear that example and encouragement is an important incitement to begin collecting for a significant number of people. Most of these received their encouragement in the form of a collecting example within the family, and the most of the rest seem to have received other kinds of encouragement, verbal and perhaps financial and spatial within the home. The flow of encouragement does not seem to have been between partners, but rather from parents, particularly mother to child. This is underlined by the 'young adult' character of many of the collections and by their tendency to belong within the 'educational', morally enhancing and socially superior categories (the three qualities are here much the same). Example can work across the family field. Once the new collector has started on his or her way, patterns of organisation, care and linkage with the world outside the home are much the same across the groups, although multiple collectors seem to use their material a little more. Similarly, the size of multiple collections matches the general norm, and so does the character of their contents.

Differences emerge not in the content but in the style of collecting, and in the emotions which it arouses. Multiple collectors are more likely to see their material as linked with their homes, and this seems in part to arise from the fact that multiple collectors tend to have their material on show in the family living room. Also, they seem to spend rather more time, but not thought, on their things. The differences should not be stressed, but multiple collectors do seem to be more likely to feel that their collections are something of a burden, by expressing higher levels of guilt, regret and lack of desire to repeat the experience. Multiple collectors were less clear about why they collected, although in answer to specific questions a liking for the objects featured most strongly, and not many were interested in memories, something which perhaps reflects the relative youth of many of them.

Without over-estimating the significance of these tendencies, it does look as if encouragement and example within a collecting family can be experienced as pressure by the individual who is being persuaded to collect. The public display of the collection in the most used room could easily be a part of this, and it links up with the traditional and 'superior' character of some of the material collected. Parental aspiration for children seems to emerge here, and is sometimes experienced by the young people, either at the time or soon after, as manipulative and tiresome rather than helpful and enhancing. If this is true, then we touch here one of the unhappier aspects of collecting practice.

Playing Away

An interesting area of the complex of relationships between collecting, family and home is the relative extent to which family collectors use their material to forge links outside their homes and families. Roughly a third of all collectors with partners make use of their collections by wearing them, driving them, or using them in various talks and demonstrations. The figures for collectors without partners are similar, but score a little higher on the usage roster. These scores are closely mirrored in the figures for the extent to which the collection links up with another hobby, and here the ethnographic evidence shows that the hobbies involved are often the talking and demonstrating already mentioned. In contrast, the scores for participation in a collectors' club are very low (5% of those with partners, 2% of those without), reflecting the relative lack of interest in this aspect of collecting which has already been noticed (pp. 54–60). Links with work score rather higher at 9% of those with partners forming a relationship between their work and their material, and 11% of those without partners doing so.

Plainly, family members are no more likely to belong to a club than are collectors in general; in fact most of those who do belong *are* with partners, but their overall percentage is low. Relationships with the work place come in at around one in ten across the board, and this is broadly true for using and linking with a hobby, but here the across-the-board percentage runs at around 33%. It looks as if family members behave much like non-family collectors in their relationship to the world outside their immediate home base, although non-family people are a little more likely to use their collecting to foster social links.

We receive a balanced impression. On the whole, family members are happy to keep their material at home and to enjoy its satisfactions within the home and with other members of the family, although a substantial proportion of them are outward-looking, and use their collection as a link with the outside world of work and social life. The pattern of non-family collectors is similar. We do not perceive non-family collectors who have their material primarily as a means to make social connections or such collectors who cower in their solitary lives making no external links; equally we do not see family collectors who never stir from the security blanket of home or such collectors who use the collections either as a means of escape or as an indication of the kind of balanced, confident individual who functions as well socially as he does domestically. The accent overall is low key, modest and unemphatic.

The question of links outside the home leads to that of those with whom knowledge of a collection is shared, and the degree of secrecy which surrounds the collecting habit. This has been the subject of considerable recent discussion, particularly in the broadcast media, who like to develop the idea that collectors are frequently secretive people who treat their collecting habit as a hidden vice. In fact, 89% of collectors with partners said that their families knew about their collections, and 76% of those without partners said that their families knew, again representing largely the youngest group. Given that some people failed to complete this section, it is likely that very few people indeed who have partners wish to keep – or succeed in keeping – knowledge from that partner. Around half (56%) of family people say their friends do not know, and two-thirds (63%) of partnerless people say that their friends do know. This is predictable, with friends to a certain extent taking the place of partners, especially among the young.

The figures plummet in the answers to the next two questions. Clearly, fairly few collectors feel that many people outside family and friends are aware of their collections: only 15% of family collectors and 23% of non-family feel that 'many people' know that they collect. But even fewer collectors are completely secretive, for in both cases only about 5% felt that nobody knew. It seems that habits in this area do not differ greatly inside and outside a context of a partner and family of one's own: most people share their practice with family and friends, some do so more widely, probably in the context of work or a demonstrating hobby, but very few are secretive in any meaningful sense of the word.

More detailed breakdowns bear out these suggestions. Women are slightly more likely than men to share knowledge of their collection with friends (58% v. 61%), or share it more widely (22% v. 15%): this comes as no surprise. The age profiles equally hold no surprises. The youngest group, and all those over 36, all share with their families to a high degree, but those between 26 and 35 are the least likely to share – although at 72% they are still likely do so. Again unremarkably, this age group are the likeliest (at 23%) to share their collection with a wide circle. The role of friends is very important in the youngest group (58%), drops in the next group (49%) and then rises steadily across the years (60%–76%) until it drops back abruptly in the oldest group (41%). This will reflect the period between 26 and 35 when many know a wide range of people and are still sorting out their close relationships of partner and friends, the period of maturity when such relationships are fixed to a large extent, and then the final phase when family – although very probably grown children – is still very important, but friends begin to die.

The patterns of sharing knowledge are the same across the habitation groups: in all the differentials most people's families and friends are aware of what they have. Interestingly, the pattern is broken in the occupation groups, where only 50% of the unemployed, 67% of the farm workers, 67% of the students and 50% of manual workers shared with their families; the students, also, had the only substantial proportion of 'nobody knows' at 33%. It seems that the proportion across the board of those who are reticent belong within these occupation groups. It is easy to see why the unemployed might wish to keep their affairs secret, and to see that students are in the process of defining themselves as separate from their families. The reticence of the two groups of manual workers seems to reflect the traditional exclusiveness of husbands in the old working class.

Connecting with practices of openness and secrecy are the feelings which the collections arouse – of guilt, of regret at having started, and of willingness to repeat the experience. The overwhelming majority of collectors report that they would wish to repeat their collecting experience if they could go back again to the beginning: around 95% say that they would repeat the experience and this figure is equally true for those in families and those without them. The figure of around 95% is similarly universally returned as the answer 'No' to the question 'Do you regret starting your collection?' Clearly, collecting is almost universally seen as something which adds interest and which enhances life. The affection with which people view their accumulations is the single fact which comes across with most force, however the data are viewed.

The question of guilt is more complicated. A fifth of the collectors in general admitted to experiencing some guilt in relation to their collecting habit. This broke down in relation to membership of a family to show that those with families were slightly more likely to feel guilty than those without (22% v. 18%). This suggests that when a family member has a collection it can cause some of the frictions, probably to do with spending money and devoting time and space, which arouse twinges of guilt in the collector. Moreover, as we shall see in Chapter 6, women are a little more likely to feel guilt than men. This translates into a certain degree of guilt being felt more by wives and mothers than by husbands and fathers, and the qualitative information certainly bears this out.

Taking all this together, we might conclude that although family members delight in their collections, they do so with a touch of guilty defiance, especially if they are women. This seems to be true, although it would probably be wrong to over-estimate the degree of guilt outside a few specific individuals. In the main, collections seem to be experienced as a genuine source of simple interest and pleasure, and to add to the satisfactions of family life rather than to its burdens.

Lone Parents

Mythology surrounds the single parent: she (as it usually is) is somebody who puts her own enjoyment before her responsibilities, and acquires a child as a means to housing and benefits on the state. Her work-shy, immoral habits threaten old fashioned values and are unravelling the fabric of society dangerously fast (Y. Roberts 1996). But, as recent research has shown, the average lone parent is a woman of 34 who has married or co-habited for a long time. She has one child, takes the family break-down very seriously, and will probably create a new, serious relationship by the time she is 40. She would like to find the kind of job which makes independence possible (Burges and Brown 1995).

There are 1.5 million lone parents in Britain, caring for 2 million children; of these 57% are women who, for whatever reason, have lost their men, 33% are women who have never been in a stable relationship, and 9% are men. Forty-two per cent are working, mostly part-time, but overall lone parents cost the country £9 billion each year in benefits. The average age of the never-partnered mother is 25. She tends to come from the poorer educated group, and far from plotting a life of lazy ease, seems to be confused, ignorant and suffering from low self-esteem. In spite of all this there is no evidence that the children of lone parents turn out better or worse than those from orthodox families (see e.g. Dowd 1996).

Those respondents who scored themselves as having children but not living with a partner came to 2% of the total replies, which is quite close to the proportion of this group in the population as a whole (approximately 2.5%). The respondent group represented 7.7% of those respondents who said that they collected. As with the lone parents in the country overall, however, the respondents presented a mixed bag of circumstances. Two were men, although whether their children were with them or their mothers was unclear. Four were older women (over 56) whose children are presumably now living independent lives. The rest, 65% of this group, were 'classic' single parents, young women with their children and without partners.

One of the men collects firearms and ammunition. He is between 26 and 35, and is employed as a clerical officer. He is an international shooter and takes part in competition pistol shooting. His collection totals up to 20 pieces. He scores himself as happy with his collecting practice, and keeps an associated collection of relevant material. He reckons to spend up to £100 on a piece. This collector represents what a significant number of collectors would wish to be. The content of his collection is typical of male accumulations, and so are his attitudes to it; his competitive success and its identity with his collected material would be envied by many men. It is a pity that we do not know if these activities contributed to the breakdown of his relationship.

The younger women all collect material like sleeping cat images, ornaments and pictures of cats, and pig images. They conform in every way to the normal patterns of female collecting. Two of the older women collect early pewter and carnival glass, and again conform to gender collecting norms and practices.

All this suggests that, although 'ordinary' family life is the norm for collectors as it is for people as a whole, those adults who constitute single parent families collect in very much the same ways as their partnered brothers and sisters. This seems to be because orthodox or traditional family life still dominates the mind-set of us all, whether we are actually in such a family or not at any given moment, and governs responses to the material world.

Conclusion

In persistent sentiment, backed up in reality by the very large percentage of the population who are experiencing or have experienced it, the notion of 'family' has three main foci: the interrelated group of blood and sexual kin centring upon the core relationship of father–mother; the home as the spatial dimension of family life; and cumulative shared experience, reaching backwards and forwards beyond a single life, which makes the dimension of family time. Across these are the fields of family life represented by internal and external relationships.

Collecting inside this network and outside it have much more in common than they have in difference, probably because family life is so very standard an experience that it has the effect of creating norms. The kinds of objects collected, the ways in which this is done, and the kinds of care taken, do not differ greatly between family and non-family collectors, although family collections tend to be rather smaller and better considered. Similarly, the balance of outside interests between the two groups is much the same.

What does show up is the importance of gift-giving in sustaining the life of the family, and the role which gifts have in the development of collections. The collections then become a record of gifts received which contributes to the families' psychological stability. Male family members participate in this as do females, but the mother/wife does so most. Again, both mother and father display their material in the living room, but the woman does so most. There is a distinct continuity of material between the generations of the family's women. All these factors together inform each other and reinforce the solidity of family personality.

It seems that most family collectors take pleasure in what they have, a pleasure which adds to their enjoyment of their lives. However, within this there are some complexities which should not be ignored. The nature of male collecting suggests that men are often not as 'at home' in their houses as their partners are (a theme more fully explored in Chapter 6). Similarly, it looks as if young people not infrequently see themselves as persuaded into collecting, usually by their mothers, for educational and social reasons. These points suggest that the link between home-making and collecting made by women can be seen as a threat to men, whose stamp is not so clearly set on the character of the family room. In relation to both partner and children, the women's urge to create personality by accumulating material can be, in their different ways, experienced as coercion and exclusion. Similar feelings may be experienced by adult men at the female tendency to pass things to each other: women would not like to live with objects gathered by their partner's father and grandfather, but men are expected to suffer the equivalent.

Csikszentmihalyi and Rochberg-Halton (1981) have shown that 'warm' families, well-balanced between inside and outside concerns, involve both concrete family objects and a certain sacrifice of personal ambitions on the part of the wife and mother. It looks as if positive collecting, as opposed to simple accumulating of objects, modifies these conditions. Once a woman considers herself to be a collector (and this is the key difference, not the type or integral meaning of the objects) she makes a statement of personal individuality. As the Paper Weight Collector put it, 'I needed to collect something in competition with my husband.' (Her husband collects guns, militaria and coins, all very male categories.) The objects themselves, with their character as gift, family history and home decorating qualities, still help to create the web of family strength and resilience. However, as a family there is a risk that it has perhaps become a few degrees cooler.

Whether this operates to the real detriment of the family probably depends upon the quality of the relationships concerned. Baekland, when considering the effects upon marriage of male fine art collecting (1981), concluded that collecting of this kind improves, or at least does not harm, a good marriage, but can easily make a poor one worse. The same in a scaled down fashion, may be true of female collecting.

6

Women and Men

One way and another, issues to do with the ways in which gender is bound up with collecting have already run through the chapters of this book. This is inevitable, because gender is an all-embracing subject which none of us, throughout all our endeavours in life, can shake off: it colours all we think, feel and do. Equally clearly, gender itself is an enormous subject, and even that aspect of it which seems to relate most directly to our material surroundings has been covered at corresponding length.

In very rough terms, the prolific literature has tended to continue to see a major difference between 'maleness' and 'femaleness' in which male individualistic, opportunist, achievement-oriented self-assertion is contrasted with female family based, emotionally warm nurturance. These qualities seem to be integral to our ideas about maleness and femaleness, and our desire to make a sharp distinction between the two (see e.g. Benn 1974). All this, it is usual to stress, is not about biological masculinity and femininity, but about cultural assumptions surrounding gender and the construction of gender roles in society. There is, however, empirical evidence that men and women do tend to describe themselves in the kinds of terms just mentioned (Storms 1979). In particular, work on gender (Beckett 1986) and moral development (Gilligan 1982) stress that women's descriptions of themselves are embedded in their links to others, especially their families, and are expressed in a 'relational mode of discourse'.

One of the things this means is that, willy-nilly, both the investigator and the collectors will share a common set of stereotypes and expectations, however consciously any, or all, of those involved may be aware of the pitfalls. This is a significant point, because, as will appear in due course, the material content of collecting appears to fall in with, and support, the conventional view of gender types, allowing for some cultural developments in the view of each gender and particularly of women's.

Another necessary caveat is the extent to which gender can, or should, be divided into two simple halves, rather than be regarded as a rainbow of appreciation and sentiments on which each individual is personally placed. This is a difficult issue in any social investigation, since it is not yet usual to include a tick box on sexual orientation in the personal information section with a questionnaire. This in itself is, of course, flippant; it would tell us little or nothing for there is no general agreement about what constitutes hetero- or homo-sexuality other than through the labelling of specific acts. Equally, we have no way – certainly no quick questionnaire way – of assessing other kinds of sexual temperament which might be relevant. More broadly based studies into the relationship between material culture and sexuality as such, and into collecting and gay groups are just beginning, and when they are completed, they should add a fresh perspective to our understanding.

Following this very brief preamble, we can outline three broad ways in which gender and collecting may inter-relate. The first revolves around the gendered, or, indeed, the sexual, meaning of collecting as such. The second is concerned with the gendered associations of collected objects, that is the gendering of collecting material content. The third considers the gendered use of collections, that is to say the style of collection control and use across the genders, the ways of creating collection culture, and the kinds of feelings or attractions which the collections support. Each of these major areas will be considered in turn, but first we must pick up the threads of the points made in earlier chapters, especially Chapter 2.

The pattern of collecting in contemporary Britain shows that there are more women collectors than men, probably in the proportion of something like 42% men to 58% women: there are roughly 16% more female collectors than male. Most of these, of both sexes, over 25, are living with partners of the opposite sex, and the numbers of these who have children are in line with the national average. Men and women collectors are distributed across the age range with peaks in youth (18–25 years old) and middle age (late 50s/early 60s). They tend to be living in the towns and suburbs, rather than in the country, or the inner cities. The pattern is, overall, in tune with the life-styles and histories typical across a broad swathe of middle England.

Collecting as a Variety of Sexual Experience

The language of collecting parallels that of sexual activity. Objects of desire are pursued with passion; collectors keep things in the closet or come out of the closet themselves as players in a particular collecting game; and possession is finally achieved. The language of sexuality itself, like that of collecting, overlaps with that of hunting and warfare: the passing scene is watched carefully and objects are finally tracked down; something is won after a long fight; and trophies are carried home in triumph. In the light of this it may seem that pursuit and capture is both a fundamental metaphor for human life and a way of staying alive. Sex, collecting and a host of other activities are not so much varieties of each other, or surrogates for each other, but rather different facets of the same basic human drive which takes its energy from the need to grapple with the external world, to achieve possession of necessary things – other humans, food, material goods – and to integrate these into an organised world-view which seems to make sense.

So far, so good; but the thrust of much of the literature on collecting has developed the view that the link between sexuality and collecting is much more specific than a general view of the human condition would suggest, seeing collecting as a specific form – indeed a perverted form – of sexual activity. With this is linked notions of the collection, or the collected object, as an element in anal-eroticism, as 'fetishistic' and as narcissistic where the collector sees a reflection of himself in his collected things. Freud's original biological drive model (most accessible in the 1963 edition of his collected works) was elaborated by Jones (1950), Abraham (1927) and Fenichel (1945). These writers were concerned to show a continuity between child-hood experiences and adult personality, and especially between the anal-erotic stage of infant sexual pleasure, which relates to sphincter control, to the production of faeces viewed as product creation symbolic of all future productive acts, and to toilet-training and its attendant struggle with adults. They also saw this as the origin of adult traits like obstinacy, orderliness and parsimony.

Jones made what he saw as the link between all this and collecting quite specific, when he wrote of

> the refusal to give and the desire to gather, . . . collect, and hoard. All collectors are anal-erotics, and the objects collected are nearly always typical copro-symbols: thus, money, coins (apart from current ones), stamps, eggs, butterflies . . . books, and even worthless things like pins, old newspapers, etc. . . . . A more deifying manifestation of the same complex is the great affection that may be displayed for various symbolic objects. Not to speak of the fond care that may be lavished on a given collection – a trait of obvious value in the custodians of museums and libraries. (Jones 1950: 430)

Fenichel pursues the relationship between success and failure in toilet-training and later attitudes to personal success. Anal conflicts include fear of loss and enjoyment of an erogenous pleasure and these may be displaced on to collecting as:

> A patient with the hobby of excerpting everything he read and arranging the excerpts in different files enjoyed in so doing (a) an anal-erotic pleasure: what he read represented food; his files represented the faeces, into which the food had been turned by him, he liked to look at his faeces and to admire his 'productivity'; (b) reassurance: the filing system was supposed to prove that he had things 'under control'. (Fenichel 1945: 383)

Lerner (1961) put these suggestions to an experimental test. He constructed a list of 22 'anally connotative' words, matched these with a similar list of neutral words, and put the whole group to 15 stamp collectors and 15 non-collectors. The stamp collectors did seem to react differently to the words in ways which suggested some relationship between stamp collecting, at least, and the anally oriented character.

The use of the word 'fetish' in relation to material culture is now a normal part of the armoury of discussion, and needs careful review. The notion of 'fetish' in the broad sense has generated a literature of its own, usefully reviewed by Ellen (1988), and discussed in relation to popular culture in the essays gathered by Browne (1980). It has encouraged the recent mounting of special exhibitions. In 1995 'Fetishism' produced by the Hayward Gallery, London, and the Royal Pavilion and Museums, Brighton, toured the country (Ades et al. 1995). The exhibition aimed to show objects charged with a strong, readily apparent power in order to illustrate the changing meanings the west has given to the concept of 'fetishism'. The earliest of these, the anthological, was represented by objects like the 'nail fetishes' from Zaire and the Congo. The second concentrated on what the Surrealist artists made of Marx's notion of fetish as the substitution of commodity relations for social relations. The third, linked with Freud's appropriation of the word as describing sexual activity which substitutes a part of the body or its clothing for the whole, concentrated upon artists like Tania Kovats, who has embalmed a ball of her own hair and her nail clippings in cubes of polyurethane (Ades *et al.* 1995). The important thing about this exhibition was that it translated abstract terms into actual material objects.

It is worth remembering that both Marx and the psychologists had borrowed the concept from early anthropologists like E.B. Tylor, just as the psychologists have made use of notions like 'totem' and 'taboo'. The standard reference works trace the word back to the Portuguese *feiticos*, meaning 'a charm', which was used in the fifteenth century to describe contemporary Christian relics, rosaries and holy medals. When they arrived on the African coast later in the same century, the Portuguese naturally applied the word to the local wooden figures, stones and so on, which were regarded as the residence of spirits. More to the purpose here, *feiticio* also means 'made by man' and carries the idea of something 'artful' or 'magically active'. It was from this web of connections that the anthropologists appropriated the word, and used it to describe material objects which were worshipped for their magical powers, believed to be inherent rather than deriving from an indwelling god or spirit.

In a very influential book on literary criticism, in many ways a very closely related field to material culture study, Terry Eagleton discusses the nature of society in early industrial Britain in Marxist vein. He says:

> In England, a crassly Philistine Utilitarianism was rapidly becoming the dominant ideology of the industrial middle class, fetishing fact, reducing human relations to market exchanges, and dismissing art as unprofitable ornamentation. (Eagleton 1983: 19)

Two pages on, he continues:

> Art was extricated from the material practices, social relations and ideological meanings in which it is always caught up, and raised to the status of a solitary fetish. (1983: 21)

Daniel Miller, in his 1987 discussion of material culture and modern mass consumption, speaks of how:

> An approach to modern society which focuses on the material object always invites the risk of appearing fetishistic, that is of ignoring or masking actual social relations through its concern with the object *per se*. (Miller 1987: 3)

The idea of fetishism in relation to collecting has been taken up in some detail by Bal (1994: 104–110). Bal starts from Clifford's suggestion that 'in the West, however, collecting has long been a strategy for the deployment of a possessive self, culture and authenticity' (1988: 218). This entails a crucial separation between object and subject, itself a characteristic of the western tradition in the long term (Pearce 1995: 160, 168). This 'merciless separation', as Bal calls it, makes for 'incurable loneliness' that compels the subject to gather things in order to create a 'subject-domain that is not-other' so that 'the act of collecting then becomes a form of subordination, appropriation, de-personification'. Objects are cut off from their context, and the desire to extend the limits of the self is entwined with the need to dominate 'which in turn depends on a further "alterization" of alterity'. This paradoxical move, Bal argues, is precisely the defining feature of fetishism in all senses of the term (1994: 105). Collections reach in to help the collector to develop a sense of self, while providing a comfortable ethical or educational alibi.

Bal discusses the visuality of fetishism by drawing attention to the technique in psychoanalysis of the use of narrative legends, in this case the child's sudden perception that the mother has no penis, and makes the metaphorical transfer from 'lack of penis' to 'fundamental, existentialist lack' (Bal 1994: 106). In Freudian theory this negative vision is crucial to the formation of subjectivity, and is therefore bound up with both gender formation and the genesis of semiotic behaviour. Through a complex sequence of symbolisation the substitute for the penis comes to stand for the whole body of which it is a part – this may be a foot or hair, or it may be something contiguous to the body like stockings or a bracelet.

The female body is put safely at several removes – a rupture which shows the violence implicit in the story – in Marx's idea of fetishism, as in Freud's. We see that the nature of visuality is deceptive, a creation of image and metaphor like any other human perception, and that therefore the objectivity which it promises is equally suspect. This subject-constructing power of objects was pushed further by Slavoj Zizek, who writes:

> we have established a new way to read the Marxian formula 'they do not know it, but they are doing it': the allusion is not on the side of knowledge, it is already on the side of reality itself, of what the people are doing. What they do not know is that their social reality itself, their activity, is guided by an illusion, by a fetishistic inversion. (1989: 10)

and again:

> The point of Marx's analysis, however, is that the things [commodities] themselves believe in their place, instead of the subjects; it is as if all their beliefs, superstitions and metaphysical mystifications, supposedly surmounted by the rational, utilitarian personality, are embodied in the 'social relations between things'. They no longer believe, but the things themselves believe for them. (1989: 10)

The function of any kind of ideology, including the material culture of the collector, is therefore 'not to offer us a point of escape from our reality but to offer us social reality itself as an escape from some traumatic, real kernel' (Zizek 1989: 10).

Taking these developments of Freud and Marx together, then, we can see collecting as an impulse within a cultural situation which is itself a mix of capitalist materialism or commodity and individual endeavour, an impulse which, with its visually impaired origin, has a fetishistic character. As Bal puts it, 'the hybrid notion of fetishism, able to account for the entanglement of agency in a political *and* individual history, should be assigned its rightful – because productive – place as the beginning of collecting seen as narrative' (1994: 110). We have here the most pertinent narratives of fetishism, as psychoanalysis, as social theory, especially Marxist theory, and as visuality, into all of which is integrated the latter-day anthropological concept of fetishism as a projected western mode of understanding others.

Bal is careful to use phrases like 'in this narrative' in order to distance herself from too close an identification with the story as she presents it. But if the little boy noticing his mother's lack of penis triggers off the whole (?western) fetishistic appreciation of the world, what happens to those who do not notice this, or do not care, notably, perhaps, little girls? The classic, but unproven and unprovable, penis complex provides the only directly sexual feature of this narrative, which otherwise has to do with our tendency to objectify the world of both material things and other people, and to build up strings of metaphorical meaning on the basis of separation and distinction. It is true that women have frequently been 'thingyfied' in this way by men, but so have slaves, labourers and certain types of servants by both men and women. No doubt there is a sexual element in this, but it belongs with the general diffusion of sexuality through our lives rather than with the specific sexual activity, or orientation to which the word 'fetish' has frequently been attached.

Probably the reason why writers like Bal and Zizek use the word 'fetish' in the broader sense, as writers like Eagleton have done before them, is partly to draw on Marx's (rather strange) use of it, and partly to harness its tacky glamour to the points they wish to make. What emerges from Bal's discussion is the helpfulness of the semiotic approach to the genesis of collecting – though not to its sexuality or otherwise in any useful way – a point which has, of course, been made several times before. The semiotics of collecting seem to relate most to the western propensity for distinctive, rather than holistic, imaginative schemes (Pearce 1995: 57–86). This has to do with the (western) capacity to create metaphorical strings of meanings and then treat them as if they had essential reality, and to express this the notion of collecting as allegory is very fruitful (see Chapter 7). But this does not cancel the need for a term which can describe the particular emotional or psychological relationship which perhaps all collectors have to towards their material to some degree, and some have to an intense degree. This is fetishistic in the early senses of the word (psychological and anthropological) and the term is best left to cover this intensity rather than being pressed into more general service where, in endeavouring to explain everything, it explains nothing.

Roger Cardinal has done collecting studies a great service in translating and publishing Baudrillard's 'The System of Collecting' (Baudrillard 1994), an essay which hitherto had been known only patchily and with difficulty in the English-speaking world. Baudrillard's essay appeared originally under the heading 'Le Système Marginal: La Collection' as a chapter in his book *Le Système des Objets* published in Paris by Gallimard in 1968. Various sections of this book, but not this chapter, have been translated and published in Baudrillard anthologies (e.g. Poster 1988) with the result that in the thirty-odd years since it was written, it has filtered into much of the discussion of material culture which has taken place during those decades. This is true for both the translated and the untranslated sections, with the result that a good deal of what Baudrillard has to say in this essay has, so to speak, been much discussed *in absentia*. It is refreshing, therefore, to have the text before us.

Baudrillard starts from the notion of the 'loved object' and the passion of personal possession, and goes on to draw a distinction between utilised objects (like a freezer used for freezing) and objects divested of their function and made relative to a subject: these objects constitute themselves as a system on the basis of which the subject seeks to piece together his world. We might suggest, at the outset, that this is an over-simplification. One can feel a passion of possession over a utilised object, and objects made relative to a subject need not be divested of their function: cars are an obvious example. In any case, all objects, including apparently utilitarian ones, operate at bottom as symbols which unite to make up a world. However, Baudrillard remarks that possession of an object is always both satisfying and frustrating because there is always the notion of the rest of its set, and he immediately relates this to the sexual sphere where the (presumed male) subject wishes to express possession through a string of objects.

Baudrillard then writes an important paragraph which deserves quoting at some length:

> The active phase of collecting seems to occur between the ages of seven and twelve, during the period of latency prior to puberty. With the onset of puberty, the collecting impulse tends to disappear, though occasionally it resurfaces after a very short interval. Later on, it is men in their forties who seem most prone to the passion. In short, a correlation with sexuality can generally be demonstrated, so that the activity of collecting may be seen as a powerful mechanism of compensation during critical phases in a person's sexual development. Invariably it runs counter to active genital sexuality, though it should not be seen as a pure and simple substitute thereof, but rather a regression to the anal stage, manifested in such behaviour patterns as accumulation, ordering, aggressive retention and so forth. The practice of collecting is not equivalent to a sexual practice, in so far as it does not seek to still a desire (as does fetishism). Nonetheless, it can bring about a reactive satisfaction that is every bit as intense. In which case, the object in question should undoubtedly be seen as a 'loved object'. (Baudrillard 1994: 9)

We see that collecting as an activity is seen to run parallel to the typical sexual history, and that Baudrillard explicitly rejects an identification between collecting and fetishism, conceived in the traditional psychological sense. But the collector is 'sultan of a secret seraglio' (p. 10) for 'the whole charm of the harem lies in its being at once a series bounded by intimacy (with always a privileged final term) and an intimacy bounded by seriality' (p. 10). After a tour through symbolic castration, Baudrillard addresses 'The Object Reconstructed: The System of Perversion', in which passion for, and possession of an object is seen as a 'discreet variety of sexual perversion' (p. 19), in which the collector, conceived as relating to the parts of a woman's body rather than to the woman herself, becomes 'the epitome of narcissistic self-engrossment, who collects and eroticises his own being, evading the amorous embrace to create a closed dialogue with himself' (p. 19). Baudrillard glances backwards to the earlier literature when he says 'we are no longer dealing with the genital order of the serial system, for which erotic activity serves only as a cover' (p. 21). The concreteness and social significance which the objects possess preserve the collector from lapsing into delirious mania, but, in Baudrillard's final words (p. 24), 'if it is true that "he who collects nothing must be a cretin", he who does collect can never entirely shake off an air of impoverishment and depleted humanity'.

A cold douche seems the necessary response to all this sexual activity. We have seen that the view taken of the relationship between sexuality and collecting ranges from the anal erotic, through varieties of fetishism – Bal's being well removed from the sexual connotations of the term – and into Baudrillard's 1968 view of collecting as perverted narcissism with anal overtones. A statement as bald as this, while robbing the writers of their undoubted subtlety of argument, also begins to show up some of the flaws in their approaches to the problem. There seem to be three of these.

The theoretically based discussions of collecting do not relate very well to what is revealed in any of the recent analyses of actual collecting in social practice, including the present one. This is not merely to say that the collectors themselves do not report on their erotic inclinations in terms of their collections, for we would not expect this, and nor is it particularly significant. They clearly do report a passion for possession and for the emotional nature of possession which needs explanation. The difficulty is that the commentators seem to be aware of only one *kind* of collecting, and that is the stereotyped one of either the connoisseur or the miser, in Baudrillard's phrase 'the rich man specialising in Persian miniatures, or the pauper who hoards matchboxes' (p. 9). In fact, this is not typical collecting: most collecting, as we have seen, is integrated into family, work and the broader systems of commerce and life cycle to a much greater extent. Again, there is the idea that collecting is a relatively rare pastime attracting maladjusted people; but as we know, it involves around a third of the population and so large a minority can scarcely be 'abnormal' in any meaningful sense. Collecting is as much a social activity as it is a form of solitary pleasure, and although this does not mean it lacks sexual content, it does mean that this should be visualised within a social, and not purely an individual, context.

A second fundamental problem with the discussions of collecting as sexual practice, as with most discussions which revolve around the psychological analysis of human life, is the extent to which humans (and collectors) are supposed to be men. In fact, as we know, at least half of all contemporary collectors are women. Are we to suppose then, that these women collectors are fetishising their material in relation to erotic distinctions made in their view of male bodies, or that they see their things as secret rooms full of toy boys? The answer is that in spite of recent work (e.g. Ramet 1996) all we seem to know about female sexuality is that it is more diffuse than male and more inclined to see erotic feeling as a flow than as a series of specific moments. Specifically, it does seem that the literature records few female fetishists in the clinical psychological sense (Ellen 1988: 218; see also Suleiman 1985). Equally, extremes of female sexual practice seem to belong largely within male fantasies, not female ones.

This was shown in a flippant way by the history of the recent 'chain lingerie letter' event in which knickers were sent out in anonymous chain letter format by women only (de Lisle 1993). One woman said she received two pairs: 'One were kinky red satin and the others were from Marks and Spencer, and came with a receipt, which I thought was very considerate.' Men apparently show initial fascination with the chain letter, which turns to boredom when told that most of the underwear involved is white, functional and decorous. Another woman commented, 'If a man gives you underwear its really for himself. Whereas from a woman you're more likely to get something you'd actually wear – not nasty and black with red ribbons.'

Finally, there seems to be a difficulty about the approach to sexual understanding which the commentators on collecting tend to take, following their use of the earlier generation of psychologists. The contemporary 'rainbow' approach to sexuality prefers to see a continuous spectrum in which erotic appreciations and activities blend in different balances in different people, and themselves inform a flow of psychic energy which can be tuned to sex itself, to violence and aggression, to ambition, and, of course, to collecting. This brings us back to where we began, but with two added suggestions. Collecting may well be seen as sexual activity, but chiefly in the sense that all our activity has an erotic base, for in the west the erotic drive is bound up with a tendency to see the world in terms of metaphorical distinctions; and, in ways which are as yet far from clear, there may be a difference between men and women.

Collecting Gender Images

As we saw in Chapter 2, the gender difference in collecting terms in relation to traditional values was very stark, and this now needs further examination. The pattern of collection content by gender is set out in Figure 6.1. Female collections are concentrated in the room ornaments, tourist material, household goods, jewellery and pop material, which the enquiries

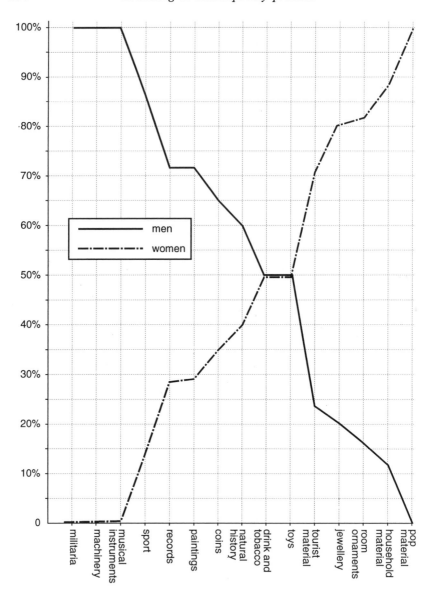

Figure 6.1   *Pattern of collection content by gender: analysis of Survey returns*

made clear involves posters and related memorabilia of pop concerts and their stars. The Decorative Plate Collector has her plates arranged to be decorative (but she only started to think of herself as a collector when her husband started to take an interest). The Decorated Promotional Milk Bottle Collector has been known to swap a plain milk bottle put on her step with a decorated one put on somebody else's. All of this material is conspicuous for its display character: it is intended to be pinned up or shown on shelves in a domestic setting, or, in the case of jewellery, on the body of the collector herself.

Male collectors concentrate in the areas of sporting material, machinery, musical instruments, militaria, and paintings. Men also make a major showing in records, natural history and coins. Many of these, in contrast to the female collections are less display material and more demonstration pieces. The musical instruments can be played, the machinery made to work and the natural history pieces made to create knowledge. Similarly, the militaria is frequently worn, often in connection with re-enactment groups. Only the paintings are gathered purely to be seen, although perhaps the coins show something of this character too. The sporting material belongs to two groups. Some of it is used during the playing of the appropriate game, and some of it functions as trophy, and as remembrance of games past, particularly those in which the collector featured as supporter rather than player. It, too, is made for display.

There are also areas of overlap. Toys are collected equally by both sexes. The male Tin Toy Collector says that as a child he could never get himself to throw anything away, while the female Owl Collector puts hers in the window in rotation in order give others enjoyment. We may suspect that there is a large emotional gulf between the model railway laid out in the loft and the collection of teddy bears set out in the bedroom. The gap narrows when the male collection of Model Buses, for example, is compared with the female Toy Cars Collector, but she makes a point of saying that she and her boyfriend collect together. However, it is true that the great majority of female toy collections involve dolls or stuffed toys, while those of men include toys with wheels.

Drink and tobacco is collected equally by both sexes in what seems to be quite similar ways. Female collections of miniature drinks bottles are quite common, and so are male collections of beer mats or (still) cigarette and cigar packets. All this material seems in part to function as 'trophy of event' and in part represents a desire to create a satisfactory set.

The nature of collected material has an important bearing on the relationship between material goods and the creation of gender image. It is immediately apparent that the great bulk of collecting is carried out within, rather than in any defiance or subversion of, traditional patterns of gender image: women collect soft, pretty, display-worthy things, and men collect metal goods with which things can be done. There is no evidence here of widespread dissatisfaction with traditional, even stereotyped, gender roles. On the contrary, people seem very happy to collect in well-established gender styles without any sense of strain, and this in spite of the fact that such an essentially private habit could be an excellent vehicle for rebellion or diversity.

Gender images in the western tradition, however, are more complex than a simple male : female dichotomy (Pearce 1995). Western tradition of the long term favours a single, and relatively simple, male image in which all men, once adult, are of equal social weight and possessed of the same range of mythic or poetic characteristics, upon which, in theory, society can rely. This is not, of course, to say that class, income or education do not have a bearing on how we view individual men, or that men as a group are not as different, or as complex, as women. It does say that, as a culture, we attach the same range of values and expectations to all adult, able-bodied males.

The same simple, one-figure, gender image does not, however, apply to women. The female image, as is well known, is refracted into a number of separate figures which create a mutually defining set of perceptions. We have the adolescent girl, and those no longer adolescent who choose still to behave like her: girlish, silly, charming, vulnerable and, at least in theory, asexual. We have the pure and virginal Madonna with her baby in her arms, no contradiction, of course, in the traditions of Christendom. We have the mature, experienced women, the figure to whom a workaday respect is given closest in kind to that given to all men; and we have the whore, threatening, fascinating and dangerous.

It is not difficult to see how the information which emerges from the Survey, as from similar endeavours, fits and reinforces this multiple picture. Figure 6.2 sets out the plot, giving the main perceived characteristics of each human type and listing a range of typical collections against them. It emerges that people relatively seldom transgress their expected collecting content. Men do not collect glass animals or stuffed pandas, nor do they accumulate sets of spice jars or Tupperware storage boxes (see Wolff 1993); women do not collect military uniforms, and, generally speaking, they do not collect what would usually be labelled 'fine art'. In other words, women do not collect men. Men do not collect mature or girlish women in their material fantasy, but they do collect the material image of the Madonna, either literally or, and more probably, in the tradition of fine art which, historically, owes a good deal to it. Both sexes collect the image of women as whore, or vamp, men through specifically erotic material, women through exotic costumes, fans, Thirties clothes and the like.

This analysis of gendered collecting habits tells us a good deal about how the sexes see each other, and sheds some light on how the erotic drive informs the collecting process. It does not, of course, tell us whether the gendering of collecting contrast is a matter of nature or nurture, and collecting studies alone are unlikely to solve this fundamental conundrum. What we do see are men and women collecting, apparently, as square pegs in square holes, with a zone of overt erotic practice – women as whore or vamp – shared by both. Here both men and women collect women as sexual objects, in what seems to be standard western cultural practice.

If the sexual, or gendered, nature of collecting as such, and the gendered content of collections, are important, equally so are the ways in which each gender approaches collecting practice and the satisfactions which they take in their material, Each of these aspects of collecting will be considered in turn.

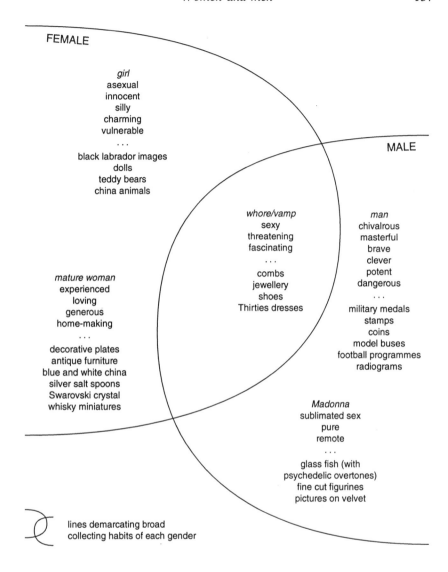

FEMALE

girl
asexual
innocent
silly
charming
vulnerable
. . .
black labrador images
dolls
teddy bears
china animals

MALE

whore/vamp
sexy
threatening
fascinating
. . .
combs
jewellery
shoes
Thirties dresses

man
chivalrous
masterful
brave
clever
potent
dangerous
. . .
military medals
stamps
coins
model buses
football programmes
radiograms

mature woman
experienced
loving
generous
home-making
. . .
decorative plates
antique furniture
blue and white china
silver salt spoons
Swarovski crystal
whisky miniatures

Madonna
sublimated sex
pure
remote
. . .
glass fish (with
psychedelic overtones)
fine cut figurines
pictures on velvet

lines demarcating broad
collecting habits of each gender

Figure 6.2   *Plot of gender types and typical collecting habits*

Gendering Organisation

As we have already seen (Figure 2.2), the distribution of collection sizes across the genders shows most of the smaller ones belong to women, and the larger ones to men. Discussions with collectors had suggested that there is a sharp distinction between the organisational formality with which men and women approach their collecting, expressed particularly in their information-gathering and recording habits. A related group of questions in

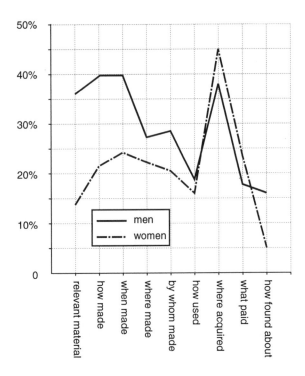

Figure 6.3   *Pattern of collectors' approaches to organisational formality by gender: analysis of Survey returns*

the Survey was directed towards throwing light on this area. These questions focused upon whether or not the collector had any interest in discovering how the pieces were made and used and by whom, whether additional material relevant to the collection itself was also gathered, and whether or not there was any interest in remembering details of acquisition and cost. Following on from this, collectors were asked if they made any kind of record of this information, and if so, how they did this.

The breakdown of the returns by gender to the first set of questions are shown in Figure 6.3. The gender distinction between those who do, and do not, collect additional relevant material is very clear: most women do not do this, to the point where for a woman to do so could be described as rare or even unusual. On the other hand, rather more than a third of men do this, although of course this means that a substantial majority (63%) do not. The message seems to be that additional material is not something which has great attraction across the collecting scene, but insofar as it appeals at all, it does so to men. These men belong in the groups that accumulate the specifically historically based collections of militaria, historical material and sporting material, because here time and place of performance are counted as very important.

Similarly, there was only muted enthusiasm for discovering the previous history of a collected piece, probably either because it was obvious (i.e. derived from a community very much like the collector's own in time and space) or because the point of the collection was the special expertise which the collector was in a position to bring to bear upon it. The same line of argument perhaps related to information about where the piece was made and by whom, which again did not arouse much recorded curiosity; again perhaps 'made by whom?' is seen as a pointless question where mass produced material is involved. However, more men than women are interested in the broad earlier history of what they have gathered. This matches the kinds of material involved. The collections of machinery, militaria, musical instruments and sporting material, the great majority of which, as we have seen, are held by men, allow the exercise of historical curiosity, while those of room ornaments, tourist material and household goods, usually held by women, offer less scope for this kind of investigation.

In opposition to this, women collectors were rather more interested than men in remembering where a piece was acquired (46% as opposed to 39% of men) and what was paid for it (22% *v.* 17%), although more men (16% *v.* 6%) wanted to remember how they found out about the piece. Clearly, this whole area does not much attract collectors at all, but when it does, it attracts women more.

In terms of record keeping, again collectors in general show little interest, with 15% overall saying that they do make records. This group is divided unevenly between the genders, with 18% of men and 13% of women scoring themselves as making records. Those who do record use proportionately broadly similar methods, across the range of cards, notebook and sheets of paper, but 17% of men favour using a computer while no women do. More than half of the men did, however, show a tendency to spend a regular time (every day, two to three times a week, once a week, once a month) looking after their collection, while of the women only 45% did so. The pattern among both sexes was to do this less often than more frequently: 23% of the men and 19% of the women looked after their material once a month, while only 5% and 3% did so every day.

All of this suggests that, in general, collectors are not very concerned to gather supporting information of any kind about the material in their collections, or to keep notes about this information or about the pieces themselves. This will come as no surprise to museum curators, who have always been aware of the reluctance of collectors to document their material and who are well aware of all the difficulties which this causes when collections arrive within a museum service. However, men are slightly less likely to suffer from the documentation malaise than women, and are consistently rather more likely than women to find out and record. The Rare Records Collector checks discographies and with very special items puts a piece of paper with information in the sleeve. The Tools from the Parish of Wray Collector gathers books and similar relevant material.

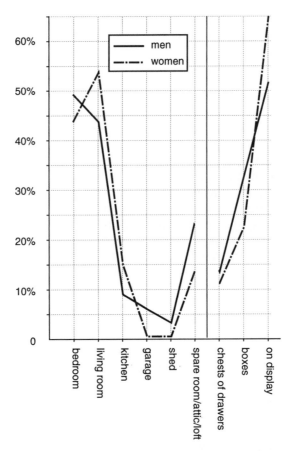

Figure 6.4 *Pattern of approaches to collection location by gender: analysis of Survey returns*

There is a chicken-and-egg feel to this. Most typical women's material – often shop-bought – does not lend itself to data-collecting, or certainly not in any traditional 'historical-research' style, whereas a distinct proportion of male collections do have 'historical' interest. This shapes the likelihood of the two genders to make records, so that attraction to particular kinds of things, and their data-gathering potential, are together a part of the same gender based difference. With this, also, is linked the desire to spend specific time working with the material, since much of this specific time will be spent writing up information, reading up the material and, of course, carrying out repair and maintenance, something which male-characterised material frequently needs more than the female equivalents.

The relationship of the genders to the appropriation and use of space is another significant area, and three sections in the Survey were addressed to it. The results of these are set out in Figure 6.4. Almost half of all collections, with little distinction of gender, are held in the collector's bedroom.

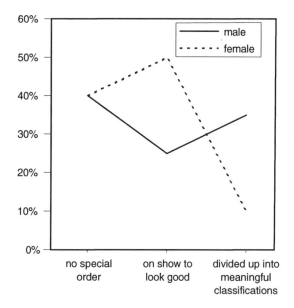

Figure 6.5   *Collections scored by approaches to ordering across genders: analysis of Survey returns*

This clearly reflects the substantial number of young collectors who do not yet have living rooms or kitchens of their own. Apart from these, women collectors show a clear tendency to have their material in the living room more than men do, and the same applies to the kitchen. The Decorative Plates Collector has hers in the living room and the Promotional Milk Bottle Collector has hers in a line on top of the kitchen units. Men, on the other hand, are more likely to keep their material in a spare room or loft. Women are more likely to have their material on show, rather than in boxes or chests of drawers, while relatively more men keep their objects in storage, although in all categories there is considerable overlap. This relates to the large group of women (50%) who have their material displayed so that it looks good, in contrast to the 35% of men who divide their material up into meaningful classifications (whether on display or not) (Figure 6.5). Only 10% of women do this, and we seem here to touch a genuine gender difference.

All of this together suggests the tendency towards a pattern of gender difference. Women favour open display, with the material in the living room, set in no particular classificationary distinctions but so that it looks pleasing to the owner's eye. The Owl Collector says 'it flows through the house and outside – but it's mainly in the living room', and she has over 500 owls. Men also show material in the living room, but also make considerable use of rooms not occupied domestically, and which do not form part of the core living space. These collections are more likely to be boxed up, no doubt largely in the unoccupied rooms, and the collections overall are markedly more likely to be organised into meaningful categories. The Model Bus Collector keeps his buses in the spare room and organises them by type of manufacturer. The young of both sexes keep their things in their bedrooms, which they frequently regard, and use, as bed-sitters.

This pattern bears on the different kinds of material which the two sexes collect, a point which has already been made. However, it may run deeper. All the evidence shows that, for very many women, their collecting and their home-making activities are essentially the same thing. 'Home' is a complicated structure of memories, attitudes and emotions embodied in material objects and their spatial distribution (see Chapter 5), and the principal decision-maker for purchases and arrangements is, almost always, the chief woman of the household, aided perhaps by her daughter(s). Naturally, therefore, her collections are going to be an integral part of her creative home-making, and what she collects is going to be the kind of material which can, by 'normal' late twentieth century standards, fit comfortably into this role.

Men, on the other hand, have a lesser home-making role. In contemporary society, they are likely to be involved in decisions about home furnishing, especially those that cost serious money, but the woman will still have the final choice about colours, patterns and designs, and virtually unfettered control over the smaller – but crucial – details regarding the arrangement of pictures, ornaments, indoor plants and so on. It may be, in part at least, because of this, that men are drawn to collect non-domestic material, and then to keep it in those places in the house which are less integrated into the living core, and to organise it in ways which are not home-specific (as on open show) but collection-specific, deriving from the material itself rather than as a part of its broader context. Men are therefore expressing their separateness in their collections, which may at once be a way of marking a desirable distinction between themselves and the domestic vortex, and a demonstration of the male's essential alienation from the home world. With this goes perhaps the individual's desire to put a personal mark of ownership or acquisition on each collected piece. Less than one in every ten collectors make a practice of doing this, but of those who do, three-quarters are male. This seems to be the top end of a kind of self-assertiveness in a mildly hostile climate which many male collections appear to embody.

Satisfactions and Pleasures

The most important piece of work on differential gender responses to material goods is that carried out by Dittmar (1991). This was a study that combined gender with social class in order to throw light upon how and why different satisfaction values are attached to things. The social backgrounds involved a gendered mix of business commuters and unemployed people in Brighton, on the south coast of England, but it is the responses by gender which interest us primarily here. The surveyed people were asked to list their five most treasured possessions and to write open-ended statements giving reasons why they considered each important.

It was hypothesised, on the basis of the broad relevant literature, that women would show much greater tendency than men to describe possessions as important because they symbolise interpersonal integration, relatedness and emotional attachment. By contrast, men were expected to show a much greater tendency to describe possessions as important because of their pragmatic, action-related meanings and because they constitute self-referent symbols of achievement. Dittmar's coding system for reasons why possessions are important is set out in Figure 6.6. This balances qualities thought to be 'intrinsic' to the object with connotations of use and feeling, where functional features are taken in the simpler sense rather than as a form of social symbolism.

The findings showed that women do indeed value objects that provide a sense of personal history and continuity. These objects also play a prominent role as symbols for personal relationships and emotional attachment. Personal history and relatedness to others are thus closely linked. Men, on the other hand, were mainly concerned with the instrumental and use-related features of possessions. Here, as elsewhere, studies of gender attitudes brought no surprises.

A rather different coding system was considered appropriate for the assessment of satisfaction values in collecting (as opposed to single objects), and this is set out in Figure 6.7. The three broad reasons relating to Intrinsic Qualities, Activity Relation and Self Expression are all considered to belong to the collected material *per se*, that is to say, that the collector primarily relates to the material rather than adding to it. The three categories relating to Memory Relation, Personal Emotion and Symbolic Value are deemed to be related to material with added value which is conferred upon it by the collector. Needless to say, the categories intermesh and overlap in many ways, and represent a relatively unsubtle appreciation of the workings of material culture; nevertheless, they do enable us to get a purchase on what the collectors themselves report of their pleasures and satisfactions.

The code headings were used to create the grid set out in Figure 6.8 where one axis embraces the contrasting positions of past memory and present/future activity, and the other represents the value perceived of intrinsic quality and the self-expression it allows, set against the value added of personal emotion and symbolic quality. Fifty randomly selected collectors were scored on this grid, allowing one point for each related activity mentioned, and one point for each phrase indicating intrinsic quality, like 'I just like them', or 'they look decorative'. One point was scored for each word or phrase, like 'they mean a lot to me', on the personal emotion scale, and one for each mention of a link with the personal past, a link with the family, a broader link with the home town and its history, which were reckoned as 'memories'. It should be noted that those

Dittmars's coding system for reasons why possessions are important

A. **Qualities 'Intrinsic' to Object**
    (1) durability, reliability, quality
    (2) economy
    (3) monetary value
    (4) uniqueness, rarity
    (5) aesthetics

B. **Instrumentality**
    (1) general utility of object
    (2) enables specific activity associated with object

C. **(Other) Use-Related Features**
    (1) enables social contact
    (2) provides enjoyment
    (3) provides entertainment or relaxation
    (4) enhances independence, autonomy, freedom
    (5) provides financial security
    (6) provides information or knowledge
    (7) provides privacy or solitude

D. **Effort Expended in Acquiring/Maintaining Possession**
    (dropped from analysis as few responses referred to it)

E. **Emotion-Related Features of Possession**
    (1) emotional attachment
    (2) mood enhancer or regulator
    (3) escapism
    (4) emotional outlet/therapy
    (5) provides comfort or emotional security
    (6) enhances self-confidence

F. **Self-Expression**
    (1) self-expression *per se*
    (2) self-expression for others to see
    (3) individuality/differentiation from others
    (4) symbol for personal future goals
    (5) symbol for personal skills/capabilities

G. **Personal History**
    (1) link to events or places
    (2) link to past or childhood
    (3) general symbol of self-continuity
    (4) long-term association

H. **Symbolic Inter-relatedness**
    (1) symbol for relationship with specific person(s)
    (2) symbolic company
    (3) symbol of inter-relatedness with particular group(s)

Figure 6.6 *Coding system for reasons why possessions are important (after Dittmar 1991: 175)*

Coding system for reasons why collections are important

---

1. **Intrinsic Qualities**
   monetary value
   uniqueness, rarity
   aesthetic/connoisseur appeal
   knowledge-holding capacity

2. **Self-Expression**
   per se, e.g. own photos
   to show some off to others
   to show individuality/differentiation from others

3. **Activity-Related**
   to use, mend, operate
   to play (as records)
   to play with (as sport)
   to belong to relevant clubs
   to deal

4. **Memory-Related**
   of one's own past
   of family past
   general sense of continuity
   general nostalgia

5. **Personal Emotion**
   pleasure in the way it looks
   has emotional attachment
   provides comfort/security/self-confidence

6. **Symbolic Value**
   of particular persons
   of particular groups

Figure 6.7   *Coding system for reasons why collections are important*

correspondents who had telephone interviews were not included, and that those in the sample who said nothing at all relevant were not scored. As in all assessments of motive, there is an inevitable degree of subjectivity in the scoring, although every effort was made to relate to what the collectors said, and to ignore what they ignored.

In the event, 23 men and 22 women were scored, and the results were interesting. In the first place, the scatter of gender scores across the axes is pretty regular: in no quadrant is there a preponderance of one or the other. Five collectors only, two men and three women, felt their collections represented both emotional qualities and activities: there was the strong feeling among the two men that it was the activity itself which attracted the feeling and the material was valued mostly as a means to an end. The expressions of simple emotion came from the three women, who wrote of loving feelings for both the activity and the things. More remarkably, only nine people

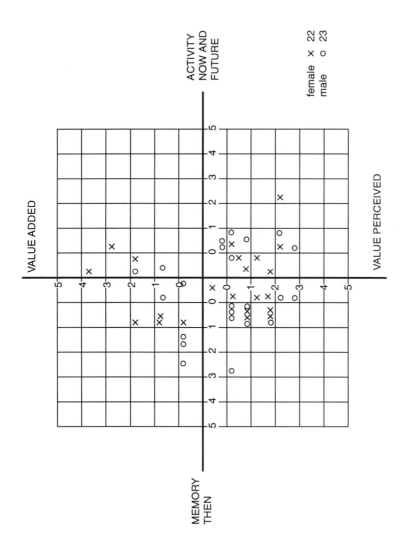

Figure 6.8 *Collections scored by gender against coding system grid: analysis of selected Survey returns*

expressed what might have been thought to be the simple combination of memory and value-added personal emotion. For neither sex, it seems, are collections frequently purely emotional in the 'memories of times past' sense. Fourteen people, seven of each sex, saw value-perceived intrinsic qualities in their material which they linked with activity value. These included the book and record collectors who valued what the material was and its capacity to be read or played.

The largest category, of 17 people, nine men and eight women, clustered in the quadrant which expressed a combination of memory attributes and intrinsic qualities. It seems that people do frequently wish to attach memory value to collected things, but they prefer to do this to things that are themselves rare, interesting or good-looking. This seems to involve partly a desire to value, and to be seen to value, things which other people would find valuable for their intrinsic qualities, and partly an anxiety to fit an honoured memory to an object which does it justice: hence the concentration on 'my grandmother's lustre ware jugs' or 'my father's army badges'.

A number of points can be made about this, admittedly small-scale, analysis. The gender picture is very mixed, and on the whole the male and female collectors do not seem to differ much in the motives they recognise in themselves. Combinations of feelings are the general rule, and in these a mixture of memory value and intrinsic value seems to predominate. Men, as much as women, clearly regard their collections as providing a desired continuity and link with the past. However, it is true that women usually express this continuity directly in terms of possessions passed down from the female blood line, usually mother and grandmother, while men take a wider view based on community and place. Very typical are the male Tools from the Parish of Wray Collector who is concerned with community history, and the female China Collector, who says simply that her pieces bring back memories of 'parents that are deceased'. Finally, there are suggestions that feelings and motives succeed each other through life: neither men nor women start to give serious memory values until their own memories start to lengthen. These findings modify somewhat those found by Dittmar in her study of individual possessions and identity. It may be that the process of collecting, as an activity of the longer term within an individual's life space, inevitably involves an element of backward-looking and remembrance value, in relation to other forms of satisfaction.

An aspect of collecting motivation related to, but rather different from, all this, is that which revolves around the desire to have material simply because it is liked, to have it to get complete sets, and to have it because it brings back memories. The overwhelming proportion of all collectors, 80% of the men and 91% of the women, wanted material because they liked it, which bears out the nature of feelings just discussed. 'Like' is, of course, a complicated world, which can cover a range of pleasures and emotions, but it is interesting that, of the three choices, most people found that this fitted their bill best. The gender balance in the desire to bring back memories was just about even, but much less, at 27% of men and 28% of women. The only major difference was in the desire to achieve sets, and here there was a male score of 16% against a female score of 5%. This particular kind of organisation emerges as a male trait, although not a particularly dominating one.

One powerful area of feeling revolves around the view the collector takes of the collection as overall a source of satisfaction and pleasure, or the opposite. Indications here were sought in a range of questions aimed at interrogating questions of regret, guilt and willingness to repeat the experience. Secrecy has been added to this group here too, although of course secrecy about a collection may mean either unhappy feelings or happy feelings hugged to oneself. The results of these questions in gender terms are set out in Figure 6.9.

People in general do not seem to feel guilty about their collecting habit, but (predictably) women feel guiltier than men, at 23% as opposed to 18%. The overwhelming proportion of all collectors would repeat the experience by starting all over again. Women's guilt is partly balanced by the 4% of men who regret ever having started, and feel their collections to be something of a burden. All those collectors who have families seem to share their knowledge with their family – willy-nilly perhaps. Similar proportions – around 60% – of both genders let their friends see what they have, and a much smaller proportion, biased towards men (22% *v*. 15%) felt that many people knew about their material. A few of both sexes kept their knowledge to themselves. The gender patterning here is quite strikingly similar.

The message from this overall suggests that, usually, collecting is a happy experience, adding enjoyment to life without too much pain. Collecting is, for most people of either sex, uncomplicated by personal mixed feelings, and it must therefore be one of the relatively small group of activities, especially those which involve material culture, of which this can be said. For nearly a quarter of the women, however, collecting is a more problematic activity, and the guilt they feel seems to have most to do with the cost of the pieces. The feeling is essentially the same as that which sometimes follows shopping, when the original elation of the buying moment is followed by shame and dislike, both of the piece bought and of oneself for succumbing to temptation.

Finally, there is the question of how the ultimate fate of the collection is seen. Forty-five per cent of the men and 36% of the women professed not to have thought of this at all. Eight per cent of men felt that a museum would be the right final home for their material but only 1% of women thought this. Most women intended either to bequeath their collections or to pass them on to family members (59%); just slightly less men felt this, at 46%. No women wished to sell, although 6% of men did. Clearly the younger members of the family are the preferred destination across the genders among those who have given the matter any thought. The low reference to museums seems to reflect a lack of confidence in the quality of much of the material and a corresponding reluctance to go to museums, perceived as 'high culture' institutions.

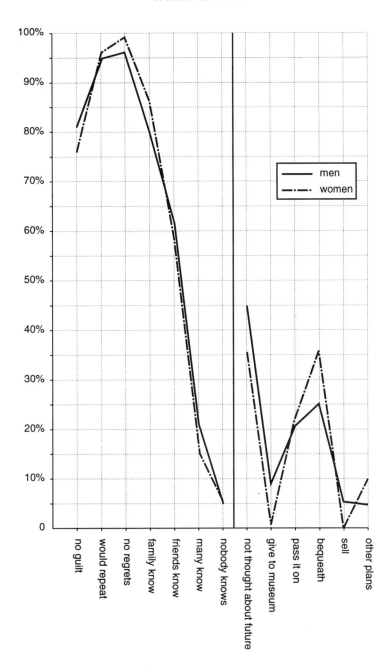

Figure 6.9 *Pattern of approaches to shared knowledge of collection, and future plans for collection by gender: analysis of Survey returns*

Conclusion

The survey has suggested a number of interesting areas of collecting practice as different and similar across the genders. Men and women do, in general, collect quite different kinds of material: the content of their collections reflects the simple male and fragmented female gender stereotypes of the western cultural tradition. Neither sex is particularly interested in information surrounding the collected pieces, but men are more interested than women; men are also rather more interested in recording their material. Young men and women both keep their collections in their bedrooms. Older men are more likely to keep theirs boxed up in the spare room, while older women have theirs on show in the family living room. By and large, men are more likely to divide up their material in an organisational scheme, women to be concerned that it looks good. Probably linking in with this, men do have a stronger wish to achieve complete sets.

Women tend to feel guiltier about their collections than men. Both sexes prefer their material to serve multiple needs, mostly a memorial role and an intrinsic one. But for women the memorial role usually relates directly to family, especially the women of the family, while for men a more community based feeling – including sentiment about their work – is involved. For women, the intrinsic role is almost always 'to look good' while men have a broader range of functional needs.

Impressions should not be overstated because the numerical basis for them is blurred and muted. Nevertheless, it does seem that women want their material to contribute to their own identity by helping to create what is seen as an attractive family home. Important memories of family events and family members, and other earlier members, invariably female, are bound up with this. Men are more interested in a collection which is set apart from the family living space, and which has a range of intrinsic qualities, particularly those which allow 'obvious' kinds of organisation and classification, reflected in the physical arrangement of boxing. Memories are embedded here also, but they are of a more general nature.

People seem to be operating within their traditional roles, and plainly this must relate, one way or another, to their sexual natures. As we have seen, however, most of what we know about human sexuality, certainly in Britain and in relation to material culture, is derived from studies of men, and tells us about male images and fantasies. The wide uses of the notion of fetishism is a case in point. Collections in contemporary study are often conceived as female, or as women-substitutes, as Baudrillard does, something that is very unhelpful given that over half of contemporary collectors *are* women. Altogether, our state of understanding is not satisfactory: it seems at least possible that the notions of man as a separate individual and woman as family member and home-maker, which is what the collecting habits seem to suggest, are either a fundamental part of the sex drive, or as fundamental as it.

How does this relate to sex/gender as the 'deep' explanation of the collecting urge, or, to put it another way, how do the speculations advanced by collection theorists marry up with our understanding of actual collectors as we can approach these through what they have, and how they report on it? Even at a popular level, collecting is being used as a topic appropriate to discussions of sexuality. An article entitled 'Why do men collect?' appeared in *New Woman* (Tierney-Jones 1996). This described men as 'just big kids' and 'inner sad bastards', using collecting as a vehicle to undermine notions of macho masculinity in a way that was, presumably, flattering to its female readers. Collecting can be harnessed to all and every kind of erotic activity, in both specific and general ways. It is part of our physical, and therefore essentially erotic, appreciation of the world.

7

Body and Soul

The previous chapters have each taken one of what may be conceived as a series of concentric rings representing the individual's interaction with the wider world through his collecting habit, beginning with that which engages with the worlds of work and consumption and moving inwards; and now we reach what might be called the heart of the matter. The point was made earlier (p. 21) that, of course, the outer circles in the complex ring are not necessarily more distant from the real concerns of any individual than the inner ones: anybody may be just as concerned with their work or their shopping as with their sexuality or, to put it more profoundly, their work or shopping may well be part and parcel of their sexuality, or of their relationship to their family. Indeed, as we have seen, the interface with the impersonal world of economic consumption, which we call shopping, transforms commodities into the gifts which are implicit in our most intimate relationships, including that with ourselves. The individual, in other words, broods over the whole operation, and it is the nature of this brooding which this chapter hopes to disentangle.

But, from the heart outwards, things are more complex than this. The whole of our tangible world is material, including our own bodies, and represents a physical continuum in which the action of collecting is a part. We therefore need to carry the discussion into the world of the body and the body of the world, in order to better understand how collecting meanings are constructed.

Together with all other facets of the material world, our physical bodies have received much recent attention from cultural theorists. The genesis of much of this has been the work of Norbert Elias, who has argued that historically culture, and particularly European culture, has to be understood as a complex interplay between body language and expression, which may be said to represent mind in matter, and the material culture which informs all social discourse. This, obliquely but powerfully, undermines the traditional western dichotomy between mind (or soul) and body, in which mind is the dominant partner, and body, animate and inanimate, the receptive, passive vehicle. Instead, a united body/soul and nature/culture becomes the place where meaning and action is generated. Here we have to understand areas like health and beauty, food, sexuality, restrictive regimes, traditions of mutilation, suffering and self-denial, and the surrounding world – fashion and taste in clothes, home furnishing and gardens – of material consumption. These issues were aired in *The Body: Social Process and*

Cultural Theory (Featherstone et al. 1991) and were followed by Shilling's valuable account of the place of the body in sociological and social psychological theory (1993), and by Falk's extended discussion of the consuming body (1994).

The body as a significant field of action became important to artists and museum installationists at the same time. In the autumn of 1993 the Tate Gallery, Liverpool displayed the work of seven artists, including Helen Chadwick and Hermione Wiltshire, who used the body as their subject. Some portrayed the whole body while others fragmented it, but all projected a sense of symbolic meaning. Similarly Marina Abramovic has produced a series of *Objects Performances*. Two at the Pitt Rivers Museum, Oxford, *Cleaning the Mirror I* and *II*, consisted of video monitors each of which showed a part of the body – head, ribs, stomach – being cleansed as a metaphor for the cleaning of the soul. *II* also showed seven different power objects – mummified ibis, Eskimo artefacts – together with images of the artist lying naked under a skeleton, so that the quick and the dead are seen together.

Our bodies are a half-way house between what (rightly or wrongly) we perceive as our essential, experiencing and remembering selves and the inanimate world of material things. Human bodies are themselves lumps of matter, an all too evident fact when we see one dead, but they are also our inescapable means of living. This hard fact has generated much speculation from (at least) the Desert Fathers onward about the nature of the relationship in philosophical rather than cultural terms. The central question is, how do we grasp ourselves as one object among others, and how is this underpinned by the ways in which we use and represent our bodies? An account of what is involved here in physiological and psychological terms is offered by Hugdahl (1996), and in terms of the nature of self-consciousness by Bermudez and his colleagues (1995). From this it is a relatively small step to a similar consideration of the cognitive processes of non-human animals (Bekoff and Jamieson 1996) and so to the political issues of animal rights.

From this two main points seem to emerge. First, the dichotomy, or duality, of body and soul needs to be abandoned in favour of a subtler appreciation of complex intermingling, an appreciation which continuing advances in genetic theory are likely to illuminate further. Secondly, we need to understand that our point of contact with the material world, that contact through which we make individual and social meaning, starts with our own bodies and extends outwards to the world of things, actual and potential. We write meanings in our hair styles, make-up and scarification, we do the same with our clothes, and we continue the process with our surroundings, especially our domestic surroundings and, within these, with our collecting habits.

All of this activity is, in essence, an exercise in appropriation, an effort to tame the 'outside' or the 'other', understood as everything with which our individual consciousness has to grapple with and live amongst. It is an effort to bring the world under control within acceptable terms. In this sense, collections are the 'extended self' both in emotional terms and in a material sense, and their role is to appropriate, or internalise, our own bodies, other people's bodies and the body of the world of consumable objects. This appropriation is managed through a process of divide and rule, through the creation of metaphorical distinctions and metonomic relationships which can structure consciousness.

This chapter will, therefore, first discuss what the collectors themselves say about the importance of their collections to them and how they feel about them. It will then consider the range of motivations which have been thrown up by the Survey overall and its discussion in this book. We will then concentrate on the bearing which the mutual physicality of our bodies and the outside world have upon these issues. This discussion will start by focusing on the transformations between bodies and collecting and collected bodies in the direct sense, and continue with a consideration of the body of the world. Finally, the concluding discussion will draw the various threads together.

How Important is the Collection?

One of the most significant questions involved in contemporary collecting revolves around how important this material extension of the body is in the collector's life. A group of questions in the survey endeavoured to get a purchase on this question. Only a fifth of all collectors felt that they thought about their collections much between the times when they were actively caring for it or adding to it, although male collectors showed a distinct tendency to do more thinking than women (28% *v.* 15%). The figure remained at around a fifth for all the various social and personal permutations, except, understandably perhaps, that all the retired people reported that they thought about it a good deal. In terms of material, the historical and musical collections, both numerically small, attracted much thought, as did the pop material. The room ornaments, toys and drink-and-tobacco material, by contrast, attract little broad attention.

How often active concern happened is a related issue. Half the collectors seem to concern themselves with their material relatively infrequently, certainly less than once a month. About a fifth do so once a month, on average, but only 15% concern themselves once a week, and only 10% more than once a week. Only a handful of collectors work with their material every day. Again, this pattern does not alter much through the social and personal parameters. In terms of material, the pattern is stable across the range of involvement, suggesting that the kind of material collected does not have a bearing on the regularity with which it is attended to.

Collectors were asked if they ever feel they 'must have' something. Predictably over half (59%) said that they had experienced this. Men apparently feel this rather more than women (63% *v.* 57%), but otherwise the pattern was stable across the variations, except that retired people felt this less than other age groups (87% said no). The opposite side of the coin to this was the 100% score for pop material collectors, which suggests that the young people, who collect this material virtually exclusively, are very prone to feel they must possess something. Otherwise (apart from the passionate few collectors of history material and musical instruments) the pattern across the material content reflects the broad picture.

Collectors were asked if they felt that the collection 'seems a part of them'. Remarkably, the Yes/No split was exactly 50/50. The difference between the sexes was trifling, and the age curve suggested a steady disengagement as the collectors grew older, although there was a peak of self-identification in the late forties/early fifties age group. The other social and personal variations do not seem to make much impact on the question. In terms of material, historical material (100%), toys (74%), records (69%) and machinery, sport and paintings (all 67%) all attract considerable self-identification, while musical instruments, militaria and pop materials (all 100% No) emphatically do not, drink and tobacco does not (80%) and nor do household goods (66%) or natural history collections (68%). The rejection of militaria is particularly interesting in view of the well-recognised dangers of taking it too seriously, and makes one wonder if, with their complete rejection, the military collectors are not protesting a little too much. In general, the material record supports the comparable gender divide.

Finally, collectors were asked how they rated the importance of their collection against a scale of four criteria (Figure 7.1). The results were very interesting, with an almost exactly four-way split between the criteria. The largest group scored their material as 'quite important', but the smallest was 'take it or leave it', so that if, for example, the two highest and the two lowest categories are added together, we have approximately 50% of collectors who consider their material to be 'important' and 50% who considered it only 'quite important' or less. Men are inclined to see their material as rather more important than women (Figure 7.1). The material plot shows that historical material and musical instruments are considered very important (100% of them), militaria is 100% 'fairly important', and pop materials 100% 'quite important', but otherwise the groups of material score fairly evenly across the categories. As before, the age profiles show a disengagement from the late forties onwards, culminating in low scores for the over 65s. Otherwise, the social and personal parameters do not affect the issue. Those who saw their material as very important usually glossed their answer, like the Foreign Doll Collector who said that the material was 'Aesthetic'.

These results do seem to hang together. It seems that around a quarter of all collectors care about their collections very much, some work and play with them once a week or more, identify with them and score them as 'very important' (Figure 7.2). Roughly the same proportion work with the collection once a month, feel their material is 'important', but still seem to identify with it. A further 20+% thought their material was only 'quite important', don't look at their collections much, and do not identify with

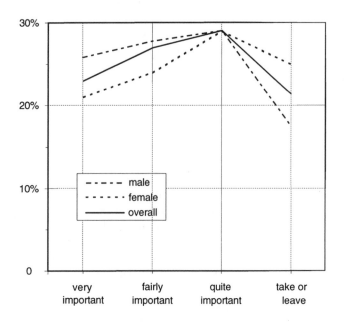

Figure 7.1 *Patterns of considered importance of the collection overall and by gender: analysis of Survey returns*

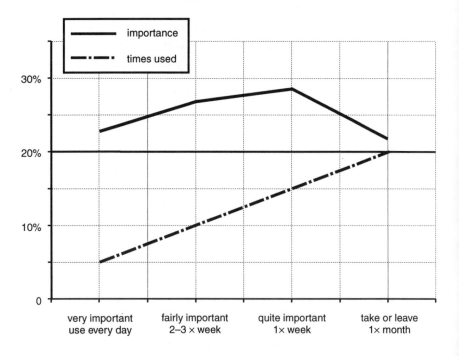

Figure 7.2 *Patterns of considered importance and time dedicated to all the collection: analysis of Survey returns*

them. The final quarter engage with their material very little, and do not seem to care about it much.

In personal terms, these splits seem to hold good across the genders, although men take their material a little more seriously, perhaps. Similarly, questions of occupation and location make little impact. The biggest break in the pattern is represented by the over 65s who seem to think about their collections a good deal but to be personally disengaged from them, a situation which fits people coming towards the final phases of their lives who have to decide the ultimate fate of their collected material. This chimes in with the answers to the question 'How do you see the future of your collection', where 88% of the over 65s said that they wished to pass or bequeath their material to somebody else. The 56–65 group scored 85% response to the same question, but below this age people had thought about the problem much less. In material terms, apart from those noted, no particular peaks and troughs occur, which suggests that in terms of feelings, the *content* of the collection is of little or no significance; any material is capable of involving any of the range of responses described.

All this seems to suggest that collecting belongs within a sliding scale of commitment to the material world. At one extreme are the anti-materialists, who claim to be un-interested in material culture and who deliberately do not accumulate. Next come those who do build up a basic life kit of household goods, clothes and personal pieces; this merges into a group with a tendency to gather accumulations of crockery, bed linen, spare machine parts and so on: these are not quite collections in any sense that would be acknowledged by their possessors. Such people also seem likely to have a few 'special objects' like a grandmother's ring or piece of furniture, and perhaps also special status objects like a three-piece suite. When the special objects start gathering to them other pieces of their own broad kind, a collection can start. This is why material can both be seen as self-identification and yet not used or referred to very often. The deliberate collectors seem to be those who care most about their material in the practical sense. The circumstances of an individual's history seem to stand behind collections which are retained but not loved. Some of these represent efforts which young people feel were inflicted on them by their elders, and others represent switches of interest or boredom, often explained by the collectors themselves as 'growing out of' a particular kind of collecting.

Collectors tend to take a deeply romantic view of their collecting. More than half (52%) feel that they started as a result of a happy accident or stroke of fate which put one particularly important object in their path, and which they acquired and then added to. As the Bead Collector said: 'I found my first one and was determined to find others.' This kind of serendipity is often talked about in the same way in which we describe the fate that brought us to our life partner. Interestingly, men feel not much less strongly about this than women. Once the crucial transformation into a collector has occurred attention to collecting may be constant (40%) or spasmodic (60% – again the sexes show little difference): collectors appear not to find this a significant distinction. What is important is the question of closure. Almost everybody (96%) declared themselves as not expecting that their collection would ever be complete. There was clearly a dread of termination assuaged either by taking a completely open-ended view of the material, or by deliberately extending the view as a conclusion seemed to loom.

Almost everybody felt that they would repeat their collecting if they had to return to the moment of choice (95%), and the same proportion (97%) said that they had no regret about their collecting habit. Most (80%) declared themselves to feel no guilt about their acquisitions, although the Noah's Ark Collector said that a 'greedy nature is abhorred'. Women were here a little guiltier than men, but otherwise the answers to these questions showed no difference across the social variants. Two-thirds of collectors (65%) found it easy to say why they liked their collection: of course this is a test of articulation as much as collecting, but obviously the ability to express what they feel comes to more people here than it would in most areas of experience. Equally, relatively few collectors (5%) are secretive about what they do, although, again, the Electric Sound/Vision Collector said 'it was bought for me – I am not interested in other people knowing I have it'. Most share their activity with their families (84%) and friends (58%), and again social variables played little part.

Even making every allowance for the efforts people make to present their best side to the world, and allowing also for the dark side of human nature, which always pairs the good, it does seem that contemporary collecting is perceived by its practitioners as without moral shadows. The creation of this extended material network into the physicality of the world beyond bodily limits usually happens smoothly and easefully. For most people it is not furtive, secretive or shameful; on the contrary, it adds to the sense of self, it gives interest and shape to experience, and it brings much pleasure.

Motives and Meanings

At the level below the conscious, or at least articulated, motives expressed by collectors we can see a series of parameters which represent individual impulses, which interact with the broader society, and which both sustain and are sustained by collected material. These are set out in schematic fashion in Figure 7.3 in relation to the broad areas of discussion into which this book has been divided, and we now need to consider how each of them operates. Like everything else in the collecting process, they are part and parcel of the perceived material reality through which we live.

Time and space are the two linked parameters within which all human activity takes place, and are aspects of its perceived physical grounding. Notions of both, and of their differing weights of significance, are socially constructed and late twentieth century British society places a very high value, and a very specific set of appreciations upon both. Space is extremely expensive in monetary terms, and this reflects the high values placed upon

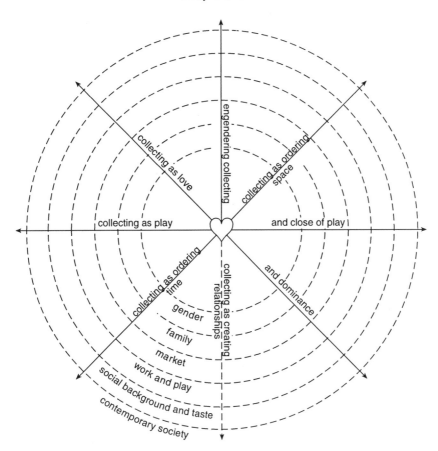

Figure 7.3 *Scheme of collector's relationships to context and chief parameters of life*

privacy and upon the scope of living space. Both are bound up with issues of quality as well as quantity. Similar considerations apply to time. Here some people, notably the unemployed, have much time to call their own but often relatively poor personal space, while for the over-employed the reverse is true. The demarcation of time, which is such a feature of the western world, has much to do with perceptions of work, family life and gender.

Collections, being material, exist in space just as their owners do. Their spatial disposition represents two distinct, albeit interwoven, elements. The first revolves around the actual placement of the material within physical space. The second involves the spatial organisation of the objects in a series of juxtapositions which create meaning. As we have seen, the allocation of personal space in which the collection can be housed is an important (sometimes very important) area of domestic politics. Young people are expected, indeed required, to keep their material in their bedrooms, upon which a door can be shut which separates these rooms from the rest of the house. The man of the house quite frequently keeps his material in an ancillary area which is not the main living space. The woman keeps hers in the main living room, or kitchen. The allotment of room to collections represents even more forcefully than sleeping or eating space the value which is placed in family terms upon the individual pursuits of the family members; and mother is paramount. In terms of the disposition which makes meaning, the genders again behave differently. Men are rather more inclined to see their material in terms of the conceptual sense which they can develop from it; women are more concerned with the affective aesthetic which it represents, and its 'home-making' qualities of pleasing appearance and comforting effect.

The placing of material, and sometimes its spatial patterning too, can have a consecrating effect upon space. A folkloristic example of this is the well-documented custom of building groups of shoes into the fabric of houses. Northampton Museums now have an index of some 900 cases across the world (Swann 1969; Dixon-Smith, personal communication). An early fifteenth century shoe was found at Tewkesbury Abbey, and when Norvic built their new factory in Norwich in 1964, they buried one of their latest models, a pair of lady's high leg boots, in the foundations. The custom seems to have both sacrificial and fertility overtones, together with the well-recognised symbolic and fetishistic content of foot and shoe. The same spirit seems to animate those collectors who insist upon particular placings of their material.

This brings us to time and its relationship to collectors' lives. We have seen how the process of collecting helps to structure the yearly cycle, and the weekly cycle and daily cycle, and is implicit in the sum of all of these which go to make up a life. It can act as a rite of passage through difficult times. The Mug Collector said she started because she acquired 'one mug that was very unusual which was given whilst I was in hospital', and she carried on from there. Again, women and men do this somewhat differently. Men use the temporal patterns which they can create as a way of creating opportunities to accumulate, and for them the progression of time serves collecting ends. For women, the passage of time *is* the collection. The material gains its souvenir character and its significance not from any intrinsic qualities, but from the encrusted significance of past transactions in which it has played a part and of which it is the only surviving element. It would be an exaggeration to say that men collect in order to organise and women in order to remember; but this brief statement has the seed of truth. Through women's collections, therefore, a home becomes a complex historical record, and we generally feel that the more it does this, the more of a home it is.

The notion that objects carry the past with them (as separable from their actual action in the past) is itself the operation of a particular symbolic way of viewing the world. Symbolic things share the assumption that an integral relationship exists between modes of being, in this case the physical collection, and what is believed to be the invisible reality of the past. Here, the objects are seen as not just simple epistemological signs – carriers of information about what happened – but rather as mystical bridges between imagination and the past regarded as eternally present and presentable through its physical traces. This looks like the Romantic concept of the symbol, seen equally in the regard for the monuments of past, and here applied to the collection of materials from a personal or family past. It is no accident that Romanticism roughly coincided with the beginnings of industrially based and imperial consumerism, and the bourgeois notion of home as we know it.

All this helps to illuminate the relationship between collecting and gender, itself a social construction seen to relate to bodily, biological givens. The genders define their differences by the ways in which they relate their collections to their homes and families. They use them to help sustain and embrace the traditional single image of men and multiple images of women, and they further this by bringing their collecting process to bear on their working and shopping lives. The most obvious feature of collecting in relation to gender is how it does follow traditional stereotypes. The great majority of collections do not show their male and female possessors stepping outside socially prescribed roles, but, quite the contrary, inhabiting them very comfortably.

The role of collecting as play and close of play is immensely significant, given the very limited control which each of us has over our lives and destinies. Practical considerations like available finances of course limit the collecting process, but within these constraints the collector has broad powers over his material. He can determine who sees it, and when, and how. He alone, if he wishes, can be allowed to touch it, or know all about it. Collecting can be used as a play of ideas within all the main parameters of life: we play with our gender roles, with our family and with our home-making persona. We exercise the kind of control playing represents when we gather material relevant to our work. We play within the commercial market, choosing among what is on offer and deciding what will be taken to be turned into something special. Play includes aesthetic and intellectual games, those plays of imagination upon material in which various kinds of 'sense' are created as the patterns form. In this way, all collections take systematic form and it is the collector's gamesmanship which determines what these forms will be.

Creating the sense of closure – and deciding when this will be – is a major part of the collecting pleasure. Danet and Katriel (1989) have distinguished five strategies which are deployed to create this sense. Completing a series or a set is of prime importance to some, and this includes the aesthetic of gathering material that 'goes' together. Filling a particular space, and creating a visually harmonious and pleasing display are an aspect of this kind of closure and completion. Manipulating the scale of objects is another strategy, involving collecting only miniatures or only very large objects. Aspiring to perfect objects is the fifth strategy. This can involve collecting only mint pieces, restoring pieces to mint condition, or continually 'trading up' so that better objects are acquired and poorer ones eliminated. All these strategies highlight the importance of tension and the release of tension in human psychological well-being. Collectors deliberately create for themselves an agenda for tension and for its manageable release. In fact, they usually do not wish to be delivered; a horror of completion is characteristically expressed and once one goal is reached, another is formed.

Issues of control, of love and dominance, are inter-linked with those of play and closure, and, like them, run back and forth across the collector's interior and exterior world. Collectors frequently express themselves as 'in love' with their material and use appropriately extravagant language to express their feelings. As Tuan has shown (1984), love is only too compatible with an associated wish to control the material world which is the object of affection. Dominance can work both ways. The collector shows his power in his ability to manipulate the meaning of his material, re-framing it at will. But objects, and the lust for objects can come to dominate the collector, and we call this obsession. The Beer Label Collector was captured by security cameras in the Public Record Office stealing labels from the archive. When he was sentenced at Kingston Crown Court, the judge said, 'You built up a mammoth collection of 30,000 beer bottle labels worth £50,000 and in my view it became an obsession.' Looking at their past life, his wife commented, 'A man's got to have a hobby, hasn't he? Something apart from his family and work' (*Telegraph Magazine* 17 August 1995).

This kind of object-dominated obsession does seem to be more common among men than women, just as technical fetishism in the psychological sense is more-or-less confined to men, and there are probably links between the two states of mind. Both are connected to an effort to control the world, by lavishing complex and powerful feelings upon a part of it, treated as a symbol of the whole.

Body Parts

The correspondences between a human body and an object (in the ordinary sense) are acute. Both occupy physical space and cannot be in two places at once; both live in time and have a measurable life span; both are of a tangible concreteness which allows for measurement, physical analysis and practical intervention. For this reason, bodies are capable of being objectified. They can be bought and sold like any other commodity, they can be viewed as objects of desire, and they have surfaces which can be decorated and dressed to provide the same symbolic field which other objects have. This is a source of much tension because, unlike other objects, they are also somehow the envelope or the dwelling of a human psyche which is itself doing the objectifying, of its own body, of other bodies, and of the object world as a whole.

Any notion of the collection as the 'extended self' has to take this corporeality into account, and the language commonly employed about collections, as always, points the way to their meaning. We habitually use the metaphor of the body to account for the character of a collection, talking about the 'corpus' of material, about the 'main body' of the collection, with its assumption of extremities, and about the 'heart' of the accumulation. The metaphor is apposite and instructive, for clearly the extended self which the collection represents is, like the human self, a physical presence which nevertheless is seen as cut off from, and distinct from, the surrounding material world. To the collector, the collection has objective reality, but it also has the kind of indwelling spirit which his own body has; for him the collection is capable of objectifying the rest of the world.

Viewed from this angle, some of the recent work on the body, particularly that of Frank (1991), illuminates the meaning and dynamic of collecting practice. Frank suggests a triangular relationship between bodily discourses, the corporeality of the physical body, and the institutions which bring these two together into social substance. In this eternal triangle, it should be noted, the only tether to physical reality is the human body itself, which, though capable of extraordinary mental manipulation, is not limitless. Everything else belongs within the bodily discourses, of, for example, fasting or athleticism, where there must be physical bodies capable of enduring the regimes necessary to tell the story, and institutions, like monasteries or sports clubs, to act as social sites.

The same triangle operates in relation to the collection body. Here, the discourses are those which have already been identified as making up the main preoccupations of the living collector, the narratives of engendering, playing, controlling, ordering time and space. The corporeality of the object world means that, like a human body, a body of collection can be isolated so that its qualities of classificatory capacity, memory carrier, display and love are drawn up into a narrative. The institutional sites where these stories are enacted are the home, the collectors' club or fair, the museum and the workplace; from here they are re-worked in contemporary fiction, in the media and in cultural studies of collecting practice.

But the body has further discernible characteristics which spring from its physical nature, and these are shared by the 'other body' of the collection. Frank suggests that bodies have four modes: control, as predictable or contingent and open to a range of possibilities; desire, either as lack through fear or anxiety, or through production; relationship to others, which is either open or closed; and a self-relatedness which is either associated or dissociated, embracing or distancing. These, in their turn, seek to articulate with four qualities or states, discipline/regimentation, domination/force, mirroring/consumption and communication/recognition, all of which are bound up with the body's physical nature (Figure 7.4). So, the disciplined body, as of the fitness freak, is predictable in its exercise of control, lacking in desire, disassociated in its self-relatedness and closed in its other-related (and probably the kind of character the earlier psychologists would have described as anal-retentive). On the other hand, a communicative body, like

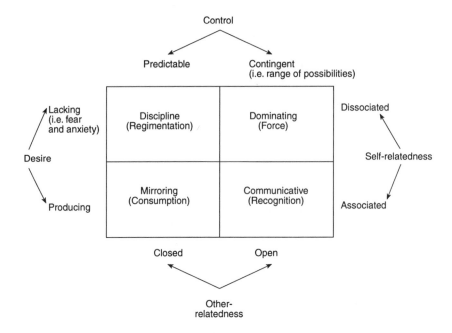

Figure 7.4   *Bodily relationships (after Frank 1991: 36–102, Figs. 1 and 2)*

that of a dancer, is contingent, open, associated and productive of desires. It is also, and because of these qualities, engaged in process rather than, as the fitness body, geared to maintain statis.

It is clear (and indeed could not be otherwise) that the collection body is equally susceptible to this kind of analysis. The collection which exists within and through its overt and conscious classification has the character of discipline. It is dissociated in its self-relatedness since it is an article of faith that classificatory principles are above and beyond the individual self, whose involvement in their construction is denied. Its predictability is seen as its *raison d'être* because its principles are seen as universally valid. Its lack of desire is equally inherent since it is a system bounded by itself, and it is closed to other-relationships because it is sufficient to itself.

Dominating collections are those which, as the collector says, 'have taken over'. These collections may be described as fetishistic, not in the general sense of the word as used by Bal (1994) and others, but in a sense rather closer to that used by psychologists, where the collected objects take on the role of shaping force in relation to their collector and become, in themselves, the source of feeling and action. The collection stimulates no desire outside itself, but that self is contingent in that it is not susceptible to predictable classification. It is closed in its other-relatedness, since it and its collector form a private universe, and closely related to the self.

Mirroring collections are those which are related to consumption, not just in the sense that all collecting is a form of consumption, but in its relationship to the world of commodities. Such collections are closed in their relationship to others because the commodity consumption is solitary. They produce desire in the collector and a central contingency of control, in relation to their most salient feature, a narcissistic concern with surfaces. In terms of the body, this implies a preoccupation with clothes and ornament; in terms of collection, it means a concern with the appearance of things. The collection's meaning is its ability to cover surfaces and to display itself. Commodity is thus consumed through the experience of the eye.

Finally, there are communicative collections. These reach through the self to others, and admit a range of possibilities. They produce a range of desires and emotions as a part of this two-way process. Collections of this kind are woven into the stuff of personal and familial relationships, functioning as presents and as markers of time and occasion. They create narratives of memory which inform present action, and as such possess the dynamic lacking in the other types.

Two further things should be said. It is, of course, perfectly possible for a collection to share two or more of these broad characteristics – collections, like people, are seldom simple. These characteristics may be present contemporaneously or serially. Secondly, there is a likely presumption that the communicating and the mirroring collections are female, while the classified and dominating collections are male. The link to the gender stereotypes in western culture is obvious, and, as we have seen, the actual collecting habits recorded for the two genders do bear out the broad distinction, providing a certain grey area is allowed for.

Written on the Body

The body itself forms a major area for the collecting process, and here the forms can be either on one's own body or on that of other people. Consequently, the way in which we treat our own body has recently been the subject of a new growth in studies that consider tattooing, scarification, body piercing and body painting, particularly in the western world. Piercing ears for earrings, in both sexes, runs back into European prehistory, and tattooing, chiefly for men, seems to have become fashionable, particularly for sailors and soldiers, as contact with the Far East increased, but tattooing for both sexes and assorted bodily piercing to take rings and studs has become an element in trendy postmodern fashion through the 1990s, and one much commented upon in the press. Similarly, body painting, especially to show tribal loyalties in sport, has now become a normal feature of the stadium scene.

This locks into the contemporary fiction scene, in which collecting also plays a noticeable role as a metaphor for life (Pearce 1997b; Wilkinson 1997). More particularly, collecting plays a deliberately ambiguous role, part metaphorical, part erotic, in the new-wave erotic popular fiction intended for women readers under imprints like Black Lace (Edgar 1997).

The same note is struck in the Gothic or Vampire fiction produced by the likes of Anne Rice and Poppy Brite, a vein which has a history as long as that of the modernist Gothic novel (Miles 1993). As Freedland says, you can tell Rice devotees, with their black clothes, their near-purple hair, and their pierced nose, ears and eyebrows (1995: 7). Rice's *Vampire Chronicles* feature conscience-stricken ghouls who debate mortality and morality, while the moment of death is dwelt upon in loving detail, with its puncturing of the skin, and draining of the blood. All this as seen as the ultimate seduction in an equation of pain and pleasure. The writing, like most of its kind, is heavy with material culture, gathered, accumulated and lusted over – gorgeous costumes, lavish settings, objects encrusted with other objects.

Detective fiction has always shared something of the same character, rooted as it is in the world of objects and their meanings in a consumer-orientated society. As Benjamin puts it

> To live means to leave traces. In the interior these are emphasised. An abundance of covers and protectors, liners and cases is devised, on which the traces of objects of everyday use are imprinted. The traces of the occupant also leave their impression on the interior. The detective story that follows these traces comes into being. (Benjamin 1969: 29)

But the reading of the material traces is in the interest of discovering how and by whom a human body was violently assaulted. Post-1960 detective fiction in the hands of P.D. James, Ruth Rendell and Elizabeth George has steadily concentrated more and more on the bleakness of the human condition and the pathologies of violence. This has culminated in the stories of Patricia Cornwell, where morbid pathology of body and mind are at the heart of the action. And yet we read these stories, as we collect body parts, for interest and escape: here as elsewhere prurience and consolation are very close together.

Bodily modification, especially in its relatively extreme and permanent ways, has its dark side, one with which contemporary body piercers are deliberately flirting. Like over-eating into grossness, or dieting into anorexia and bulimia, body modification has its pathological side. As Favazza has discussed recently (1995), people have cut their skin and put holes in their bodies for 20,000 years or so, and generally this self-mutilation is culturally sanctioned, even if damaging, like the removal of the clitoris practised in much of Africa. But in as much as 1% of the population the mutilation does not form part of a socially recognised rite of passage and is associated with mental illness. These skin cuttings and burnings, biting off of finger tips, even castration and self-blinding, are deviant forms of a distinct syndrome of dyscontrol, Favazza argues, that begins in adolescence and is often associated with eating disorders. They are an expression of pain and confusion, and in many cases, the self-mutilation is a desperate attempt to avoid suicide. Favazza reckons that 50% of chronic female self-mutilators also have a history of anorexia or bulimia.

Contemporary western practices of body piercing and skin dying seem to span these two extremes. Within much youth culture the acquisition of body rings and studs has become a rite of passage into the group, with all the psychological and anthropological weight which the phrase implies. As such, they provide a mechanism for the establishment of a kind of equilibrium. Group solidarity is spiced with the acknowledgement that self-mutilation involves experimenting with a previously forbidden body-side of life, seen as enlarging the boundaries of experience and expressing something of the suffering and bondage in the human condition. Equally pertinently here, the accumulating of nose rings or tattoos forms one phase in a continuum which links the collecting of features created on one's own body with the collecting of other people's body parts.

Body parts seem to be one of the commoner focuses of collecting. This ranges from whole preserved human bodies and parts of such bodies, to simulacra of body parts like false eyes and false teeth, to the traces or symbols of bodily action like hand and foot prints, lavatory paper and prostitutes' trade cards. It continues too in the collecting of material which is held to be directly representational of the physical body, like the rusty nails and animal bones collected as human blood and bone by the Bone and Rusty Metal Collector (Pearce 1995: 317). Peter the Great of Russia had a large collection of human teeth personally pulled by himself, all docketed and numbered (Purcell and Gould 1992), and Clare Rayner, we are told, collects glass eyes. Martin (1997: 230) records a collection which emerged during the People's Show project:

> *Sarah*: I collect my fingernails and hair.
> *Martin*: Why?
> *Sarah*: I am in awe of the fact that we eat food and it turns into skin, bone etc. I would like to collect my skin if it peeled off. I have collected large pieces that have peeled off from sunburn in the past. When I was a little girl I collected my toenail clippings, but my mother threw them out, she said they were nasty and smelly, I was extremely upset.
> *Martin*: What about dust, that's mainly dead skin?
> *Sarah*: I don't collect that because it's too difficult and ephemeral, but if it was possible I would collect that too.

The same kind of impulse probably helps to compel those who collect representations of the human body in little. The many Doll Collectors, and even the Robertson Golly Badges Collectors, have their shadowy side.

This collecting area embraces all the bodies and body parts acquired by archaeologists and anthropologists in many parts of the world, much of which was, and some is still, held in private hands, although much is now in the world's major museums. This kind of collecting seems to have its genesis around the 1830s (Daly 1994; Dawson 1934: 178) in the fascination exercised over the west by the mummified remains of Ancient Egypt, from which has developed a significant cultural strand in popular fiction and film (see also Gautier 1858, 1908, and Bernal 1987). Christianity, and some other faiths, have a long history of the collection and preservation of bodily relics, regarded as tangible references of a metaphysical presence. Interestingly, this has its secular and 'rational' counterpart. The preserved body of Jeremy Bentham, who died in 1832, aged 84, remains on public display in University College, London, which he had helped to found. He is seated in a large wooden case with a glass front, wearing his own clothes and with his stick 'Dapple' in his hand. A wax head has replaced his own, which is kept in a mummified state in a small box nearby (Marmoy 1958). Such public manifestations of the same preserving and collecting impulse, like those in important public museum collections, give a legitimacy and a comfort to similar private collectors, while drawing on the same cultural motives.

What seems to be at stake in this cultural complex which spans a range of fiction, film and other aspects of popular culture, as well as collecting, is the notion of self and identity. The body parts are metaphors for the bodies from which they come and therefore slot into the collector's (or reader/viewer's) classificatory system which has to be built up upon a sequence of perceived metaphorical distinctions. But the body parts of others bear a metonomic relationship to the collectors' own bodies also, and therefore can summon up the whole human being together with his or her authentic context. When the dead are raised in this fashion what was a collected object becomes a free agent so that the pieces oscillate between being subjects in their own right and objectifications of the collecting subject. In the same way, the collector changes his role in relation to them, ceasing to be the subject and becoming the object of his own collection. As the accumulated fantasies show, we evidently find the physical embodiment of pity and terror, shot through as it always is with voyeuristic horror and malice and linked with sudden reversals in the idea of the self, capable of delivering a powerful and valued emotional charge.

Enough has been said to render a similarly detailed discussion of clothes collecting, another major attraction for collectors, unnecessary. Clothes are so intimate with our bodies that they carry the shape, scent and personality of their owner. Accordingly, to collect and wear them (as most collectors do) stimulates the same fantasies of transference that the body parts do. We only 'become other people', the desire behind dressing up, by allowing ourselves to become objectified by the lifeless metonymic fragments of some past now endowed through contact with our living bodies with a new subjectivity. The object becomes the subject, and the collector is himself collected.

The Body of the World

We have suggested that, on a number of levels – attention to body surface, psychic and social use of the collection as body – the collection represents both an extension of the physical body of the collector and a kind of tangible *alter ego* which forms a body outside the body. It is, of course, clear that we can only interact directly with the material culture of the world in a bodily way, and belated attention to this obvious fact is now generating work which begins to deal, for example, with left-handedness in relation to objects (Saddler 1997) and with the enormous area of working tools and how we use them (Silven-Garnert 1995). All of these areas, in their turn, can and do give rise to collecting practices.

In the same way, we can only appreciate material which lies further beyond the immediate range of our direct bodily assimilation through the techniques of bodily appropriation by eye and hand. To 'run an eye' over something means to look at it and to assess it; and it is no accident that 'eyeing' has both sexual and covetous overtones. To handle something is, in every sense, the beginning of possession. We live in a world which presents these opportunities for appropriate action – also a physical impulse – at every turn, and the collector responds by making off with what he can. The language of material culture in operation overlaps constantly in complex ways with that for our other main proprietorial activities, having sex and eating food (Pearce 1997b).

The nature of this appropriation is at the heart of the collecting body. Collections are made through a species of colonialism, most obviously when the collecting is directed towards material which is self-evidently 'other' in relation to the collector, but actually equally so in terms of all material; at one extreme we might cite Roman coins as an obvious Other to all contemporary Britons in time and place, and at the other we might see the toby jugs collected on the owner's own holidays. Appropriation under the sign of colonialism has received much attention lately, particularly through the work of Gayatri Chakravorty Spivak (e.g. 1993) and the essays edited by Chambers and Curtis (1995). It is now obvious to us that even such apparently innocent collections as these are the result of complex colonial constructions. The Roman Empire is conceived as 'like' us, and more particularly 'like' the British Empire, seen as a civilising force. The coins upon which, in general terms, modern British coins have been modelled, have a spurious familiarity which re-inforces the collector's prejudices and consoles his doubts. The toby jugs utilise an icon of bonhomie and good fellowship to help people feel good about their holiday and their home which houses its physical remembrances. The politics of location are working powerfully in several directions, simultaneously creating different levels of construction.

In these, and all other, collections, the collector is re-figuring older and 'other' material in terms of metonomic relationship to his own life, one which is part parasitic, part supportive. In physical terms, he is using his bodily techniques of seeing and feeling, which are implicit in the materiality of both, to absorb the collection into his bodily system, to consume it and to feed upon it. But, of course, the material has no intrinsic relationship to the collector other than that created by him. The relationship between collector and collected must therefore be metaphorical, that is, with its separateness bridged by an imaginative effort. The most useful word for this relationship is perhaps 'allegory', to the notion of which we must now turn.

Allegory is an ancient device, and discussions of its definitions have an equally distinguished history back to the Latin rhetoricians. In *The Origin of German Tragic Drama* Walter Benjamin suggested that allegory is the process both of transforming things (the 'given' of the world) into signs (so allowing them to acquire meaning) and a way of showing that the things of the world are by nature transitory by rendering the physical world as an aggregation of signs. For Benjamin, allegory is a mode of experience, which allows us to understand that the truth is absent because in allegory 'the image is only a signature, only the monogram of essence, not the essence itself in a mask' (Benjamin 1977: 14; see also Cowan 1981). The allegoric sign expresses the need for an absolute presence – essential truth – which is always absent. As Paul de Man puts it 'Allegories are always allegories of metaphor and as such, they are always allegories of the impossibility of reading' (De Man 1979: 205).

Benjamin and De Man are of course discussing written texts, but what they say holds equally true for those material texts which we call collections. Here again 'things', the given of an individual world in the most tangible (and often in the most literal) sense, are transformed by the collector into signs which signify intellectual, aesthetic or historical meaning. Simultaneously the collector has turned the physical world into an aggregation of such signs, negative or positive, actual or potential, with his access and selective process creating the distinctions between them. This is inevitably transitory, because whatever classic modernist thinking may have held, all these signs are capable of constant re-figuring in different hands and minds, just as their material relationships to one another can be altered freely. Collecting is indeed a mode of experience in which the meaning created shows the footprint not the foot, the signature not the essence, for an object from elsewhere, past or distant, cannot recreate the context from which it has come, but lives in a context which comes from collection.

Allegory is therefore capable of holding together two realms of meaning; it is able simultaneously to create metonomic groups of signs with internally consistent patterns of meaning which embrace the world-view of the narrator, and to relate this structure of meaning to the rest of the world for which it stands metaphorically. So a collection of snail shells organised according to classic taxonomic principles has its metonomic meaning in that all the elements fit together into a greater whole which produces knowledge; but at the same time it is a metaphor for all the other snail shells which are not collected and whose meaning is not produced there. Similarly, a collection of beer mats has an intrinsic history in that they are a sign for the collector's drinking activities, but they are a metaphor for the evenings spent with friends in the pub. In this sense all the meanings implicit in any collection can be understood, whether that meaning is a matter of personal history, scientific knowledge represented by systematic juxtaposition or the simple (or not so simple) lust for acquisition. Collected objects have a nature which is neither quite metaphor nor quite metonomy, for which allegory, which implies a narrative construction, is a helpful term. And, like all stories, allegories can be written and re-written.

As we have just noted, contemporary collecting perforce operates in the postmodern world in which any logocentric relationship between signs and an ultimate meaning is severed. There is essentially an unregulated proliferation of signs which every collector creates anew for himself. Indeed, the capacity of collecting to permit this is one of its great pleasures. Because a normative base-line of reference in meaning, value, taste and so on is experienced as lacking, the collector is free to attribute whatever significance he likes to his material, and endeavour as much as he wishes to persuade others of his point of view. Here – in choice of objects, meaning attributed to them, and ways in which other people are brought into this frame – rests the personality of the collector and the constraints which drive him.

Conclusion

We have discussed the ways in which people understand the significance of their collections to them, and seen that this spans a range of importance. The ways in which these importances work across the real world of shopping, work, home and family, and gender translate into a sequence of parameters which operate in every personality. What ties together the real world of daily life, the tangible world of material culture and the personality of the collector is their bodily existence. The collector's body is the field for his activities, whether these are upon his own person, or consumed by him through seeing and touching.

The world then becomes a sequence of bodily appropriations in which the collector feeds upon material objects by constructing allegories through them which are bridges between the metonomy of the construction and its metaphorical relationship to the rest of the world. These material allegories become the extended body of the collector, his way of absorbing the alien. The outer edge of the collected imaginative pattern becomes the collector's skin, demarking himself from the outside. And because in a postmodern world all meanings are on offer, the collector can, if he wishes, change his appearance as often as any shape-shifting magician.

8

Contemporary Collecting

The starting point for this study was the appreciation of the scope and significance of collecting as a contemporary phenomenon. An activity which, at a given moment, is engaging the attention of around 30% of British adults must have a significance which ramifies across life as it continues to be lived. Accordingly, this book has endeavoured to trace the meaning of collecting across the experience of the collectors, and in order to do this, it has cut the seamless web of experience up into the broad areas which are normally recognised in the social sciences as capable of manageable discussion. These are the direct engagement in economic production which we call work and its opposite, play or leisure; the direct engagement in economic consumption which we call shopping and gift-giving; life in the family and home; gender; and notions of the self. These discussions were framed by an initial chapter which considered the class structure of the collectors, and the similar 'class' or value structure of the material which they collect.

Main Conclusions of the Survey

It will be helpful to re-capitulate the main conclusions about collecting which emerge from each of the main areas of experience. I shall group together work, leisure, shopping and giving as representing the face of the collector turned outwards to the world, and family and home, gender and the self as the face of the collector turned inwards towards intimacy because this does seem to reflect a certain distinction in the quality of personal experience as it is reported by collectors, although it does not, of course, necessarily rank experience in any order of significance or 'importance'.

For about 10% of the collectors, their work and their collecting are directly related. These people tend to be under 35, and are largely the younger professionals, and those still engaged in formal education, although there are a number of individual exceptions to the general trend. Many of these people actually use their material during the course of their daily work. These relatively young people are very flexible in their mental categories and see the distinction between work and play as fluid and blurred.

By contrast, the number – both men and women – who belong to collecting clubs is low at about 5%, and generally comprises those within the blue collar workforce. This seems to reflect a mind-set which keeps work and leisure very separate, and consequently requires a specific leisure-time forum in which to show the collection off. However, what the men, in particular, bring to the club often does have links with their job, like John Watts, who belongs to the Leicestershire Collecting Club, who was a working electrician all his life and who collects early household electrical plugs and similar pieces.

It emerges that among collectors, although differing attitudes to this relationship are perceptible across age and class background, we do not, broadly, see alienated workers, but people for whom their work experience is pleasurable and emotionally valuable, and convertible into the collecting process. For most people, however, collected material is not a part of their working lives in the sense that they use it to make, or help to make, a living by dealing in collectibles. When they engage in car boot sales and the like, they tend to buy rather than sell, and to do so as a piece of occasional fun rather than as a matter of working routine. There are, of course, dealers, who also collect – in fact probably most dealers would say that they did – but these appear as a very small group indeed in the collecting population overall.

The bulk of collectors recruit material by purchasing it in standard commercial outlets: 86% say their purchasing is an important method of adding to their material. Much of this is mass produced material of the type that slips down into the rubbish category, and a familiar argument would suggest that collectors are being manipulated into purchase through productional and promotional strategies implicit in developed forms of capitalism; that most of the shoppers are women merely emphasises the exploitative nature of the operation. This line of argument is seen to be particularly true of the larger chain stores, but is also the aim of the smaller concerns who mix in with the giants in the bright new shopping malls and centres.

However, the mesh of this market thinking is hardly ever fine enough to catch the mixture of motives and desires which actually animate the purchaser. In fact, marketing tends to lag behind shopping trends, which is one reason why the smaller and more flexible outlets can do so well. Collectors often seem to succeed in appropriating the commercial market, by choosing the egg cups or the scarves for reasons which would be hard for an outsider to guess at, and it is the action of these motives, as they emerge into the practice of collecting, which turns impersonal economics into personal culture.

The mechanism for this transformation is frequently that of gift-giving, in which the object destined for a collection takes on the role of gift. Sixty-seven per cent of the respondents said that they added to their collections through this way, and even when collectors buy things for themselves, they frequently express the transaction as 'a present from me to me'. Gifts are a traditional way of turning the profane into the sacred, and are closely embedded in the recurrent practices of social (including work) and family life.

'Family life' as it is lived seems to mean three things: the group of sexually- and blood-related kin, the home in which family life takes place, and the cumulative shared and remembered experience which transcends an individual life. The information suggests that women, as wives, mothers and daughters, participate more in family gift-giving networks than do men, and that the core living areas of the family home are more likely to show off the woman's collection than they are the man's. This may have the effect of making men feel more excluded or peripheral to family and home than they otherwise would. Csikszentmihaly and Rochberg-Halton (1981) have shown that 'warm', well-balanced families involve both concrete objects and a certain willingness on the part of the women to be self-effacing. If this is true, female collecting may modify family life in a way experienced as 'colder' by the rest of the family; perhaps female collecting, like every other statement of female self-construction, is seen as a threat to traditional family values. However, it is unlikely to be a major threat. Women's collections usually have intrinsic gift, family history and home-decorating qualities, which means that they can be absorbed by the family structure.

This brings us to gender as a parameter of collecting. Generally speaking, and for reasons that we can speculate about, people collect within, rather than in opposition to, the standard gender stereotypes, particularly in terms of what they collect. This is broadly true, even if the analysis of individual collectors can sometimes show a degree of fuzziness in their relationship to traditional gender roles. Digger's analysis of the Tie Collector (Digger forthcoming), using Fuzzy Quantifiers shows this very well (Figure 8.1). The Tie Collector presents his behaviour very carefully, saying that his expertise in embroidery and sewing was 'learnt in the Army' as a way of legitimising his access to traditional female skills. He also claims to be unable to darn a sock or sew on a button, despite these being traditional 'squaddie' skills.

Women tend to collect in ways which are thought to enhance the appearance of the family home, and commemorative material linked with family history is an important aspect of this. Accordingly, the collected material is spread around the home, and arranged so that it looks good, rather than follows a preconceived ordering. Men are often interested in a collecting style in which the objects appear to have intrinsic qualities which lead to classification, and so to organised display or storage, frequently away from the family living spaces. Male collections tend to have a broad range of functional needs. This matches the findings of Belk and Wallendorf who found that women tend to collect self-referential and decorative material, while male collecting is geared more to control and domination. Women's collections represented 'achievement in the world of connection to other people – achievement of sentiment' (Belk and Wallendorf 1992: 251).

For each individual, the collecting process operates across each of these large parameters of experience, and helps him or her to make them 'make sense', that is to say, helps in the construction of a personal narrative of selfhood and recognisable, individual identity. Since the collector, the

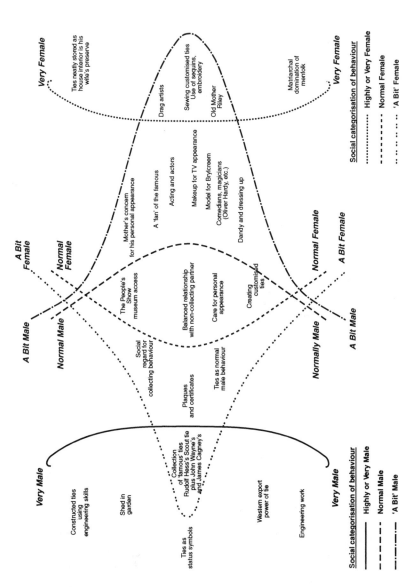

Figure 8.1 *The gender behaviour of the Tie Collector using Fuzzy Quantifiers (after Digger forthcoming)*

collected objects and the world of experience are all physically embodied, the word becomes a sequence of bodily appropriations in which the collector produces a series of allegories which bridge the gap between the metonomic consumptions of looking and touching, and the metaphoric otherness of the alien universe.

All this collecting activity takes place within the broader social framework, the nature of which was the subject of Chapter 2. Women are rather more likely to collect than men; collecting peaks in early adulthood and again around the later fifties and earlier sixties; and the proportion of collectors who live in 'normal' family and work situations mirrors that in the general population. Collectors are revealed as quite 'normal' people who engage in a particular practice, rather than the deviants of popular and media mythology (and 'serious' fiction).

The very broad middle class was over-represented in the replies, but the population spectrum was represented well enough for some general principles to emerge. In the areas of habit, feeling and action there is little or no difference in the approaches taken to collecting practice by the different socio-economic groups. Similarly, the content of the collections does not reflect social distinctions, because the same kinds of material, both 'valuable' or 'authentic' and 'rubbish' or 'inauthentic' are collected across the social scene. Unlike almost all other cultural practices, collecting in style and content does not seem to operate in a series of gear changes which reflect the *habitus* of the different social groups. The big distinction in collecting practice is not by class, but by gender.

Collecting in Contemporary Society

How we understand contemporary collecting as a social phenomenon has much to do with the ways in which contemporary society as a whole should be understood. It seems clear that, from perhaps around 1970, people began consciously to collect recent or contemporary material most of which had been mass-produced. This kind of collecting dominates the collecting scene today. The materials include all the familiar types which have been discussed here: the egg cups, spoons, animal figures, plates, old radios, Dinky toys and so on. So far as we can see, this kind of collecting was new around 1970; before that people had endeavoured to collect not near-contemporary 'rubbish' but objects to which traditional values adhered, such as coins, stamps, natural history specimens and historical material. It is often claimed that the actual percentage of collectors in the population started to rise about the same time. This takes us into uncharted territory for which the evidence is lacking, but there is a *prima facie* case for doubting if, in 1890, for example, or in 1930 anything like 30% of the population at any one time would have described themselves as collectors.

The growth in numbers (if such really exists) can be explained in terms of the general growth in prosperity, with its greater commitment to material accumulation of all kinds. The shift in the character of the objects of desire requires a different kind of interpretation. Many commentators (e.g. Martin 1996) have seen in the new collecting orientation one sign, or symptom, of the postmodern nature of contemporary society. As Martin puts it, 'The burgeoning of postmodern collecting is indicative of a *fin de siècle* sensibility in the late twentieth century' (Martin 1996: 6).

Postmodernism is deemed to involve an attack on autonomous, institutionalised art which denies its grounds and purpose. Art is seen not as a higher form of existence deriving from individual creative genius, but as present everywhere. There is no longer a valid distinction between 'high' or 'serious' art and mass popular art or kitsch (Featherstone 1991: 124). The relevance of this to collections of popular, mass-produced material is obvious. Postmodernism is seen as developing an aesthetic of the body which exalts the surface of things instead of their content, to prefer appearance to meaning. This has a bearing on the succession of one fashion in clothes to another, as differences in spectacle but not in understanding. Plainly, contemporary collected material can be seen as surface rather than content, and much of it shares the nature of fashion. Similarly, as Chapter 7 discussed, there is a kind of continuity between the body surface of the collector and the material he collects.

Attention to surface, and the negation of artist 'value', leads inevitably to the denial of the meta-narrative, the grand foundational story upon which the characteristic modernism narratives of science, religion, humanism and history are grounded (Featherstone 1991: 124). Knowledge henceforward should emphasise the qualities of irony, layered meaning, incoherence and discontinuity. The deliberate collecting of kitsch material in a camp style does exactly this. This, in turn, leads to fragmentation of culture in which time becomes an unrelated series of presents, and a sense of reality disintegrates into sequences of unrelated images, qualities cultivated by the makers of pop videos. Aesthetic experiences take their place as the prime carriers of meaning, and, as Baudrillard put in the interview which Kellner quotes (1995b: 329), 'all that remains to be done is to play with the pieces'.

Playing involves the transformation of 'reality' into images which operate in a perpetual present; these images are not brought together in narrative sequences, or, if they are, the narratives are idiosyncratic and individual, rather than hitched onto hitherto universally understood signs. So, collections are organised according to individual whim, seen as an authentic record of particular experience, rather than an affirmation of received values. In much the same way, the aesthetic of collecting favours a mode of perception which sees meaning in the individual understanding of the relevance of shapes, colours and juxtapositions.

The question really is, not is all this true, for collecting as for other social phenomena of the late twentieth century, since clearly it is, but does it truly represent a cultural break with the past, or are we looking at a different kind of event? This question itself has two faces: first, has society since around 1960 itself fractured and transformed into something quite different to what went before; and secondly, to what extent have individual attitudes and habits correspondingly changed?

The first is a very large question, and much canvassed. Much of the argument concerns the nature of the family. An influential group of sociologists concentrates upon perceived or quantifiable change in family life. Dench, for example, sees family relationships under threat from an insistent individualism that puts personal choice first, reducing the family to a matter of self-interest. If duty to the family gets in the way of career or pleasure, then so much the worse for the family, and hence the steep rise in divorce, instability of relationships and damaged children. Much importance is given to the role of women, and the acceptable relationship between the sexes: female freedoms, in particular, are seen to deprive men of their responsibility, and therefore civilising role, and a coherent (or modernist) family based society is the principle casualty (Dench 1996a, b). With this kind of argument is often connected an appreciation that society has actually changed less than the chattering classes think or wish. The 'silent majority' argument produces statements like 'the claim that *all* women want to pursue "careers", and are only held back by the "glass ceilings" imposed by men, is yet another myth . . . The primary commitment for many women is often still not to work but to their traditional role in rearing a family' (Obelkevich and Catterall 1994b: 3).

As we have seen in Chapters 2 and 5, the great majority of collectors, both male and female are living their lives through and within a traditional family organisation in which heterosexual partners live in a home with their own children, even though some of the children may belong biologically to only one of the partners. This should dispose of the stereotype of the lone collector operating as a social alien, but brings forward the interesting question of the relationship of collecting to family life. Families which are rich in objects that relate to the history and internal integrity of the family – as most women's collections do – are 'warm' environments, in Csikszentmihalyi and Rochberg-Halton's (1981) helpful term; this is to say that such collections promote family stability and well-being, through the encouragement of a 'feel-good' factor in the home. However untraditional the contents of such collections may be in terms of classic values – and, again, they usually are of this nature – their operational tone is not postmodern, but on the contrary, as modernist as may be. The female Owl Images Collector, for example, became interested in owl images because an owl was the crest of her maternal grandmother, and the Photographs Collector's great-aunt modelled for Julia Margaret Cameron. The (male) Match Boxes Collector believes that collecting runs in a family, saying 'I was born a collector like my grandmother before me', and adding that his wife, son, aunts, daughters and grandchildren all collect. In these, as in most, examples, the importance of the female line is clear. Such collections help to promote family values and all that this implies. But, as Csikszentmihalyi and Rochberg-Halton, Dench and Obelkevich and Catterall all admit, this family 'warmth' is achieved by a willingness on the part of women to see the family as their chief role in life.

For men, and perhaps for some women too, collecting may be an assertion of individuality in the face of too much togetherness. Male collections do seem often to be physically and mentally apart from the family heart, but we do not know whether this is a deliberate response intended to create distinctiveness, or acquiescence in a standard situation which always places the man somewhat apart from his wife and children. The Tram Collector, who comes from London and is interested in the transport culture of the area, says some people think he is weird: his favourite piece is four views of the Elephant and Castle junction taken between 1931 and 1946. However, an interest which strikes others as 'weird' is in itself so traditional a male predicament that a collecting – or any other leisure – response to it can hardly be described as postmodern in style.

The notion of 'traditional predicament' leads us into the question of the novelty or otherwise of those attitudes, and to a certain extent practices, which are called postmodern. A body of opinion argues that the supposed break between modern and postmodern is less extreme than sometimes supposed, and that this becomes clear when the analysis of contemporary society is put within a historical context. As Featherstone puts it, 'the origins of these sensibilities [manifest in phenomena like postmodernism] should be regarded as part of the long-term process of numeric growth and increase in the power potential of specialists in symbolic production which can be traced back to the Romantic movement' (1991: 125). This Featherstone links with the growth of consumer culture and the production and circulation of consumer goods (p. 126). The same point is made by Campbell (1987) in relation to the effect of Romantic longings, and by Kellner in relation to the operation of capital:

> Rather than postmodernity constituting a break with capital and political economy as Baudrillard and others would have it, wherever one observes phenomena of postmodern culture, one can detect the logic of capital behind them. (1995b: 257)

It has been suggested, indeed, that European history has seen a number of swings between 'postmodern' aspiration and its digestion by the contemporary equivalent of 'modern', to such an extent that a revolutionary discourse can be regarded as a Braudelian *mentalité* of the long-term in European culture (Pearce 1995: 370).

Implicit in this analysis is a view of the contrasting notions of value taken by the 'middle class' or 'service class' (or whatever is the approved term of the day) and by the 'working class' or the 'lower class', or even the 'underclass'. It is a truism that bourgeois culture and popular culture contrast in some fundamentally significant ways. The first appeals to values of taste and quality which are embodied in structures of authority and power, and prefers culture cast in traditional accessible forms like figurative art and narrative literature, while the second has little interest in abstract ideas of form and feels personal content to be more important; the first links its taste to traditional values, and is anxious about revisions of meaning, while the second places most weight on personal preference to which questions of 'taste' do not apply, and takes for granted the idea that you can place whatever meaning you like on your own things. These distinctions become most obvious in the twentieth and nineteenth centuries, but can be traced back into the eighteenth, precisely to that period when modern consumerism began, falteringly at first, to get under way and when Romanticism began to develop within the bourgeoisie as an intellectual and emotional response to it.

The significance of this in contemporary society perhaps rests in the composition of the 'new' middle class. There is a growing body of evidence relating, for example, to the very large number of common law relationships which the increased bureaucracy of the First World War revealed, which shows that in its attitude to the marriage tie, to illegitimacy, to stable work and to the nurturing of a physical home, the urban poor, during the earlier twentieth and nineteenth centuries, took what commentators today would characterise as a postmodern view, and what contemporary commentators called feckless, irresponsible, irreligious. Like present postmodernism, this privileged satisfaction above public duty, and, in relation to personal possessions, assumed that meaning consisted in whatever significance might be generated by personality and circumstance, rather than by external valuation (which, of course, most of the material culture held by such people did not possess to any worthwhile degree).

The economic logic of later capitalism has meant that in northern Europe and north America – exactly those areas where contemporary collecting is so significant – a significant proportion of the huge middle class has been recruited from this earlier urban (and, to a lesser extent, rural) poor. The family histories of many of those now in the very broad 'managerial' group would show a rise from the under class into, and sometimes through, the upper working or lower middle class, over the last three or four generations. But while the economic prospects of this group have improved, their mindset, or *habitus* to employ Bourdieu's phrase, has not changed so much, and in particular attitudes to the personal enjoyment of material goods, in the home, or as collections, has not altered. The mentality which sees objects as meaning whatever one wishes them to mean, as opposed to one which places them within socially endorsed hierarchies, remains, and helps to give us the collections of traditionally valueless material which we observe.

This process did not happen in isolation. Historically, the immediately relevant line runs back again to the Romantic writers, who themselves drew on the anarchic carnivalesque of popular village and urban tradition. The carnivalesque was brought into the cultural mainstream and is now visible in shopping malls, pop videos and consumer spectacles of all kinds. Media technology, itself a product of this broad development, produces a spiralling class of cultural intermediaries who construct symbolic goods for a market which expands with what it feeds upon. One consequence has been to offer to the 'new' middle class a cultural landscape in which it is at home, one where the aestheticisation of personally related content is more important than outward-looking form, and meta-narratives based on hierarchical values do not exist; one which is, in a word, postmodern.

The relevance of this to contemporary attitudes to material culture in general, and to collecting in particular, is obvious. It lends itself to the gathering of objects with nostalgia value for the individual, and hence to the collecting of material from the 1950s and 1960s which is so marked a feature of the collecting scene. Such collections demonstrate a particular interest in a personal past linked with a large lack of interest in a 'historical' community or national past. Similarly, it encourages and validates the symbolic valuation of 'rubbish' providing it can absorb personal memories, effective links, or simply likes. From this perspective the People's Show phenomenon represents a successful foray into the museum as a classical location of 'modernist' higher bourgeois culture by those whose traditions are different. The car boot sale becomes a contemporary manifestation of the carnivalesque, one much in tune with the theme.

The Individual as Collector

The argument here has suggested that attitudes identified as postmodern have been implicit in the unfolding of north European, and particularly British, culture since the later eighteenth century and have as much to do with traditionally anarchic attitudes as they do with sudden cultural novelties. This has resulted in an appearance-centred, personally related symbolic frame, of which contemporary collecting is a part. The next issue, therefore, is how all this is used to construct an individual identity. Eagleton describes the notion of the essential self as 'the humanistic fallacy' (1983: 207–213), and as the classic expression of humanism it has a long history in European thought, emerging as one of the key ideas of the Enlightenment, and so into the Romantic movement and its aftermath. But in fact, as Kellner points out (1995b: 231–233), modern notions of the individual embodied tensions between the idea of the substantial self, the innate and self-identical essence which constitutes the person, as offered by Descartes and so by Kant and Husserl, and that of the self and identity as an existentialist project, a creation of the authentic individual, as with Kierkegaard, Nietzsche and Sartre.

Postmodern thought has picked up on one idea of the self as project, but in turn problematises the constructivist notion by arguing that subject identity is itself a myth. The subject has disintegrated into a disjointed, fragmented and discontinuous flux which finds its expression and location in contemporary media culture, with its pastiche, superficial images and implosion of forms. Heritage sites share this character with television and so do shopping malls and much of the popular material culture which is taken into contemporary collections. Postmodern identity, then, is constituted through game playing, and, in contrast to the seriousness of modernist identity which functioned through the public persona of job, fatherhood and citizen, revolves around leisure, looks, consumption and fun. Correspondingly, identity can be changed as easily as a suit of clothes, as one responds to fashion and mood swings. Hence, among other things, the sexual ambiguities on offer in Boy George, Michael Jackson, Prince and Madonna.

Yet postmodernist reports of the death of the subject may be premature. The frequently strong and important links between collecting and paid job argue for a certain stability in the individual's view of himself. The Electrical Collector is a telecommunications engineer, the Hornby Train Collector is an engineer, and the Model Ambulance Collector is an ambulance technician: all of these suggest considerable pride and identity capital invested in what might be called an 'old fashioned' way, in callings with strong *éspirit de corps*. In more contemporary terms, as Kellner puts it, it is media culture that more and more provides the materials and resources to constitute identities that 'people appropriate' (1995b: 259). In the same way people appropriate popular material culture, which shares the same postmodern values of pastiche, self-reference and disconnected image as the visual media, and use it as an area of investment in which a subject individuality can be built up. The form and image of much collected material is clearly superficial but it can be endowed with content and narrative which produces meaning and identity. Choices are made among the polysemic natures of the objects which result in some material being collected, while other is rejected, and the objects of inclusion are constructed into a greater whole.

Meta-narratives may be under a cloud, but smaller ones are still alive and well, and may be found in every collector's psyche. For Lacan, human reality is 'profoundly elusive and not amenable to systematic articulation' (Crowther 1994: 78). The crucial moment is when the child encounters its own image in objects which mirror its appearance, which enables the child to project an 'imaginary unity of self'. For Lacan 'this projection of a "spectacular ego" proves to be a decisive trait in all modes of human awareness. We project fantasies of unity and completeness onto situations and phenomena which do not have such unity' (Crowther 1994: 78). The individual looks at the mass of material dots and joins up those which he wishes to make his picture, and in terms of a lived life the precise philosophical position of what he does makes little impact. This, of course, means that the poetic of collecting is frequently closer to slang than formal diction, but this will not worry those whose cultural roots are not, in any case, with the educated or aspiring classes with whom the modernist narratives of correctness really resided. The trashy and the vulgar are neither here nor there, when narratives of individuality rest not in these qualities or their opposites, but in their character as gift, holiday souvenir or interesting item of early technology.

In parallel with this popular carelessness towards perceived value runs a line of deliberate material subversion which as a fashionable market trend has had its own influence upon events. The Punk Rockers of the late 1970s deliberately used rubbish as a fashion statement intended as a comment upon the nature of society. Jamie Reid's graphics for the Sex Pistols used cut-out, blackmail type, newspaper, and black plastic bin liners were turned into mini-skirts and tee shirts. Poly Styrene and the band X Ray Spex made explicit statements in songs like 'The Day the World Turned Dayglow' and 'Plastic Bag'. The plastic bag and the safety pin took on the symbolic value of identity, or loss of it. The pins were made to look as if they were pushed through flesh, and so link with fashionable notions of mutilation, tattoos and exotic face paint.

Punk also turned to second-hand clothes from charity shops and what would have been termed 'kitsch' objects like plastic sandals and cheap sunglasses, using them as statements of the intrinsic worthlessness of such goods and so of the society which consumes them. But two points here are crucial. Punk may be a central site of postmodernist action, but it has a history: it can be positioned within a tradition of black humour, camp and mocking comedy which runs back into the nineteenth century, and which partakes of a 'postmodern' flavour. Secondly, the assertion of worthlessness created cultural value: the operation of the bricoleur is not new, and like the Punk Rockers, this subversion has the unintended effect of creating fresh symbolic material value, which then finds its way into the mainstream.

The process by which collected rubbish becomes received culture has been explored by Thompson (1979) and Pearce (1995). In the workings of punk and camp we can see the process happening through self-conscious interventions in the cultural scene, just as some collectors deliberately do so in ways which are intended as social comment, and with the same ultimately impotent effect: what was subversion becomes valued mainstream as culture shows its capacity to subvert the subverters. Even the female 'Objects in the Shape of a Male Willy' Collector may live to see her 20 or so penises acquire an extended cultural value. Most collectors, although perhaps influenced by the subversive tradition (to a lesser or greater extent), enter into the process unwittingly. But the effect is the same, and today's holiday mementoes become tomorrow's museum collection.

Collecting in Contemporary Practice

At the beginning of this book, we suggested that Barthes's hierarchy of signification would place this study in its epistemological position (Figure 1.1), and that the shift in focus from *collection* studies to *collecting* studies (Figure 1.3) would structure its fields of interest. In Barthes's terms, collecting appears as an exercise in denotation–meta-language (level 2), in which an object and its first range of meanings become the signified to which a new signifying meaning is attached. This meta-linguistic entity enters the rhetoric of a particular contextual ideology that is both social and individual. 'Ideology' should be understood as the making of meaning, the generation of significance with reference to past and future which can structure several and collective understanding as daily life unfolds. Levels 4, 5 and onwards embrace the meta-language of the analyst and makes the obvious, but necessary, point, that we can never escape ourselves. It is worth noting that the process also happens in reverse, so that the efforts of the consumer (both analyst and collector) influence the 'real' world in the bottom level, a process reflected in the transformation of (some) rubbish which we have just discussed.

The interesting events in collecting take place at levels 2 and 3, and its analysis has been framed at level 4 in a style aimed at unravelling its social and individual ideology; the framing of the analysis, it goes without saying, is also a part of the epistemological process. The operation of ideology, or the making of meaning, is seen as process in which individual and social context appear as active participants. In this sense, collecting is a constructive act, and interest centres upon reflexive, exploratory study aimed at discovering how ideas about the big human questions are generated through listening to what collectors themselves say about their activities. As Csikszentmihalyi and Rochberg-Halton put it:

> Meaning, not material possessions, is the ultimate goal in [people's] lives . . . People still need to know that their actions matter, that their existence forms a pattern with that of others, that they are remembered and loved, and that their individual self is part of some grand design beyond the fleeting span of mortal years . . . The battle for the value of life is fought in the arena of meaning. (1981: 145)

The role of collecting in the effort to make meaning within collectors' lives must not be over-estimated. As this study has shown the obsessed collector is the anomaly, and most collectors take a relaxed, low-key, unemphatic approach, even while taking their collection seriously as a focus of their lives. There is a strong sense that collecting is usually an undestructive, even safe, way of generating meaning, which might be another way of saying that its postmodernist tendencies of polysemantic self-reference are easily reconciled with a social structure which, in spite of recent assaults, is still largely modernist in tone. This helps to explain why so many collectors are living in 'normal', i.e. modernist, families and yet within this structure are making familial and personal meaning by collecting mass produced, traditionally (modernistically) valueless material. Ancient practices of gift exchange and recent ones of eclectic shopping are appropriated into this framework, and so are traditional assumptions about employment and the nature of gender.

The resulting reification of feelings, history and relationships, which is almost universally reported as a positive and pleasurable experience, can be seen as the idea of the romantic, in Campbell's sense, working itself out in the late twentieth century society. Here, in many, or all, aspects of life, the distinction between private and public is confused, and so also that between sacred and profane. We are all symbols of ourselves, and objects which, in so many ways, are our *alter egos* are equally symbols of themselves. Collecting becomes a simple, effective way of merging these symbols into broader and deeper meaning.

The last word should be with a collector, and one whose whimsical view of himself characterises much of the collecting process. The collector describes himself as collecting 'stones and rock from different places, i.e. mountain summits, places of interest, other countries, beaches etc.' He has between 21 and 50 stones but did not think of himself as a collector 'until recently – I assumed I just had a pile of old rocks'. The collection is kept attached to slips of board and sometimes information about the pieces is recorded on a sheet of paper, although 'only rarely' is time spent on the material. The first pieces were flint stones taken from Hyde Park, and for the collector each piece appears to be different and to bring back memories of the locations where they were found. The collector's two favourite pieces are volcanic pumice from Mount St Helens ('collected within weeks of the eruption') and a fragment of the Berlin Wall. He is aged between 36 and 45, was born in Manchester, relies on graphic design/lecturing for a living, lives with a wife and has three children. He put his address as 26 Stones Drive. He adds:

I've just realised the connection between my collection and address – interesting?

Appendix

The Contemporary Collecting in Britain Survey

Methodology of the Survey

The priorities of the Contemporary Collecting in Britain Survey were to achieve a representative sample of the whole of the adult British population (including England, Scotland and Wales but excluding Northern Ireland). A good response was important for the work to be representative of the total population. The method had to be one which allowed a relatively large number of questions to be asked, including demographic questions.

Both the specific conduct of surveys and general issues surrounding information-gathering from a living population have been the subject of much consideration over the past few years. Sapsford and Jupp (1996), Fink (1995a, b), Fink and Kosecoff (1985), Creswell (1995) and Lewis-Beck (1994) have all discussed the problems surrounding the theory and practice of survey work and offered working solutions (although Fink's useful *Survey Kit*, 1995a, came out too late to be useful in this project). Qualitative research (Denzin and Lincoln 1994; Silverman 1993), naturalistic enquiry (Erlandson et al. 1993) and ethnographic approaches (Hammersley 1992) have all been the subject of specialised methodological discussion. In addition to this general literature, investigation into contemporary collecting practice has generated its own methodological discussions. Naturalistic enquiries have been considered by Belk, Sherry and Wallendorf (1988) and Wallendorf and Belk (1989), ethnographic writing by Joy (1991), interviewing by Kremer (1992) and general issues by Belk (1991) and Holbrook (1991).

It should be noted that most of this work relates to North America, where successful approaches to information-gathering are likely to be somewhat different from those in Britain, as a result of the differing social scene. Constraints on the Survey included a limited research budget; the need for the project to be managed completely over a two-year period to ensure the smallest possible gap between information-gathering and publication; and a desire to keep the methodology and presentation of results as simple as possible.

For all these reasons, and, importantly, because it had been used very successfully by Merriman in a broadly related field (Merriman 1991), the postal survey method was chosen, organised according to the Total Design Method (TDM) described by Dillman (1972, 1978, 1983). Postal surveys are inexpensive and (relatively) uncomplicated and probably achieve a more genuinely hands-on sample than personal interviews. Similarly, they may have less built-in bias. Dillman's work shows that with careful preparation the return rate for postal surveys can be as good as that for interview surveys. Postal surveys do pose issues of length and complexity of the questionnaire, problems on attitudinal data, relevance to recipient and absence of the interviewer, but these tend to be matched or balanced by equivalent difficulties in other methods (Merriman 1991: 144–146).

Accordingly, the organising principles of TDM were adhered to here. Each recipient received three mailings: first a hand-addressed and hand-stamped quality white envelope containing a copy of the questionnaire, a pre-paid and addressed envelope for its return, and a hand-signed letter on standard University of Leicester crested paper explaining the project; secondly a reminder post-card; and thirdly another white envelope like the first containing a duplicate copy of the questionnaire, pre-paid return envelope and a different letter on the same writing paper with ink signature. The questionnaire was produced as a folded A3 sheet giving four A4 pages and, after much debate, it was printed on cream paper. Copies of the questionnaire and the two letters are included at the end of this Appendix. The objective of all this, as of all TDM-based surveys, was to produce something as unlike commercial mail shots as possible in order to encourage responses, and labour-intensive though it was, it was worth the effort.

A particular problem in this survey was the delicate nature of the enquiry as it related to people's possessions and homes. The high level of house burglary prompted the worry that recipients might distrust the Survey on general grounds, or even wonder if it had criminal connections. For this reason, the lack of connection between address and returned questionnaire was stressed. As the Survey progressed the organisers received some fifteen telephone queries intended to verify its *bona fides*, including two from police forces who had been alerted by recipients, but all were satisfied by the answers they received. The final return rate of 57% showed that the time and effort expended on the TDM approach was well justified.

Formulation of the Questionnaires

The objective of a survey questionnaire is two-fold: to gather what is seen as useful information, and to persuade recipients to complete and return it. These two aims are not entirely in harmony, and every questionnaire represents a balance between them. An initial draft questionnaire was put together in the light of broad questions relating to collecting and following discussion with those involved in the People's Show Project; in addition, three separate workshops aimed at designing such a questionnaire were held with postgraduate museum studies students at Leicester. The questions were designed to elicit material relating to collecting practice primarily, and therefore concentrated not on the content of the collection, but on areas like how it was acquired, maintained and viewed. It should be noted that the arrangement of the questionnaire was intended to be as user-friendly as possible, and that therefore discussion of the various aspects in this book does not follow the questionnaire's order.

As a result, a final draft was prepared and piloted with a group of 43 different students in June 1993. The pilot questionnaires were analysed according to the software which was to be used in the analysis of the full-scale survey (see below). As a result of this, a number of changes were made to the questions, to their organisational relationships and to the format of the questionnaire, which brought it to its final form. This form embraced both multiple choice questions, the ticked answers to which could be examined statistically, and invitations to comment, intended to evoke qualitative information. In the event, most recipients answered both types of question, although a difficulty was created by a tendency to tick more than one box in the multiple choice answers.

The final section of the questionnaire covered demographic variables (see below).

The Survey

Following Merriman's work, the electoral register was chosen as the most suitable sampling frame. The main determinant of size was the number of sub-group analyses (i.e. size of cross-tabulation cells) to be performed. Following Merriman (1991), Hoinville and Jowell (1978: 61) and Sudman (1993), a sample of 1500 was deemed to be appropriate.

Sampling was carried out in the library of electoral registers held by the Office of Population Censuses and Surveys in London. The number of electoral constituencies totalled 633. They were grouped by county in alphabetical order, with the English first and the Scottish last. A systematic sampling system was applied to ensure every member of the sample population had a statistically equal chance of selection. To arrive at the sample total of 1500 people 100 constituencies were randomly selected and from each constituency 15 polling districts were selected, again randomly. One person was then pulled from each polling district to give the total of 1500.

To start the selection procedure a random number of 29 was selected from tables. This yielded Cambridge, Cambridgeshire as the first constituency. As 100 constituencies were required the total number of 633 was divided by 100 to give 6.33 as the sampling interval; this was then rounded up to 7. The next constituency was therefore number 36, Chester, and so on. This method yielded 91 constituencies and the remaining 9 were selected randomly using number tables. To obtain the polling districts, in each constituency, the total number of polling districts was divided by 15 to gain the sampling interval – rounded up again to the nearest whole number. The next random number was then chosen and 15 districts selected by fixed interval. Finally one address was selected from each polling district by using the random number tables.

The random number tables, however, only covered numbers 01 to 99 and as the number of people in each polling district was often larger than 99 it was necessary to ensure that every person had an equal chance of selection. This was achieved by raising each subset of 15 random numbers by multiples of 100 for those polling districts with more than 99 people. For instance, the random number for the first polling district in the first constituency was 87 and the 87th person was selected. For the second polling district in the first constituency the random number was 02 so it was increased by a multiple of 100 to 102 and the 102nd person selected. For the third polling district in the first constituency the random number was 69 so it was increased by a further multiple of 100 to give 269 and so on. For the next constituency there was a return to the original figure and an increase by multiples of 100, 200, 300 etc. again. If the number of people was smaller than the figure to which it had been raised then there was a reduction by the appropriate multiple of 100. If the polling districts contained 99 people or less but the random number was still too large then the tables were pursued until a number that could be used came up. About 25% of the 1500 addresses required conversion to a full postal address. A combination of phone directories, post code directories and the post codes enquiry line were used in an attempt to fill the gaps.

The first wave of 1500 questionnaires was sent out by first class post between Friday 16 July and Friday 23 July 1993. The second mailing, the postcard, went out on Thursday 19 August and Friday 20 August 1993. The final mailing went out between Friday 10 September and Friday 17 September 1993. By 31 October 1993, the designated cut-off date, 948 forms had been received, of which 836 were usable, a response rate of 57%. The response rate to a survey is calculated according to fixed guidelines, summarised by Hedges (1977: 5). Out-of-scope mailings, including those sent to vacant, demolished or non-residential addresses, and to people who have moved out of the country, are deducted. For the purposes of this survey those whose questionnaires were returned stating that they were in hospital long-term or in retirement homes were deemed out of scope because collections cannot be maintained in such circumstances; similarly those returned as addressee deceased were deducted. Another 14 forms had been received after 31 October 1993, but these did not form part of the analysis. Table A.1 gives details of the survey response rate. Given the property-related sensitivities of this survey, the achievement of a 57% response rate is most respectable. It is broadly comparable to Dillman's response rate of 62% (1978: 56) and close to the response normally achieved by personal interviews (see, for example, NOP 1982).

Following the return of the forms, telephone interviews were organised with those people who had stated on the questionnaire that they would be willing to participate in such an interview. Thirty-one people had so stated, but four of these proved to be unobtainable, and eventually 27 such interviews were conducted. These maintained the question format of the questionnaire, but followed up individual questions in greater detail. These

Table A.1 *Contemporary Collecting in Britain Survey: survey population and response rate*

Sampling popluation	all persons eligible to vote in private households in Great Britain (excluding Northern Ireland)	
Sampling frame	Electoral Register	
	(No.)	(%)
Addresses selected from Register	1500	
Found to be out of scope	17	
Assumed to be out of scope	15	
In scope addresses	1468	100
Response rate	836	57
Non-respondents	632	43
Of which:		
Number of individuals from whom no response at all obtained	520	
Replies received but Questionnaire not completed	112	
Of these 112, the following reasons for non-completion were received		
Refusal/not interested	29	
Moved house	33	
Incomplete address	5	
Not prepared to disclose personal information	3	
Dog ate form	1	
Not known	41	

interviews have informed discussion in the book, but have been eliminated from the statistical analyses.

Data Analysis

After considerable discussion with the University of Leicester Computer Centre, the decision to use SPSS software was taken. SPSS is one of the most popular packages for analysis of questionnaire material and has been used successfully by many in the university working on social science related projects. SPSS is available on the Mac, Irix and PC systems. It was decided to use the Macintosh, as the graph facility, Cricket Graph, can be used in conjunction with SPSS. SPSS ver. 4 was used for data entry, and SPSS ver. 6 for data translation and production.

Before the data could be entered for analysis in SPSS it had to be coded. SPSS works much more effectively with numeric values and therefore each answer required a numeric code. A format of using a 1 to signify yes, 2 for no, 0 for no response, and values between 1 and 6 for multiple answer questions, was worked out. In order to do this, the questions relating to collection type by content and occupation required categorisation. The categories finally decided upon are listed on p. 28 (Table 2.2) and p. 31

(Table 2.3). Each question on the questionnaire was cross-tabulated against all of the demographic variables to yield a run of bar charts showing comparative percentages. The categories of collection type by content were similarly cross-tabulated against the questions on the questionnaire. Selective use was made of all this analysed data, and in many cases the bar charts were re-cast as graphs to maximise the information each one could show. It should be noted that in each case, unless specified, the figures show the respective percentages of those who answered the relevant questions and not percentages against the Survey as a whole. However, it must be remembered that some respondents scored more than one answer to some questions, and this habit explains some of the apparent anomalies. After reflection, these were not removed because they represent collecting realities. Generally, figures over x.5 were rounded up: this sometimes causes apparent anomalies.

Sources of Bias

As noted previously, the Survey is concerned only with adult collectors, so the restriction of the electoral registers to those over 18 years was no difficulty. However, the registers have their own difficulties. Butcher and Todd (1981) have shown that around 4% of eligible people will not be listed, and these exclusions tend to be concentrated among Commonwealth citizens or those about to attain voting age. A further bias is caused by the length of time the register has been in operation and population mobility. By the time in the year each annual register comes into force (16 February), it has been estimated that about 3% of electors will have moved house and by the end of its currency about 12% will have moved. Since this survey was conducted between July and September, about 6% of electors may have moved, accounting for perhaps 5% of the non-responses (allowing for those represented by postal returns) (Hoinville and Jowell 1978). Similarly, this survey approach excludes all those living in institutions rather than private addresses. The sampling method also ignores the differing sizes of the constituencies, and means that individuals in small constituencies had a greater chance of selection.

Discussion in Chapter 1 concentrated upon the characteristics of those returning the questionnaire and the characteristics of the population as a whole (pp. 25 and Table 2.1). Because of the need to keep names and addresses and responses completely separate, it was not possible to telephone a sample of the non-responders in order to form a view of the personal characteristics of this group. Goyden has shown that males are more likely to return questionnaires than females, that occupation and education have a strong effect on response rates, and that the response is about 13% lower in urban areas than others (1982). As noted in Chapter 1, these biases do indeed show up in the present survey. There is no way of knowing whether these non-responders are likely to be collectors or non-collectors: non-collectors might be more likely not be bother with the form, but collectors might be wary of replying for security reasons. In any case, they have of course been excluded from the statistical analysis.

It is sometimes considered appropriate to account for non-respondents in the analysis of a survey by weighting the sample so that it emulates the characteristics of the general population. Merriman (1991: 157) chose the system of weighting by access to vehicle as the one which produced a sample profile most nearly representative of the whole population. After careful consideration, no weighting was undertaken in the analysis of the results presentation of the present survey. Instead, the imbalances were noted in the initial discussion (Chapter 1) and borne in mind thereafter: this seems the clearest way of presenting the survey results.

Acquiescence bias was not felt to be a major distorting feature of this survey, since the initial questions – of collection possession and so on – involved facts not opinions, and the opinions expressed related directly to the personal view taken of these specific facts. However, the small group of people who viewed their material differently as a result of receiving the questionnaire has been noted (Table 1.1).

The principal demographic variables used have been sex, age, racial allegiance, community, occupation of main family wage-earner, access to a car, and possession of partner and children. The first four of these present no difficulties, except that heterosexual/homosexual orientation did not emerge from the gender/partner questions. The term 'partner' was used instead of 'spouse' (in any case too much like a tax return) or 'husband/ wife' in the hope of capturing the wider range of relationships. However, there is no way of knowing how committed these relationships were (or how long-term) or how the children scored related to them. In practice, all of these relationships had to be treated as if they were 'standard' marriages and families: in fact, there is no reason to suppose that they are much (or any) less stable than formal marriages and the families which result from them. The percentage of replies received from individuals scoring themselves as other than white was very low, too low to merit separate consideration in the statistical analysis. This broad issue is pursued on pp. 29–31.

The questions about occupation and access to car were intended to give information about the class, or socio-economic group of respondent. In this regard, 'access to car' did not prove to be useful, because young collectors in the 18–25 age group and women over 65 tended not to have access, regardless of social position, while those in other age groups almost all did, again regardless of class. Occupation of respondent (or respondent's bread-winner) is generally regarded in survey work as the best indication of socio-economic class, and this proved to be the case here. Difficulties revolved around some evasive replies (as 'retired') and some which gave an inadequate level of detail, but the information received was sufficient for a meaningful analysis. It is generally acknowledged that this is both a very crucial area and a very difficult one to penetrate.

Some of the demographic variables were found to have greater explanatory capacity than others. Sex, age, socio-economic status and family circumstances turned out to be the most revealing of collecting practice, and are therefore cited more frequently than car access, community and racial allegiance.

Department of Museum Studies
University of Leicester
Contemporary Collecting
Project

Please tick the box that applies to you. Tick more than one box if you like. Please also write what you like for the other questions. If you have more than one collection, please choose one and answer for it.

Do you collect anything?

Yes ☐   No ☐

If No, then please turn to the back page, fill in the 'background' section and return the form.

We would like to know the history of your collection.

What do you collect? _____

_____

How many items are there in your collection?

1 - 10 ☐   11 - 20 ☐   21 - 50 ☐   51 - 100 ☐   over 100 ☐

Have you   collected constantly ☐   collected off and on ☐

If you have ticked the last box, why did you stop and then start again? _____

_____

When did you start to think of yourself as a collector? _____

_____

Do you belong to a collectors club?   Yes ☐   No ☐

We would be interested to know how you got your collection

Did you get some of your collection

by purchases ☐   as birthday/Christmas/other presents ☐   swapping with others ☐

belonging to a collectors' club ☐   informal contacts ☐   other ☐

If purchase, was it from

shop ☐   auction ☐   car boot /jumble sale/market ☐

other private collectors ☐   mail order from magazine ☐   other ☐

What do you reckon to spend on a piece?

5p - £1 ☐   £1.05 - £5 ☐   £5.05 - £10 ☐   over £10 ☐

1

Do you

seek out pieces actively ☐   wait for pieces to appear ☐   are you offered. pieces you don't want? ☐

How do you look after your collection?

Are you interested in remembering

where you acquired each piece ☐   what you paid for it ☐   how you found out about it ☐

Are you interested in finding out

how the objects were made ☐   when ☐   where ☐

by whom ☐   how they were used in the past ☐

Do you make a record of any of this..yes ☐ no ☐

in a notebook ☐   on a card ☐   on a computer ☐   on a sheet of paper ☐

Do you think about it much between times? ....yes ☐ no ☐

Do you put a personal mark of any kind on each piece? ....yes ☐ no ☐

If yes, what do you put? _____

Do you collect material relevant to your collection, eg newspaper articles?...................yes ☐ no ☐

Do you spend time collecting and looking after your collection

every day ☐   2 or 3 times a week ☐   once a week ☐

once a month ☐   other ☐

If 'other', how often? _____

Where do you keep your collection?

in your bedroom ☐   living room ☐   kitchen ☐

garage ☐   shed ☐   spare room/attic/loft ☐

Is your collection

in chest of drawers ☐   boxes ☐   on display eg on shelves ☐

Anywhere else? _____

How is your collection arranged?

no special order ☐   put on show so that it looks good ☐   divided up in a particular way ☐

What way? _____

Who knows you collect?

family ☐   friends ☐   wide range of people ☐   nobody ☐

2

Who do you show your collection to especially? _____

Why? _____ When? _____

What do people seem to think of you? _____

We would like to hear why you collect

Do you collect

just because you like them ☐   to get complete sets ☐   because they bring back memories ☐

If memories, then what memories? _____

Any other reasons? _____

Is it easy to say why you like them? ....yes ☐   no ☐

Can you put down some reasons, eg they look decorative/may be an investment? _____

_____

Were you encouraged to collect because you found one thing and carried on from there? .....yes ☐   no ☐

What thing? _____

Where did you get it? _____

because it linked up with your home? ....yes ☐   no ☐

how? _____

because you were encouraged by somebody? ....yes ☐   no ☐

who? _____

Does your collection link up with another hobby or activity? ....yes ☐   no ☐

What hobby/activity? _____

Does your collection have anything to do with your work? ....yes ☐   no ☐

What? _____

How do you feel about your collection?

How important is it to you?

very important ☐   fairly important ☐   quite important ☐   take it or leave it ☐

Does it seem a part of you? ....yes ☐   no ☐

Do you use your collection at all? ....yes ☐   no ☐

how? _____

3

If a piece turned out to be very valuable, would you sell?...yes ☐ no ☐

Will your collection ever be complete? ....yes ☐ no ☐

Why, or why not? _____

Do you have a favourite piece? What is it? Why? _____

_____

Do you sometimes see something you must have?..yes ☐ no ☐

Does it ever make you feel guilty? ....yes ☐ no ☐

Why? _____

Do you wish you had never started?...yes ☐ no ☐

Would you do it again? ....yes ☐ no ☐

What will you do with it in the end?

      sell it ☐   pass it on to somebody ☐   bequeath it to somebody ☐

give it to a museum ☐   not given the matter any thought ☐   other ☐

If 'other', what _____

We would like to have a little background about you

sex   male ☐   female ☐

age   18-25 ☐   26-35 ☐   36-45 ☐   46-55 ☐   56-65 ☐   over 65 ☐

Do you think of yourself as   white ☐   Afro-Caribbean ☐   Asian ☐   other ☐

Do you live in   big city centre ☐   big city suburb ☐   large town ☐   small town/village ☐

Where were you born (please given town and county)? _____

What is/was (if retired) the occupation of the main wage-earner in your family? _____

Do you have access to a car? ....yes ☐ no ☐

Are you living with a partner?..yes ☐ no ☐

Do you have children? ....yes ☐ no ☐

Does anybody else in your family collect? _____

THANK YOU VERY MUCH FOR YOUR HELP

If you would not mind a follow-up contact, please put your name and address below.

_____

_____

If you object to your name and address being held on computer, please tick box ☐

4

UNIVERSITY OF LEICESTER

105 PRINCESS ROAD EAST · LEICESTER LE1 7LG · ENGLAND

DEPARTMENT OF
MUSEUM
STUDIES

DIRECTOR AND
HEAD OF
DEPARTMENT
Professor SUSAN PEARCE
MA (Oxon), PhD, FSA,
FMA

TELEPHONE
0533 523963
(Direct line)
FACSIMILE
0533 523960
TELEX
341198 LEICUN G

15 July 1993

Dear Collector

Collecting is now recognised to be a very important activity, which a great many people share. Each collection, however, is unique, and therefore very interesting in its own right. I am hoping to gather information about collecting in Britain today, and so I am writing to you and sending you a copy of our questionnaire.

You have been randomly selected. You may feel that your collection is a very private matter, but I assure you that there is no link between your name and address and the questionnaire which accompanies this letter. I hope that you will complete the questionnaire and send it back to me in the pre-paid envelope provided, but I have no way of knowing who you are, or where you live. There will be no follow-up unless you express a wish for this at the end of the form.

Collections can be all kinds of things. If you collect glass frogs, or hotel soaps, or carrier bags, or football souvenirs, I do hope that you will fill in the questionnaire. If you think that you do not collect anything, it would be helpful if you still returned the questionnaire with a 'no' response to the first question.

I am sure that you are a very busy person, but in the interests of research I would be grateful if you could complete the questionnaire and return it to me.

I look forward to hearing from you.

Yours sincerely

Susan M Pearce (Professor)
Director

UNIVERSITY OF LEICESTER

105 PRINCESS ROAD EAST · LEICESTER LE1 7LG · ENGLAND

DEPARTMENT OF
MUSEUM
STUDIES

DIRECTOR AND
HEAD OF
DEPARTMENT
Professor SUSAN PEARCE
MA (Oxon), PhD, FSA,
FMA

TELEPHONE
0533 523963
(Direct line)
FACSIMILE
0533 523960
TELEX
341198 LEICUN G

5 August 1993

Dear Collector

A short while ago you will have received from me a letter and
questionnaire about collecting.   As I said in my previous letter, the
responses are entirely anonymous, and so therefore this follow up
letter is going to all the original addresses.

If you have already completed your questionnaire and sent it to me,
can I thank you very sincerely for the effort which you have put in,
and the contribution which you have made.

If you have not yet filled in your questionnaire I would be very glad if
you would do so.   I enclose a second copy and a second pre-paid
envelope in case this is helpful.

Thank you if you have already sent back the form. If you have not
yet done so I look forward to hearing from you.

Yours sincerely

Susan M Pearce (Professor)
Director

Bibliography

Abraham, K., 1927, *Selected Papers on Psychoanalysis*, Hogarth Press, London.

Ades, D., Mack, J., Malbert, R. and Shelton, A. (eds.), 1995, *Fetishism: Visualising Power and Desire*, Lund Humphries, South Bank Centre, Royal Pavilion, Brighton.

Adlmann, J. von, 1970, *Selections from the Exhibition: Kitsch, the Grotesque Around Us*, Wichita Art Museum, Wichita, Kansas.

Adlmann, J. von, 1973, 'Kitsch: the Grotesque Around Us', *Museum News*, 52, 1: 19–21.

Adorno, T. and Horkheimer, M., 1977, *Dialectic of Enlightenment*, trans. J. Cumming, Verso Books, London.

Alsop, J., 1982, *The Rare Art Traditions: the History of Collecting and its Linked Phenomena*, Thames and Hudson, London.

Appadurai, A. (ed.), 1986, *The Social Life of Things*, Cambridge University Press, Cambridge.

Aristides, N., 1988, 'Calm and Uncollected', *American Scholar*, 57, 3: 327–336.

Atticus, 1995, 'Filth Peddlers in the Guise of Art', *Sunday Times*, 11 June: 26.

Baekland, F., 1981, 'Psychological Aspects of Art Collecting', *Psychiatry*, 44: 45–59.

Bal, M., 1994, 'Telling Objects: A Narrative Perspective on Collecting', in Elsner and Cardinal 1994: 97–115.

Barthes, R., 1985, *The Fashion System*, trans. M. Ward and R. Howard, Jonathan Cape, London.

Bascom, W., 1979, 'Changing African Art', in Graburn 1979: 303–319.

Baudrillard, J., 1975, *The Mirror of Production*, Telos Press, St Louis.

Baudrillard, J., 1988, *Selected Writings*, Stanford University Press, Stanford, CA.

Baudrillard, J., 1993, *Symbolic Exchange and Death*, trans. Iain Hamilton Grant, Sage, London.

Baudrillard, J., 1994, 'The System of Collecting', in Elsner and Cardinal 1994: 7–24.

Bazin, G., 1967, *The Museum Age*, trans. J. Cahill, Wang and Wang, New York.

Beckett, H., 1986, 'Cognitive Developmental Theory in the Study of Adolescent Identity Development', in S. Wilkinson (ed.), *Feminist and Social Psychology: Developing Theory and Practice*, Open University Press, Milton Keynes, pp. 15–27.

Bekoff, M. and Jamieson, D. (eds.), 1996, *Readings in Animal Cognition*, Massachusetts Institute of Technology, Boston, MA.

Belk, R., 1988, 'Possessions and the Extended Self', *Journal of Consumer Research*, 15: 139–168.

Belk, R., 1991, 'The History and Development of the Consumer Behaviour Odyssey', *Highways and Buyways*, 1991: 1–12, Association for Consumer Research, Provo, Utah.

Belk, R., 1993, 'Materialism and the Making of the Modern American Christmas', in Miller 1993a: 75–104.

Belk, R., 1995a, 'Studies in the New Consumer Behaviour', in Miller 1995a: 59–95.

Belk, R., 1995b, *Collecting in a Consumer Society*, Routledge, London.

Belk, R., and Coon, G., 1993, 'Gift-giving as Agapic Love: an Alternative to the Exchange Paradigm Based on Dating Experience', *Journal of Consumer Research*, 20: 393–417.

Belk, R. and Wallendorf, M., 1992, 'Of Mice and Men: Gender Identity in Collecting', in K. Ames and K. Martinez (eds.), *Material Cultural of Gender/Gender of Material Culture*, University of Michigan Research Press, Ann Arbor, pp. 1–11.

Belk, R., Sherry, J. and Wallendorf, M., 1988, 'A Naturalistic Inquiry into Buyer and Seller Behaviour at a Swap Meet', *Journal of Consumer Research*, 14: 449–470.

Belk, R., Wallendorf, M. and Sherry, J., 1989, 'The Sacred and the Profane in Consumer Behaviour: Theodicy on the Odyssey', *Journal of Consumer Research*, 16: 1–38.

Belk, R., Wallendorf, M., Sherry, J. and Holbrook, M., 1990, 'Collecting in a Consumer Culture', *Highways and Buyways*, Association for Consumer Research, Provo, Utah.

Belk, R., Wallendorf, M., Sherry, J., Holbrook, M. and Roberts, M., 1988, 'Collectors and Collecting', *Advances in Consumer Research*: 548–553.

Benjamin, W., 1969, *Illuminations*, ed. Hannah Arendt, trans. H. Zohn, Schocken, New York.

Benjamin, W., 1977, *The Origin of German Tragic Drama*, trans. John Osbourne, New Left Books, London.

Benn, S., 1974, 'The Measurement of Psychological Androgeny', *Journal of Consulting and Clinical Psychology*, 42, 2: 155–162.

Benn, S. and Graus, G. (eds.), 1983, *Public and Private in Social Life*, Croom Helm, London.

Bermingham, A. and Brewer, J. (eds.), 1995, *The Consumption of Culture 1600–1800*, Routledge, London.

Bermudez, J.L., Marcel, A. and Eilan, N. (eds.), 1995, *The Body and the Self*, Massachusetts Institute of Technology, Boston, MA.

Bernal, M., 1987, *Black Athena*, Free Association Books, London.

Bloom, L., 1991, 'People and Property: A Psychoanalytic View', in Rudmin 1991: 427–444.

Bonner, F., 1995, *Economic Discourses on Television: the Peculiar Case of the 'Antiques Road Show'*, Pavis Centre, Open University, Milton Keynes.

Bourdieu, P., 1977, *Outline of a Theory of Practice*, Cambridge University Press, Cambridge.

Bourdieu, P., 1984, *Distinction: A Social Critique of the Judgement of Taste*, trans. R. Nice, Harvard University Press, Cambridge, MA.

Brewer, J. (ed.), 1994, *Early Modern Conceptions of Property*, Routledge, London.

Brewer, J. and Porter, R. (eds.), 1993, *Consumption and the World of Goods*, Routledge, London.

Browne, R. (ed.), 1980, *Objects of Special Devotion: Fetishes and Fetishism in Popular Culture*, Bowling Green University Popular Press, Ohio.

Burges, L. and Brown, M., 1995, *Single Lone Mothers: Problems, Prospects and Policies*, Policy Studies Institute Research Paper, Policy Studies Institute, London.

Burkert, W., 1985, 'Offerings in Perspective: Surrender, Distribution, Exchange', in T. Linders and G. Nordquist (eds.), *Gifts to the Gods*, Uppsala Studies in Ancient Mediterranean and Near Eastern Civilization: 15, University of Uppsala Press, Uppsala, pp. 44–50.

Butcher, B. and Todd, J., 1981, *Electoral Registration in 1981*, HMSO, London.

Campbell, C., 1987, *The Romantic Ethic and the Spirit of Modern Consumerism*, Blackwell, Oxford.

Campbell, C., 1993, 'Understanding Traditional and Modern Patterns of Consumption in Eighteenth-Century England: a Character Approach', in Brewer and Porter 1993: 40–54.

Campbell, C., 1995, 'The Sociology of Consumption', in Miller 1995a: 96–126.

Caplow, T., 1982, 'Christmas Gifts and Kin Networks', *American Sociology Review*, 47: 383–392.

Caplow, T., Bahr, H., Chadwick, A., Hill, R. and Williamson, M., 1983, *Middletown Families: Fifty Years of Change and Continuity*, Bantam Books, New York.

Carman, J., 1990, 'Commodities, Rubbish and Treasure: Valuing Archaeological Objects', *Archaeological Review from Cambridge*, 9, 2: 195–207.

Carrier, J., 1993, 'The Rituals of Christmas Giving', in Miller 1993a: 55–74.

Carrier, J., 1994, *Gifts and Commodities: Exchange and Western Capitalism Since 1700*, Routledge, London.

Chambers, I. and Curtis, L. (eds.), 1995, *The Postcolonial Question*, Routledge, London.

Cheal, D., 1988, *The Gift Economy*, Routledge, London.

Chodorow, N., 1978, *The Reproduction of Mothering*, University of California Press, London.

Chodorow, N., 1980, 'Gender, Relation and Difference in Psychoanalytic Perspectives', in H. Eisenstein and A. Jardine (eds.), *The Future of Difference*, G.K. Hall, Boston, MA, pp. 25–50.

Clifford, J., 1986, 'Objects and Selves – an Afterword', in G. Stocking (ed.), *Objects and*

Others: Essays on Museums and Material Culture. History of Anthropology, vol. III, University of Wisconsin Press, Madison, WI, pp. 236–246.

Clifford, J., 1988, *The Predicament of Culture*, Harvard University Press, Cambridge, MA.

Cook, G., 1992, *The Discourse of Advertising*, Routledge, London.

Cooper, C., 1996, 'Hot under the Collar', *Times Higher Education Supplement*, 21 June: 15.

Copp, J., 1995, 'Collectomania '95', *Collecting Now, Journal of the Leicestershire Collectors' Club*, August, No. 4: 11–15.

Coren, A., 1993, 'The Old Curiosity Show', *Radio Times*, 2 April: 14.

Costa, J.A. (ed.), 1994, *Gender Issues and Consumer Behaviour*, Routledge, London.

Cowan, B., 1981, 'Walter Benjamin's Theory of Allegory', *New German Critique*, 22: 109–122.

Crandall, R., 1980, 'Motives for Leisure', *Journal of Leisure Research*, 12: 45–54.

Creswell, J., 1995, *Research Design: Qualitative and Quantitative Approaches*, Sage, London.

Crowther, P., 1994, 'Lacan and Zizeh', *Art and Design*, March/April (9): 7–13.

Csikszentmihalyi, M. and Rochberg-Halton, E., 1981, *The Meaning of Things: Domestic Symbols and the Self*, Cambridge University Press, Cambridge.

Curtice, J., 1994, 'Political Sociology 1945–92', in Obelkevich and Catterall 1994a: 31–44.

Daly, N., 1994, 'That Obscure Object of Desire: Victorian Commodity Culture and the Fictions of the Mummy', *Novel: A Forum on Fiction*, 28, 1: 24–51.

Danet, B. and Katriel, K., 1989, 'No Two alike: Play and Aesthetics in Collecting', *Play and Culture*, 2: 253–277.

Dannefer, D., 1980, 'Rationality and Passion in Private Experience: Modern Consciousness and the Social World of Old-Car Collectors', *Social Problems*, 27: 392–412.

Dannefer, D., 1981, 'Neither Socialization nor Recruitment: the Advocational Careers of Old-Car Enthusiasts', *Social Forces*, 60: 395–413.

Dawson, W., 1934, 'Pettigrews' Demonstrations upon Mummies. A Chapter in the History of Egyptology', *Journal of Egyptian Archaeology*, 20: 170–182.

Debord, G., 1977, *Society of the Spectacle*, Black and Red Press, Detroit.

de Lisle, R., 1993, 'Brief Encounters with Chain-Mail', *The Independent*, 12 December: 13.

De Man, P., 1979, 'The Rhetoric of Temporality', in C. Singleton (ed.), *Interpretation: Theory and Practice*, Johns Hopkins University Press, Baltimore, MD, pp. 173–210.

Dench, G., 1996a, *The Place of Men in Changing Family Cultures*, Institute of Community Studies, London.

Dench, G., 1996b, *Transforming Men: Changing Patterns of Dependency and Dominance in Gender Relations*, Transaction Books, London.

Denzin, N. and Lincoln, Y. (eds.), 1994, *Handbook of Qualitative Research*, Sage, London.

Derrida, J., 1992, *Given Time I Counterfeit Money*, trans. P. Kamuf, University of Chicago Press.

Derrida, J., 1995, *The Gift of Death*, trans. David Wills, University of Chicago Press.

Digger, J., forthcoming, 'The People's Shows at Walsall', in K. Moore and S. Pearce (eds.), *Museums and Collecting*, Athlone Press, London.

Dillman, D., 1972, 'Increasing Mail Questionnaire Response in Large Samples of the General Public', *Public Opinion Quarterly*, 36: 254–257.

Dillman, D., 1978, *Mail and Telephone Surveys: the Total Design Method*, John Wiley, New York.

Dillman, D., 1983, 'Mail and Other Self-administered Questionnaires', in Rossi et al. 1993: 236–245.

Dittmar, H., 1991, 'Meanings of Material Possessions as Reflections of Identity: Gender and Socio-Material Position in Society', in Rudmin 1991: 165–186.

Dittmar, H., 1992, *The Social Psychology of Material Possessions: To Have Is To Be*, Harvester Wheatsheaf, London.

Dittmar, H., Mannetti, L. and Semin, G., 1989, 'Fine Feathers Make Fine Birds: a Comparative Study of the Impact of Material Wealth on Perceived Identities in England and Italy', *Social Behaviour*, 28: 159–171.

Dorfles, G., 1969, *Kitsch: The World of Bad Taste*, Universe Books, New York.

Douglas, M. and Isherwood, B., 1979, *The World of Goods: Towards an Anthropology of Consumption*, Allen Lane, London.

Dowd, N., 1996, *In Defense of Single-Parent Families*, New York University Press, New York.

du Gay, P., 1995, *Consumption and Identity at Work*, Sage, London.

Durks, N., Eley, G. and Ortner, S. (eds.), 1987, *Culture-Power-History. A Reader in Contemporary Social Theory*, Princeton University Press, Princeton, NJ.

Durost, W., 1932, *Children's Collecting Activity Related to Social Factors*, Bureau of Publications, Teachers' College, Columbia University, New York.

Eagleton, T., 1983, *Literary Theory: An Introduction*, Blackwell, Oxford.

Edgar, K., 1997, 'Old Masters and Young Mistresses', in Pearce 1997a: 80–94.

Eichenbaum, L. and Orbach, S., 1982, *Outside In . . . Inside Out*, Penguin Books, London.

Eisenstein, H. and Jardine, A. (eds.), *The Future of Difference*, G.K. Hall, Boston, MA.

Eliot, T.S., 1954, *Selected Poems*, Faber and Faber, London.

Ellen, R., 1988, 'Fetishism', *Man*, 1988, 23: 213–235.

Elsner, J. and Cardinal, R. (eds.), 1994, *The Cultures of Collecting*, Reaktion Books, London.

Erlandson, D., Harris, E., Skipper, B. and Allen, S., 1993, *Doing Naturalistic Inquiry: A Guide to Methods*, Sage, London.

Falk, P., 1994, *The Consuming Body*, Sage, London.

Fardell, R., 1995, 'The People's Show Festival at Harborough Museum', *Museological Review*, 1, 2: 72–76.

Favazza, A.R., 1995, *Bodies Under Siege: Self-Mutilation and Body Modification in Culture and Psychiatry*, Johns Hopkins University Press, Baltimore, MD.

Featherstone, M., 1991, *Consumer Culture and Postmodernism*, Sage Publications, London.

Featherstone, M., Hepworth, M. and Turner, B. (eds.), 1991, *The Body: Social Process and Cultural Theory*, Sage, London.

Fenichel, O., 1945, *The Psychoanalytic Theory of Neurosis*, Norton, New York.

Fink, A. (ed.), 1995a, *The Survey Kit*, Sage, London.

Fink, A., 1995b, *A Survey Handbook*, Sage, London.

Fink, A. and Kosecoff, J., 1985, *How to Conduct Surveys*, Sage, London.

Fleming, D., Paine, C., Rhodes, J. (eds.), 1993, *Social History in Museums: A Handbook for Professionals*, HMSO, London.

Frank, A.W., 1991, 'For a Sociology of the Body: an Analytical Review' in Featherstone et al. 1991: 36–102.

Freedland, J., 1995, 'Feeding Frenzy on Bitter Rice-Paper', *Guardian*, 6 July: Screen 7–8.

French, H., 1995, 'Burial in Ghana is a Dead Trendy Business', *Guardian*, 28 December: 9.

Freud, S., 1963, 'Character and Anal Eroticism', in P. Rieff (ed.), *Character and Culture*, Collier, New York.

Gautier, T., 1858, *Le Roman de la momie*, Paris.

Gautier, T., 1908, 'The Mummy's Foot', in *Stories by Gautier*, trans. P. Hearn, Dutton, New York, pp. 52–70.

Gilligan, C., 1982, *In a Different Voice: Psychological Theory and Women's Development*, Harvard University Press, Cambridge, MA.

Girling, R., 1994, 'Roses Round the Modem', *Sunday Times: Rural Living*, 17 March: 3.

Glancey, M., 1988, 'The Play World Setting of the Auction', *Journal of Leisure Research*, 20: 135–153.

Glennie, P., 1995, 'Consumption within Historical Studies', in Miller 1995a: 164–203.

Goldman, R., 1992, *Reading Ads Socially*, Routledge, London.

Goyden, J., 1982, 'Further Evidence on Factors affecting Response Rates to Mailed Questionnaires', *American Sociological Review*, 47(4): 550–553.

Graburn, N. (ed.), 1979, *Ethnic and Tourist Arts*, University of California Press, Berkeley, CA.

Greaves, W., 1991, 'Hugh Scully's Private Passions', *Radio Times*, 26 January: 21.

Griemas, A.J. and Rastier, F., 1968, 'The Interaction of Semiotic Constraints', *French Yale Studies*, 41: 86–105.

Hall, R., 1994, *Sociology of Work: Perspectives, Analyses and Issues*, Pine Forge Press, Thousand Oaks, CA and London.

Hammersley, M., 1992, *What's Wrong with Ethnography?*, Routledge, London.

Hebdidge, D., 1985a, *Hiding in the Light: On Images and Things*, Routledge, London.

Hebdidge, D., 1985b, *Subculture: The Meaning of Style*, Methuen, London.

Hedges, B., 1977, *Presentation of Response Rates*, Methodological Working Paper No. 1. Social and Community Planning Research, London.

Hermann, G. and Soiffer, S., 1989, 'For Fun and Profit: an Analysis of the Urban Garage Sale', *Urban Life*, 12: 397–421.

Hodder, I., 1986, *Reading the Past*, Cambridge University Press, Cambridge.

Hodder, I. (ed.), 1987, *Archaeology as Long Term History*, Cambridge University Press, Cambridge.

Hoinville, G. and Jowell, R. (eds.), 1978, *Survey Research Practice*, Heinemann Educational Books, London.

Holbrook, M., 1991, 'From the Log of Consumer Researcher: Reflections on the Odyssey', *Highways and Buyways* 1991: 12–47, Association for Consumer Research, Provo, Utah.

Hoole's Guide to British Collecting Clubs, 1992, Adwalton Publications, Bradford.

Hugdahl, K., 1996, *Psychophysiology: The Mind–Body Perspective*, Harvard University Press, Cambridge, MA.

Jameson, F., 1991, *Postmodernism: On the Cultural Logic of Late Capitalism*, Verso Books, London.

Jennings, C., 1993, 'Fever Kitsch', *Independent: Magazine*, 7 August: 30–32.

Jewson, N., 1991, 'Inner City Riots', *Social Studies Review*, 5, 3: 170–174.

Jones, E., 1950, 'Anal-Erotic Character Traits', in *Papers on Psycho-Analysis*, 5th edn, Baillière, Tindall and Cox, London.

Joy, A., 1991, '"Beyond the Odyssey", Interpretations of Ethnographic Writing in Consumer Behaviour', *Highways and Buyways*, 1991: 216–238, Association for Consumer Research, University of Utah, Utah.

Kelley, J., 1982, *Leisure*, Prentice Hall, Englewood Cliffs, NJ.

Kellner, D., 1989, *Jean Baudrillard: from Marxism to Postmodernism and Beyond*, Polity Press, Cambridge.

Kellner, D. (ed.), 1994, *Baudrillard: A Critical Reader*, Blackwell, Oxford.

Kellner, D., 1995a, 'Advertising and Consumer Culture', in J. Dowing, A. Mohammadi and A. Sreberny-Mohammadi (eds.), *Questioning the Media*, 2nd edn, Sage, London, pp. 329–344.

Kellner, D., 1995b, *Media Culture: Cultural Studies, Identity and Politics between the Modern and the Postmodern*, Routledge, London.

Koenig, J., 1993, 'Editorial: Welcome', *Baby Boomer Collectibles*, 1, 1 (Oct.): 6.

Kopytoff, I., 1986, 'The Cultural Biography of Things; Commoditization as Process', in Appadurai 1986: 64–91.

Kremer, R., 1992, 'Meaningful Materialism: Collectors' Relationship to Their Objects', unpublished PhD thesis, Faculty of Graduate Studies, University of British Colombia.

Kron, J., 1983, *Home-psych: the Social Psychology of Home and Decoration*, Crown Publishers, New York.

Kuhn, T., 1970, *The Structure of Scientific Revolutions*, 2nd edn, Chicago University Press.

Kuper, A., 1993, 'The English Christmas and the Family: Time Out and Alternative Realities', in Miller 1993a: 157–175.

Lancaster, B., 1995, *The Department Store*, Leicester University Press, London.

Law, C., 1994, 'Employment and Industrial Structure', in Obelkevich and Catterall 1994a: 85–98.

Lerner, B., 1961, 'Auditory and Visual Thresholds for the Perception of Words of Anal Connotation', Doctoral dissertation, Ferkauf Graduate School of Education, Yeshiva University, New York.

Lewis-Beck, M. (ed.), 1994, *Research Practice*, Sage, London.

Linders, T. and Nordquist G., 1985, *Gifts to the Gods*, Uppsala Studies in Ancient Mediterranean and Near Eastern Civilizations, 15, University of Uppsala Press, Uppsala.

Linnell, P., 1995, *Simply Switch On . . .*, Albion Press, South Wigston, Leicester.

Lovatt, J., 1995, 'A People's Show *Means* a People's Show', *Museological Review*, 1, 2: 66–71.

Lovatt, J., 1997, 'The People's Show Project, 1994', in Pearce 1997a: 196–254.

Macdonald, D., 1952, *Against the American Grain*, Random House, New York.

Maisel, R., 1974, 'The Flea Market as an Action Scene', *Urban Life and Culture*, 2: 488–505.

Marcuse, H. (ed.), 1964, *The Democratic and the Authoritarian State: Essays in Political and Legal Theory*, Free Press, Glencoe, IL.

Marmoy, C.F.A., 1958, 'The "Auto-Icon" of Jeremy Bentham at University College, London', *Medical History*, 11, 2: 1–10.

Martin, P., 1995, '"I've got one just like that": Collectors, Museums and Community', *Museological Review* 1, 2: 77–86.

Martin, P., 1996, 'Tomorrow's History Today? Post-Modern Collecting', *History Today*, February: 5–8.

Martin, P., 1997, 'Contemporary Popular Collecting in Britain: the Socio-Cultural Context of the Construction of Identity at the End of the Second Millennium AD', unpublished PhD thesis, University of Leicester.

Mauss, M., 1954, *The Gift*, Free Press, Glencoe, IL.

Merriman, N., 1991, *Beyond the Glass Case: the Past, the Heritage and the Public in Britain*, Leicester University Press, London.

Miles, R., 1993, *Gothic Writing 1750–1820: A Genealogy*, Routledge, London.

Miller, D., 1987, *Material Culture and Mass Consumption*, Blackwell, Oxford.

Miller, D. (ed.), 1993a, *Unwrapping Christmas*, Clarendon Press, Oxford.

Miller, D., 1993b, 'A Theory of Christmas', in Miller, 1993a: 3–37.

Miller, D. (ed.), 1995a, *Acknowledging Consumption*, Routledge, London.

Miller, D., 1995b, 'Consumption as the Vanguard of History', in Miller 1995a: 1–57.

Morgan, R., 1993, *£500 A Week From Car Boot Sales*, Imperia Books, London.

Morley, D., 1995, 'Theories of Consumption in Media Studies', in Miller 1995a: 296–328.

Morris, M., 1988, 'Things to Do with Shopping Centers', in S. Sheridan (ed.), *Grafts: Feminist Cultural Criticism*, Verso, London.

Mossman, S., 1997, *Early Plastics*, Leicester University Press, London.

Moulin, R., 1987, *The French Art Market: A Sociological View*, trans. A. Goldhammer, Rutgers University Press, New Brunswick, NJ.

Muesterberger, W., 1994, *An Unruly Passion: Psychological Perspectives*, Princeton University Press, Princeton, NJ.

Muncie, J., Wetherall, M., Dallos, R. and Cochrane, A. (eds.), 1995, *Understanding the Family*, Open University/Sage, London.

National Museums of Denmark, 1991, *Museum Europa: Presentation of the Exhibition*, National Museums of Denmark, Copenhagen.

Newton, T., Handy, J. and Fineman, S., 1995, *'Managing' Stress: Emotion and Power at Work*, Sage, London.

NOP (National Opinion Poll) Market Research 1982, *A Report on a Survey Carried Out for the English Tourist Board on Museums*, NOP Market Research Ltd, London.

Oakley, A., 1976, *Housewife*, Penguin, Harmondsworth.

Obelkevich, J. and Catterall, P. (eds.), 1994a, *Understanding Post-War British Society*, Routledge, London.

Obelkevich, J. and Catterall, P., 1994b, 'Introduction: Understanding British Society', in Obelkevich and Catterall 1994a: 1–8.

Olmsted, A., 1991, 'Collecting: Leisure, Investment or Obsession?', in Rudmin 1991: 287–306.

Parsons, T., 1959, 'The Social Structure of the Family', in R. Anshen (ed.), *The Family: Its Function and Destiny*, Harper and Row, New York, pp. 25–50.

Peach, C. (ed.), 1996, *The Ethnic Minority Populations of Britain*, vol. 2, *Ethnicity in the 1991 Census*, HMSO, London.

Pearce, S., 1992, *Museums, Objects and Collections*, Leicester University Press, London.

Pearce, S., 1995, *On Collecting. An Investigation into Collecting in the European Tradition*, Routledge, London.

Pearce, S. (ed.), 1997a, *Experiencing Material Culture in the Western World*, Leicester University Press, London.

Pearce, S., 1997b, 'Foreword: Words and Things', in Pearce 1997a.

Pearce, S., forthcoming, 'Symbols of Ourselves: Our Relationship with Objects', in *Material Memories*, Victoria and Albert Museum, London.

Poster, M. (ed.), 1988, *Jean Baudrillard: Selected Writings*, Polity Press, Cambridge.

Purcell, R.W. and Gould, S.J., 1992, *Finders, Keepers*, Hutchinson Radius, London.

Radner, H., 1995, *Shopping Around: Feminist Culture and the Pursuit of Pleasure*, Routledge, London.

Ramet, S. (ed.), 1996, *Gender Reversals and Gender Culture: Anthropological and Historical Perspectives*, Routledge, London.

Roberts, J., 1996, '"The Gardens of Dunroamin": History and Cultural Values with Specific Reference to the Gardens of the Inter-War Semi', *International Journal of Heritage Studies* 1, 4: 229–237.

Roberts, Y., 1996, 'Holding the Baby', *Sunday Times: Magazine*, 28 July: 18–25.

Rochester, N., 1995, 'Gudgies', *Collecting Now, Journal of the Leicestershire Collectors' Club*, April/June, No. 3: 11.

Rojek, C., 1996, *Decentring Leisure: Rethinking Leisure Theory*, Sage, London.

Rosenberg, B. and White, D.M., 1957, *Mass Culture*, Free Press, Glencoe, IL.

Rossi, P., Wright, J. and Anderson, A. (eds.), 1993, *Handbook of Survey Research*, Academic Press, London.

Rudmin, F. (ed.), 1991, 'To Have Possessions: A Handbook of Ownership and Property', *Journal of Social Behaviour and Personality*, Special Issue, 6, 6.

Saddler, N., 1997, 'A Sinister Way of Life: A Search for Left-Handed Material Culture', in Pearce 1997a: 140–153.

Saisselin, R., 1984, *Bricobracomania: the Bourgeois and the Bibelots*, Rutgers University Press, New Brunswick, NJ.

Sapsford, R. and Jupp, V., 1996, *Data Collection and Analysis*, Open University/Sage, London.

Scanlon, J. (ed.), 1996, *Inarticulate Longings: The Ladies Home Journal, Gender, and the Promises of Consumer Culture*, Routledge, London.

Sewell, B., 1991, 'Are Collectors Deranged?', *The Art Newspaper*, No. 5, February: 4.

Shanks, M., 1996, *Classical Archaeology of Greece: Experience of the Discipline*, Routledge, London.

Sherry, J.F. (ed.), 1995, *Contemporary Marketing and Consumer Behaviour*, Sage, London.

Shields, R. (ed.), 1992, *Lifestyle Shopping: The Subject of Consumption*, Routledge, London.

Shilling, C., 1993, *The Body and Social Theory*, Sage, London.

Silven-Garnert, E., 1995, 'The Body and its Material Extensions: Practice and Meaning in the Work of Professional House-Painters', *Ethnologia Scandinavica*, 25: 67–78.

Silverman, D., 1993, *Interpreting Qualitative Data*, Sage, London.

Singleton, C. (ed.), 1969, *Interpretation: Theory and Practice*, Johns Hopkins University Press, Baltimore, MD.

Smith, R., 1994, 'Elements of demographic change in Britain since 1945', in Obelkevich and Catterall 1994a: 19–30.

Spivak, G.C., 1993, *Outside in the Teaching Machine*, Routledge, London.

Stewart, S., 1984, *On Longing: Narratives of the Miniature, the Gigantic, the Souvenir, the Collection*, Johns Hopkins University Press, Baltimore, MD.

Stocking, G. (ed.), 1986, *Objects and Others: Essays on Museums and Material Culture, History of Anthropology*, vol. III, University of Wisconsin Press.

Stoller, M., 1984, 'The Economics of Collectible Goods', *Journal of Cultural Economics*, 8: 91–104.

Storms, M., 1979, 'Sex Role Identity and Its Relationships to Sex Role Attitudes and Sex Role Stereotypes', *Journal of Personality and Social Psychology*, 37, 10: 1779–1789.

Strinati, D., 1995, *An Introduction to Theories of Popular Culture*, Routledge, London.

Sudman, S., 1993, 'Applied Sampling', in Rossi et al. 1993: 145–194.

Suggitt, M., 1993, 'Collecting Methods: the Antique Trade', in Fleming, Paine and Rhodes 1993: 181–6.

Suleiman, S.R. (ed.), 1985, *The Female Body in Western Culture: Contemporary Perspectives*, Harvard University Press, Cambridge, MA.

Swann, J.M., 1969, 'Shoes Concealed in Buildings', *Northampton Museums Journal*, 6: 9–21.

Thompson, M., 1979, *Rubbish Theory: the Creation and Destruction of Value*, Oxford University Press, Oxford.

Thomson, R.G., 1996, *Freakery: Cultural Spectacles of the Extraordinary Body*, New York University Press, New York.

Tierney-Jones, 1996, 'Why Do Men Collect?', *New Woman*, April: 94.

Tuan, Y., 1984, *Dominance and Affection*, Yale University Press, New Haven, CT.

Wallendorf, M. and Belk, R., 1989, 'Assessing Trustworthiness in Naturalistic Consumer Research', *Interpretative Consumer Research*, 1989: 69–84, Association for Consumer Research, University of Provo, Utah.

Wallendorf, M., Belk, R. and Heisley, D., 1988, 'Deep Meaning in Possessions', *Advances in Consumer Research*, 15: 528–530.

Wallmann, S., 1984, *Eight London Households*, Tavistock Press, London.

Walvin, J., 1996, *Fruits of Empire: Exotic Produce and British Taste, 1660–1800*, New York University Press, New York.

Weatherill, L., 1996, *Consumer Behaviour and Material Culture in Britain, 1660–1760*, Routledge, London.

Wilkinson, H., 1997, 'Mr Cropper and Mrs Brown: Good and Bad Collectors in the Work of A.S. Byatt and Other Recent Fiction', in Pearce 1997a: 95–113.

Wilkinson, S. (ed.), 1986, *Feminist Social Psychology: Developing Theory and Practice*, Open University Press, Milton Keynes.

Willcut, J. and Ball, K., 1978, *The Musical Instrument Collector*, The Bold Strummer Ltd, New York.

Wilson, E., 1989, *Adorned in Dreams*, Virago, London.

Wolff, I., 1993, 'Don't Ask Why, Just Put a Lid On It', *The Independent*, 12 December 1993: 5.

Wooliams, A., 1995, 'I'm Just an Old-Fashioned Boy', *Best of British Magazine*, Sept./Oct. 1995: 8–9.

Worcester, R., 1996, 'Socio-Cultural Currents Affecting Heritage Site Consideration: The Impact of Human Values on People's Attitudes and Behaviour', *International Journal of Heritage Studies*, 1(4): 207–218.

Yates, F., 1964, *Giordano Bruno and the Hermetic Tradition*, Routledge, London.

Zizek, S., 1989, *The Sublime Object of Ideology*, Routledge, London.

Index

toys, 32, 34, 44, 56, 58
  gender and, 135
  self-identification and, 155
  use of, 56
transport, access to, 26, 32, 54–5
Tuan, Y., 162

use of collections, 56–9, 70, 117, 119

values, 8, 9, 14, 80
  class and, 179–80
  market and, 91–3
  paradigms of, 37, 38
  traditional, 35–44, 176
visuality, 129, 130

waiting for items to appear, 74, 76, 77, 115
Walker, J., 15–16
Wallendorf, M., 174
'warm' environment, 97, 124, 178
White, D. M., 36

Wichita Art Museum, 35
women, 124, 126, 133, 136, 150, 178
  and care of collection, 140
  collections of, 100, 133–4, 135, 136
  in Collectors' Clubs, 60, 70
  family and, 178
  gift giving and, 85, 112, 174
  images of, 136, 161
  inheritance of collections, 107
  mail order and, 84
  shopping and, 81–2
Wooliams, A., 4
work, 24, 27–8, 49, 52
  and consumption, 50
  insecurity of, 50
  links with collecting, 53–6, 72, 119, 172–3, 182
  new practices of, 50
works of art, 31, 40, 43, 56, 58
wrapping of presents, 90–1

Zizek, S., 129